W9-DFL-411

TO DANCE THE DANCE

A Symbolic Interactional Exploration of Premarital Sexuality

LEA'S SERIES IN PERSONAL RELATIONSHIPS
Steve Duck, Series Editor

TO DANCE THE DANCE

A Symbolic Interactional Exploration of Premarital Sexuality

F. Scott Christopher

Arizona State University

2001

LAWRENCE ERLBAUM ASSOCIATES, PUBLISHERS
Mahwah, New Jersey   London

Lawrence Erlbaum Associates, Inc., Publishers
10 Industrial Avenue
Mahwah, NJ 07430

Cover design by Kathryn Houghtaling Lacey

Library of Congress Cataloging-in-Publication Data

Christopher, F. Scott
    To dance the dance: a symbolic interactional exploration of premarital sexuality / F.
Scott Christopher
        p. cm. — (LEA's series on personal relationships)
    Includes bibliographical references and index.
    ISBN 0-8058-3710-8 (cloth: alk. paper)
    1. Premarital sex. 2. Teenagers—Sexual behavior. 3. Adolescent psychology. 4.
Symbolic interactionism.   I. Title. II. Series.

HQ35.C5285 2000
306.73—dc21

                                                                    00-044247

Books published by Lawrence Erlbaum Associates are printed
on acid-free paper, and their bindings are chosen for strength
and durability.

Printed in the Untied States of America
10 9 8 7 6 5 4 3 2 1

Contents

Preface

When I was first introduced to symbolic interaction theory in graduate school, I had an office-mate who owned a large wall hanging depicting a couple dancing with wild, joyous abandon. As I explored how symbolic interactionism could be used for examining premarital sexuality, my thoughts often returned to the picture of the couple. Dance seemed to be the perfect metaphor for introducing how sexuality and symbolic interaction could be integrated. Picture two young, single adults dancing sensuously with each other, their bodies closely intertwined. Both are dressed seductively in tight-fitting clothes that show off their athletic bodies. Their feet follow an intricate, intertwining pattern as they flow across the floor. A tango plays, a dance well known for its sexual and romantic tension. The partners alternately lead or follow by subtle cues without exchanging words. Instead, they convey meanings by the press of a breast, the closeness of the hips, a look of the eyes.

Other couples dance by this couple. At first glance it appears that all follow the same pattern of steps. Closer inspection reveals differences across couples. One couple has problems negotiating the intricate dance and eventually leaves the floor—angry and blaming each other at their failed attempt. Another couple bumbles, laughs at their flawed efforts, and continues, enjoying each other's presence. Others deviate from the established pattern of steps, showing off their own distinct flair. These couples have danced together many times before, using previous opportunities to negotiate a style completely their own.

Dance is a useful analogy for introducing the examination of premarital sexuality from a symbolic interactional perspective because there are so many parallels between the two. Similar to sex, one can dance alone, but its full capacity for meaning and pleasure is best realized with a partner. Individuals prepare for dance or sex by dressing in a particular manner—often to send signals to a partner about their masculinity or femininity. Couples can dance or engage in sex for pleasure and/or as an expression of romantic attachment. The question of romantic attachment, however, is often intricately tied to both sex and dancing.

Both involve patterns of interaction or a series of steps between the partners. In dance, these patterns form recognizable dances such as the tango, the waltz, or the rumba. In sexual expression, these form roles such as the seducer, romantic partner, or sexual predator. These interactional patterns are learned through socialization from the larger society, but many couples deviate from these established patterns and develop their own unique style of role interaction. Nonverbal exchanges are essential elements of both dancing and sexual interaction as they are primarily nonverbal in nature. This may make it difficult for a person to know specifically what is meant when his or her partner lightly brushes his or her arm, gives a kiss, or even suggests coitus. Only when a couple develops a relational history is it likely that such messages will be correctly interpreted most of the time. In this book, I explore the dance of premarital, heterosexual, sexual expression in society and how people learn the steps of that dance.

Before exploring that dance, however, I need to address a number issues. First, this book is heterosexually biased. This was a purposeful choice. The literature on homosexuality is not as well developed and the task of integrating the research on heterosexual, premarital sexuality was daunting enough by itself. Second, an ethnic bias toward the White middle class exists. The only chapters that consider ethnicity are chapters 3 and 4, which focus on early adolescence. Ethnic differences have received serious attention by scholars solely for this particular developmental stage. Thus, this same limitation influenced the present work. Third, I believe that engaging in sexual intercourse and becoming a parent is not desirable for early adolescents. My choice of language in the chapters on adolescence reflects my personal bias and beliefs. Readers will find, for example, that I describe first coitus and premarital pregnancies in terms of "risk" and in other writings I emphasize the need to prevent such pregnancies (Christopher, 1995).

ACKNOWLEDGMENTS

It is important that I acknowledge the contributions of those who helped with the writing of this book. Heartfelt thanks go to Steve Duck for his patience and careful editing, and to Sally Martin and Mark Roosa for reviewing individual chapters. Their helpful insights resulted in numerous improvements in what you will read. Karen Dubner, Lori Weaver, and Sara Jacobs Carter get marks of distinction for supplementing the articles that served as a foundation for this work. Special thoughts go to Fonda, my wife, and Michaela, my daughter, for their support in this endeavor. Finally, I extend deeply felt gratitude and appreciation to Jacqueline Voss who first introduced me to Symbolic Interaction Theory and whose inspired teaching played a major role in my career, and to Rodney Cate who opened my eyes to the importance of research. Now let us begin the dance.

—F. Scott Christopher

1

First Steps:
Symbolic Interactionism
and
Premarital Sexuality

Paul, a 4-year-old, walks in on his mother as she is changing clothes. He notices her vulva, points, and says "Mommy where is your thing?" His mother mumbles something about boys and girls being different while blushing and shoos Paul out of the room.

Rachel's 14-year closest friend, Heather, went "all the way" with her boyfriend John last Friday night. In Rachel's bedroom, Heather shares her experience. Her telling highlights the romance of the evening and how close she felt to John afterward. Elsewhere, John relates his version of the encounter to five of his friends while they cruise the streets. He talks about Heather's tight body, how willing she was, and that he gets "horny" just thinking of their next time together.

When Luke and Jody began dating, they hit it off right away. They soon stopped dating others and spent all available time together. While celebrating their 4-month anniversary at Jody's apartment, they professed their growing love for one another. Neither said anything after sharing their feelings. Instead, they kissed, removed each other's clothing, and "made love" for the first time.

Shivering, Wendy lies in bed, tears falling across her cheeks. She berates herself for being "so stupid" by going over to Roscoe's apartment after the movie. He seemed like a nice guy, but after a couple of beers he wanted to do more than kiss. When she protested, he became enraged, tore her clothes, and forced himself on her. She replays the incident in her mind over and over, attempting to comprehend what happened to her.

Experiences such as these have inspired social scientists to investigate different dimensions one of most basic qualities of being human, our sexuality. The experiences differ from one another in meaningful ways. Paul wanted an understanding of how men and women are physically different. Heather and John socialized their respective friends by relating their unique perspectives of their shared sexual encounter. Luke and Jody's joining in intercourse helped build their relationship. Wendy's dating partner used sex to dominate and violate her. Differences also exist in that in each experience the individuals are at different developmental stages, Paul at childhood, Heather and John at adolescence, and Luke, Jody, and Wendy at young adulthood.

In many ways, empirical investigations into the development of our early life sexuality are similarly segmented. Researchers typically focus on a single developmental period, use a limited number of variables, and make conclusions about what these variables reveal about sexual experiences for individuals at that developmental stage. Moreover, the choice of what to study often represents the discipline of the researchers. Past sociological work, for instance, focused on the relationship of peer influences, family structure, ethnicity, and social class to adolescent coital transitions. More psychologically oriented investigations centered on premarital sexual attitudes, self-concept, and locus of control for the same developmental group. Such choices characterize the study of human experience in general and should not be judged harshly. Scholars make difficult decisions when designing their studies. They balance limited resources, time, and research participants' willingness to comply with their demands against a strong desire to understand this very complex part of life.

At the same time, however, the ability to understand premarital sexuality continues to be limited by this segmented approach. Past reviewers of the empirical literature have either combined findings of dissimilar developmental stages, such as early adolescence and young adulthood, or ignored certain types of experiences, most often childhood sexuality or sexual aggression in dating relationships. Except for the limited view put forth by introductory human sexuality texts, no review to date has concurrently included literature on childhood, early adolescence, older adolescence and young adulthood, and sexual aggression in dating. In many ways, this results in boxes of knowledge being stacked against one another as if they are unrelated to one another.

A more fruitful approach is to concurrently examine these literatures so that continuities, commonalties, and distinctions can be identified. Thus, my first goal in writing this book was to review the empirical literature on sexuality before marriage. I wanted to highlight the unique, sexually related experiences of individuals from childhood to young adulthood. There are a number of benefits to taking this formative approach. By acknowledging developmental differences and changes, a more integrated understanding of how sexuality develops emerges. It also allows a better understanding of what is known and not known about premarital sexuality at different stages of development. New and important directions for scholarly investigations can thereby be revealed. Moreover, a fuller understanding of premarital sexuality can lead to better efforts at preventing some of the unwanted outcomes that can occur from sexual exploration before marriage including sexually transmitted diseases, unplanned pregnancies, and sexual exploitation.

To this end, four of the chapters in the book review research findings for different developmental stages and for different types of experiences. Chapter 2 examines those childhood experiences that lay the foundation for later sexual expression.[1] Children are openly curious about sexual issues. They strive to understand the origins of babies, the physiological differences between boys' and girls' bodies, and what it means when men and women interact in romantic ways. Preadolescents spend time in same-sex groups discussing the meaning of behaviors that contain sexual or romantic underpinnings. This chapter delves into these issues. Chapter 3 progresses to the next developmental stage. It focuses on researchers' findings on early adolescent sexuality and it begins with a review of the scope of adolescent sexual activity. After this review, it continues by considering specific influences on sexual expression for this developmental stage including the role of the individual, family, peers, and partners.

Chapter 5 moves forward by concentrating on research findings for older adolescents and young adults. It begins with an in-depth review of the relational experiences that are significantly tied to sexual intimacy at these developmental stages. The importance of commitment, intimacy,

---

[1]I do not review the literature on child sexual abuse as this was beyond the focus and purpose of the book.

conflict, and communication is established and different forms of influencing one's dating partner are investigated. The focus of this chapter, however, is not solely on the dyad. The relative influence of parental, peer, and individual variables is examined. Not all sexual interaction in dating is a positive experience. Sexual aggression can result when the sexual wishes of dating partners are discrepant with one another and it is not an uncommon experience among those who date. Chapter 7 scrutinizes the literature on this form of aggression. It opens with an examination of the frequency of sexual aggression in dating. I follow this by postulating that there are two broad forms of sexual aggression, *sexual assault* involving the threat or use of force, and *sexual coercion* exemplified by verbal coercion (but without threats of force), pressure, and manipulation. Cultural, social, dyadic, and individual factors associated with sexual assault and coercion are then explored.[2]

Although the reviews of these related literatures serve as a foundation for this book, the empirical findings by themselves are insufficient to provide the unity that I hoped to gain. What is conjointly required is a theoretical orientation that integrates the literatures. Although other scholars have proposed frameworks to explain premarital sexuality (i.e., Buss, 1998; Hobgen & Byrne, 1998), for the most part these have been focused on singular phenomenon and often ignored entire classes of variables shown by empirical investigations to be important. For instance, social exchange theory can potentially explain why a couple first engages in intercourse and continues to do so in a relationship (Sprecher, 1998). However, it is more difficult to explain how supportive parenting is related to adolescents' coital decision making using this particular framework. Thus, my overall goal for this book is to propose a unifying theory of premarital sexuality.

To introduce this theory, I ask that you consider again the four experiences of the individuals who opened this chapter. Although they differ from one another, they also share an important commonality. In each instance, the individuals create or search for meaning in their sexuality. Four-year-old Paul learns from his mother that talking about one's sexual body parts can lead to embarrassment. Heather and John use their respective friends to help establish unique meanings for their shared coital experience. Luke and Jody engage in sexual intercourse as an expression of their newly found love. Wendy attempts to comprehend why Roscoe

---

[2]The appedix provides a brief review of methodological, statistical, and path model concepts used in the book for readers who would find this helpful.

would use sex to dominate her. Symbolic interactionism, with its emphasis on the development of shared meaning, represents a theoretical framework that is encompassing and flexible enough to integrate the different empirical literatures I review. The following is a brief description of symbolic interaction theory and the constructs I use in the book.[3]

SYMBOLIC INTERACTIONAL CONSTRUCTS

There are a number of basic assumptions that form the foundation of symbolic interaction theory. Five of these are central to the model I propose. They are as follows:

1. Individuals strive to create and maintain meaning in their environments.
2. Meaning is created and modified in interactions between people.
3. Individuals are self-directed in their behavior rather than simply reactive to their environments.
4. Individuals are self-reflective; they can examine their actions as an object separate from themselves.
5. Individuals' behavior is motivated by how they view themselves (Hewitt, 1991; Longmore, 1998; Stryker & Statham, 1985).

According to the first assumption, people look at *objects* in their environment and assign meaning to them. Individuals create meaning in this way. The most basic examples of this assumption originate in how people name physical objects in the environment such as articles of clothing, furniture, or rooms in a house. However, many of these objects take on additional, special meanings because they represent shared experiences with someone close, serve as reminders of important life hallmarks, or are otherwise paired with salient life events. In such instances, the objects come to represent or symbolize this specially assigned meaning and a singular status is bestowed on them. Assigning symbolic meaning is not limited to physical objects. People also examine behavior, organize it into sequences or *social acts*, and create meaning for these acts. Because of this, the same behavior may take on different meanings depending on who is involved and the meaning they impart on the behavior. A kiss from a mother, for example, means something entirely different than a kiss from a lover!

---

[3]See Longmore (1998) or Stryker and Statham (1985) for more in-depth descriptions.

Assigning meaning usually does not take place in a social vacuum. Applying the second assumption, that meaning is created and modified in interactions between people, allows one to see how objects and behavior develop a shared meaning between people. Couples often communicate with one another by *gestures*—sequences of behaviors that have a joint meaning. Hence, a surreptitious touch to the breast or genitals in public can convey an interest in later engaging in sexual intercourse with a partner. The creation of shared meaning is not limited to dyads. For example, preadolescent boys often share pornographic materials in group settings (Thorne & Luria, 1986). This experience undoubtedly includes group discussions where the viewed pornography is dissected into specific objects and behavioral acts, and meaning is created for both. Boys with previous exposure to pornography may "instruct" those with less experience in what certain things mean. This process likely results in sexual themes being assigned to certain modes of dress, eye glances, body parts, and dyadic exchanges that are transmitted across groups by more experienced boys.

Individuals organize behavioral acts into coherent, meaningful entities. These entities are an essential component of *social roles*. Social roles occur in complementary pairs such as boyfriend–girlfriend, parent–child, best friend–best friend. In common parlance, and among scholars who subscribe to *role theory*, a *role* is "a cluster of duties, rights, and obligations associated with a particular social position (or . . . status)" (Hewitt, 1991, p. 93). Put more simply, if someone is a steady dating partner (a *social position* or *status*), he or she will be required to follow certain *behavioral norms* or behavioral expectations—such as only dating the partner, engaging in sexual intercourse, and making statements of affection. In turn, this individual can expect similar behaviors from the corresponding dyad partner. From the perspective of role theory, roles originate in the larger society and are often referred to as *social scripts*. *Socializing agents* such as parents, peers, and dyad partners teach and reward correct role behavior and punish deviations from common role expectations and norms.

In contrast, symbolic interactionists take the perspective that roles are negotiated through dyadic interaction. Roles begin with knowledge about the role positions of the individuals involved. Individuals then use this knowledge to organize and give meaning to the situation in which they find themselves. The knowledge allows individuals to assess possible and acceptable ways of acting (Hewitt, 1991). This development of roles involves two interrelated processes. The first is *role making* where individuals focus on their own possible behaviors and consider how these behaviors will fit into their social context and their interaction with a role partner. The second is *role taking* where the individual tries to see the proposed interaction from the partner's point of view.

Actual *role enactment* is an outcome, in part, of the interaction of the dyad members who form the role pair as they engage in role making and role taking. According to the third theoretical assumption, that individuals are self-directed in their behavior, individuals choose behavioral sequences when engaging in a given role. Across time, this contributes to dyadic partners developing role expectations for each other. Developing these role expectations for one's self and partner often requires a couple to negotiate what constitutes acceptable behavior. One form of *role conflict* occurs when one's expectation about how one's partner should behave are out of synch with that partner's self-expectations. It is through this overall process of developing and enacting roles that shared, symbolic meanings of gestures and other behavioral sequences are created.

Stryker and Statham (1985) provided an in-depth comparison of these two theoretical orientations—role theory and symbolic interactionism—and conclude that both offer insight into the nature of roles. I share this position in this book. Specifically, I posit that parents and peers act as socializing agents especially during childhood and early adolescence. Both developmental periods are characterized by learning about sexual roles and possible behavioral repetoirs that contribute to the content of these roles. Individuals bring these preconceptions to bear when they enter into sexual relationships. I further speculate, however, that dyadic partners create their roles within these learned parameters. Thus, I make use of constructs from both theories.

The fourth theoretical assumption that I listed states that individuals are *self-reflective*. Stated another way, individuals have the capacity to examine themselves as a separate object. One can consider one's own actions, feelings, beliefs, and experiences separate from oneself. Cooley called this concept "the looking glass self" (Hewitt, 1991). This very powerful concept gives rise to a number of interrelated constructs. Central to these is the theoretical construct of *self*. The self is where individuals build an identity of who they are. It includes a hierarchical grouping of the various role positions that individuals perceive themselves as filling (Stryker & Statham, 1985). A young woman, for example, may see herself as concurrently holding the positions of romantic partner, friend, daughter, student, and waitress to name a few. Each of these positions includes corresponding, self-held role expectations connected with a specific position. They also include a *self-evaluation* or *self-concept* component where individuals evaluate how well they perform in their given roles. Each role has a separate evaluation. For example, the same young woman may spend much of the week devoted to her studies, yet also feels that she has ignored her boyfriend. She may feel quite good about her scholastic achievements, but guilty about the lack of time spent with someone for whom she cares. This example also illustrates *intraindividual role conflict* where one's role expectations for two or more roles oppose one another. The young woman is unable to fulfill her own simultaneous expectations for being a student and a girlfriend and experiences this form of role conflict.

The idea of a self gives rise to the construct of *social self* where one examines and creates one's concept of self in a social context. Put more simply, individuals consider the reactions of others to their own possible role enactments. A sexually inexperienced teenage boy, for instance, may seriously contemplate caressing his girlfriend's vulva for the first time. He may see her as a willing partner or as someone who will stop him from fulfilling his wishes. This process is characteristic of the social self.

Two sources of social reactions are considered when constructing the social self. The first source comes from individuals who are salient influences in an individual's life—*significant others*. Significant others are those people whose opinions and evaluations are valued by the individual. Parents, dating partners, and close friends are likely included in this group. The second source comes from a more general view of how a category of *generalized others* may react. This group of individuals is often less defined. For instance, a young man may contemplate the jealousy of others in a club if he were to show up with a strikingly attractive date. His sense of the "others" in this reverie may lack specific personalities; nonetheless, their opinions are considered and may eventually influence his choice and treatment of a partner in a dating role enactment.

The final assumption identified, that individuals' self-perceptions motivates their behaviors, flows from the previous assumption. It capitalizes on the multidimensional construct of *self* by stating that the process of *self-reflection* influences individuals' choices about their role enactment. For example, if a young man's definition of *self* includes the role position of "religious person," then his *self*-perceptions will most likely lead to a sexual role enactment characterized by limited sexual involvement. In contrast, if another single man's *self*-identity revolves around the position of "player," his sexual role enactment will include seduction, game playing, and attempts to manipulate his partner. Thus, one's perceptions of *self* play key roles in the behavioral choices one makes.

I use, and more fully explain, these concepts in the chapters of the book that explicate the theoretical model. More specifically, whereas chapter 2 reviews the literature on childhood experiences with sexuality it concludes with a theoretical model that conjectures about the role of parents, peers, and the media in childhood sexual knowledge and feelings that form the initial sense of one's sexual self, a sense of self that carries over into adolescence. In chapter 4, I integrate the early adolescent sexuality literature using symbolic interactional concepts. Parents, close friends, and other adolescents are hypothesized to have unique socialization influences on early adolescents' sexual selves and social selves. I hypothesize that these forces come to bear on the development of early adolescents' role expectations that, in turn, eventually influence their sexual role enactments.

In chapter 6, I build on the theoretical framework used for early adolescence to posit about how parents, peers, and individual variables uniquely influence the sexual self of later adolescents and young adults. The model is then expanded to posit about the interrelationship of dyadic experiences and sexual role enactment. Finally, in chapter 8 I use the model developed in the earlier theory chapters to integrate the body of literature on sexual aggression.

Thus, as is hopefully obvious at this point, the book is organized such that a review of a particular literature is followed by the application of symbolic interaction theory to this literature in an attempt to integrate the corpus of its findings. The next chapter focuses on to childhood experiences with sexuality—experiences that lay the foundation for later sexual development.

2

Childhood:
Early Influences
on
Adolescent Sexuality

Children do not enter into adolescence with a blank sexual slate.[1] The popular conceptualization that they do is a holdover from Victorian times and research has refuted such a premise. Nor do they enter into this developmental stage with their sexuality fully developed. The development of one's sexuality is a lifelong process, with adolescence serving as a critical period in its formation, growth, and exploration. In fact, children come to adolescence with just over a decade's life experience; an experience that includes a decade's exposure to sexual messages from parents, peers, the media, and teachers.

Very little is known about children's sexuality because, with a few exceptions, scholars have assiduously ignored this area of research. Some have relied on Freudian constructs and beliefs. Briefly, Freud suggested that personality development is the outcome of early childhood experiences that are driven by a psychosexual energy. Furthermore, Freud

---

[1]My use of the concepts *child, early adolescent, older adolescent,* and *young adult* refer to specific developmental stages. Advancement from one stage to the next is more a function of developmental competencies than chronological age. If pressed, I would state that early adolescence begins somewhere between ages 11 and 13, older adolescence between the ages of 15 and 16, and young adulthood between the ages of 18 and 20.

believed that after the personality is formed, at around the age of 6, children experience a latency stage characterized by little interest in sexuality. The small amount of existing research shows that Freud was correct in speculating that children are actively interested in and make conceptualizations about sexual matters (Goldman & Goldman, 1982). This interest, however, does not noticeably lessen at any point during childhood. In fact, curiosity, inquisitiveness, and a wish to understand sex seem to be the norm throughout childhood (Goldman & Goldman, 1982).

Investigators have only just begun to empirically establish connections between normal childhood sexuality and adolescent sexuality. For instance, longitudinal work by Okami and his colleagues suggests that engaging in child sex play and exposure to parental nudity are unrelated to such harmful adolescent outcomes as experiencing sexual problems or drug use. In fact, these early sexual encounters appear to be associated, albeit weakly, with a decrease likelihood of contracting sexually transmitted diseases and fathering a child before marriage for sons (Okami, Olmstead, & Abramson, 1997; Okami, Olmstead, Abramson, & Pendleton, 1998). This singular investigation suggests links between childhood and adolescent sexual experiences. It would be naïve to think that richer connections that are more diverse would not also be present when early developmental events in the cognitive, social, and affective realms have been shown to affect later development. Before hypothesizing about such links, it would be helpful to examine what researchers have discovered about sexuality during these early stages of development.

Examining the development of sexuality in children needs to begin with certain cautions about how the concept of *sexuality* is defined for this age group. Although children will sometimes engage in behaviors that give them physical pleasure, and will often ask questions that either directly or indirectly focus on sexual information, children should not be viewed as "sexual" in the same way as adults or adolescents are viewed as sexual. Children have yet to learn the full, culturally assigned meaning given to certain body parts, behaviors, words, and sexual forms of interpersonal interactions (Thorne & Luria, 1986). This knowledge deficit contributes to the view of children as asexual innocents. At the same time, children are capable of tactile pleasure, eager to explore their world, and soon learn that sexual matters carry a special significance in our culture (Goldman & Goldman, 1982; Victor, 1980).

Children's capacity for pleasure is evident in their exploration of their own, and others' bodies. Boys experience erections in utero (Calderone, 1983), and infant girls are capable of vaginal lubrication (Victor, 1980), so it is not surprising that some infant and preschool children masturbate (Gundersen, Melas, & Skar, 1981; Whitfield, 1989), possibly to orgasm (Kinsey, Pomeroy, & Martin, 1948). Children not only show an interest in their own genitals, but are also interested in others'. Games of "doctor" or "nurse" are common during childhood (Gundersen et al., 1981; Okami et al., 1997; Victor, 1980) and are usually used to compare and contrast genitalia. Preschool teachers report that children frequently initiate contact comfort and intimacy from significant adults in their world. Sometimes this contact will evolve into attempts to explore parts of the adults' body linked to their sexuality (Gundersen et al., 1981).

Children's curiosity extends to other areas of sexuality, such as where babies come from, how it is decided that one is male or female, and what the special relationships between men and women are. Children look to their mothers as the primary source of information for answers to these and related questions. To a lesser degree, peers, the media, and sex education teachers serve as knowledge sources (Goldman & Goldman, 1982; Thorne & Luria, 1986). Two separate processes influence children's understanding of the sexual information they receive.

Capitalizing on Piagetian theory, the first reflects normal stages of cognitive development that characterize any child's understanding of the world, including his or her sexual conceptualizations (Goldman & Goldman, 1982). More specifically, the thoughts of children between the ages of 2 and 6 involve *preoperational thinking*. At this stage, children typically are egocentric, unable to reverse their thoughts, can focus only on one aspect of a problem at a time, and have problems with how "things" transform from one state to another. As a result, it may be difficult for them to comprehend how the baby they can readily see began as a sperm and an egg. Pictures or movies can help them visualize this process. Children's thinking during the elementary school years reflects *concrete operations*. They can now perform mental operations and use logic as long as it involves concrete objects from their environment. Within this stage, children gain the ability to classify objects and reverse their thinking. The limitations of this stage become obvious when parents have the "birds and the bees" talk but fail to speak in human terms, instead referring only to plants and animals. Children typically leave these talks with ideas that people behave sexually in ways similar to plants and/or animals. If the parent's talk was short on details, the child will happily and logically fill in any gaps, albeit inaccurately, from his or her own concrete experiences. Adolescents' thinking evolves toward *formal operations*. At this stage, thinking includes abstractions, possibilities, a growing comprehension of the steps of problem solving, and the ability to formulate hypotheses. Hence, the tenor of their thinking becomes similar to adults, but is still limited by a lack of actual life experiences. The effects of this cognitive stage on adolescent sexuality are quite notable and are explored in later chapters.

The second influence on children's sexual understanding is our culture's bias toward restricting children's exposure to any type of sexual information. Specifically, parents confronted with children's exploratory behavior or sexual questions usually react with avoidance, or even worse, punishment (Victor, 1980). Furthermore, although parents will spend long hours with their children teaching them about table manners, how to manage friendships, and proper hygiene, they typically limit discussions about reproduction to a single talk (Allgeier, 1992). Parents are not forthright about the information they give during this single discussion. They rarely describe sexual intercourse as it happens between men and women (Goldman & Goldman, 1982; Roberts, Kline, & Gagnon, 1978) and often rely on vague mechanical descriptions or plant analogies. To children whose thinking is very concrete at this point in their life, these explanations are confusing and leave them to develop their own, usually inaccurate, understanding of how reproduction occurs (Goldman & Goldman, 1982).

An examination of these understandings is instructive because it shows how children make interpretations about sexual and reproductive issues using whatever information is available to them. Goldman and Goldman (1982) delineated six forms of understanding after interviewing more than 800 children ages 5 to 15. *Geographers* are cognitively simplistic; they explain reproduction only by stating that the baby is inside the mother. *Manufacturers* picture babies as inserted into the mother by some nonsexual mechanism after they have been assembled outside the mother's body. *Agriculturists* probably make use of parents' plant analogies, they believe babies are the product of seeds planted in the soil. *Reporters* know reproductive facts, but are incapable of explaining them. *Miniaturists* conclude that the sperm or egg contain a fully developed, but very tiny baby that simply needs to be put in the mother to mature. Finally, *realists* possess a basic understanding of the reproductive process. Generally, most U.S. children lack an understanding of basic reproductive facts until age 11. As is shown here, this is not the result of a cognitive deficit but rather is due to parents' unwillingness to provide factual information.

Parental reluctance to provide information may be due in part to parents' discomfort (White, Wright, & Barnes, 1995), and in part to a mistaken belief that children are not capable of understanding sexual information. Research by Goldman and Goldman (1982) questions the validity of the assumption that children cannot comprehend sexual information. They compared children of different ages from Australia, England, North America, and Sweden. This comparison is noteworthy as Sweden is one of the most sexually open societies in the Western world (Allgeier, 1992; Weinberg, Lottes, & Shaver, in press). They found that the children from the English-speaking countries were considerably delayed in their understanding of sexual and reproductive issues when compared to the Swedish children. This delay was not due to differences in cognitive abilities. The North American children demonstrated the highest Piagetian abilities, but were the lowest in sexual thinking.

Parents in our society seem to be unaware that children learn about sexuality through different types of experiences. Children are just as receptive to nonverbal signals of discomfort and unease as they are to verbal signals of evasion. Hence, although parents may congratulate themselves about getting out of a "sticky" conversation about some sexual issue, the child correspondingly learns that certain life experiences are either not spoken about, or are linked with uncomfortable feelings. Similarly, if parents wait for children's questions about sexual issues, while initiating discussions about other important life matters, children may eventually feel that parents do not want to talk about sexual matters. Such family conversation rules are learned through repetition and most likely provide a powerful context for children's understanding of their own sexuality. Furthermore, although researchers have yet to examine this issue, these rules possibly limit the degree of influence parents have later in their children's development when adolescents begin engaging in sexual activity that carries a much greater risk of severe lifelong consequences.

Parents are not the only agents of sexual socialization. As children begin to attend school at age 6 or 7, they develop friendships with other children. These friendships provide additional influences on the sexual development and identity formation of children. Thorne and Luria's (1986) extensive field observations of elementary school children provide insight into how these influences operate. This insight begins with an understanding about how boys and girls differ in their friendship patterns. Boys interact in large cohesive groups that are active, competitive, aggressive, and take up large amounts of space during play. Boys' groups tend to build toward heightened and intense moments of shared arousal and excitement that reinforce their activities. Girls interact in shifting alliances of two and three individuals at a time. Girls are more likely to engage in turn-taking, stress cooperation, and focus on being nice. There is little casual mixing between boys and girls; gender segregation is the usual rule during unstructured time.

These gender-specific interaction patterns provide the context for certain types of sexual learning during the elementary school age years (Thorne & Luria, 1986). Emotional arousal in boys' groups is often brought about by rule breaking. A common form of rule breaking is using "dirty" words, which boys use casually and in ritualized games that emphasize their forbidden quality. They additionally engage in rule breaking by sharing pornographic materials in all-boy settings. These materials provide explicit examples of what is considered arousing by society. They contribute to boys' sexual fantasies and attitudes. The emotional arousal that accompanies rule breaking reinforces the all-male, interpersonal context that the boys are playing to in their transgressions. Hence, these incidents make concurrent contributions to boys' developing sexual self, male identity, and friendship bonds. They are also apt to lay the groundwork for peer influences on sexual behavior during adolescence.

Girls' groups are far less likely to engage in rule transgressions and are more likely to experience adult control when they do (Thorne & Luria, 1986). Instead, girls experience dyads and triads that shift in their membership. The emphasis within these small groups is not on rule breaking, but on who is and who is not a friend, how to be a good friend, and how to dissolve and maintain relationships. Best friends share secrets, feelings, and engage in overt displays of physical intimacy, especially when compared to boys. Friendship bonds are often built upon giggling sessions where guarded information is exchanged. Romance stories, instead of pornography, are shared during these interchanges. Although it is plausible these stories contain some sexual content, most likely they lack the specificity common to boy's interactions. These experiences provide girls with far more experience in intimacy, emotional management, and relationship skills.

Contrasting the two experiences demonstrates different sequences in the development of early sexuality (Thorne & Luria, 1986). Boys experience the sexually explicit before exposure to intimate interactions. For girls, the reverse is true. They gain practice in intimacy skills before exposure to the sexually explicit.

Boys and girls of elementary school age use ritualized activities to experience a measure of cross-sex interaction (Thorne & Luria, 1986). Opposite sex, third parties serve as go betweens for same-sex groups to test the romantic interests of individuals. Messages are delivered by these third parties in a way that individuals receive them in a group. The immediate peer group provides the appropriate meaning for and agenda behind these messages. Their interpretations have a distinct sexual overtone and are used to help define sexual scripts characteristic of emerging adolescents.

Boys and girls of this age also engage in cross-sex teasing rituals. These include boys and girls chasing one another, frequently with a "threat" of kissing the person if caught. Same-sex peers are often called on for help when the chase ensues. When kissing or touching results from these chases, the individual who is "caught" is seen as polluted in some way (given "cooties") by the group, the individual, or both. These activities make additional contributions to developing sexual scripts, the importance of which is best stated by Thorne and Luria (1986):

> rituals of teasing, chasing, and pollution heighten the boundaries between boys and girls. They also convey assumptions which get worked into later sexual scripts: (1) that girls and boys are members of distinctive, opposing, and sometimes antagonistic groups; (2) that cross gender (sex) contact is potentially sexual and contaminating, fraught with both pleasure and danger; and (3) that girls are more sexually-defined (and polluting) than boys. (pp. 187–188)

A THEORETICAL MODEL

Using these findings from children as a basis for theoretical implications for adolescent sexuality carries a certain level of risk and must be done with the realization of the limited scope of this body of research. Knowledge and science, however, progress on hypotheses and therefore I advance several. These hypotheses are based on the heretofore largely untested assumption that normal early childhood experiences lay a salient foundation for the development of adolescent sexuality.

First, parents are the primary sexual socialization agents of their children, and many parents reflect the larger society's feelings that sexual information should be kept from children for as long as possible. This parental orientation contributes to children developing an understanding of sexuality that is permeated with a sense that it is forbidden, mysterious, and conceivably rewarding; and large-scale ignorance and misconceptions about sexual issues for the child. These messages and misconceptions become an integral part of the sexual script that children take with them into adolescence.

Second, parental evasions, incomplete descriptions, active distancing, and reluctance to take charge of teaching their children about sexuality are hypothesized to establish family sexual discussion rules. These rules regulate the flow of sexual information within the family. All family members are aware of these rules even if they are not explicitly stated. Because of their evolution and repetition for more than a decade, these rules are difficult to change, even when parents perceive a need, such as when puberty triggers worries about future sexual activities. Furthermore, when family discussion rules restrict children's access to parents as sources of sexual information, the rules weaken parental ability to influence adolescent sexual involvement because parents' directive role in sexual matters during childhood was correspondingly weak. When parents fail to cultivate family discussion rules that allow them to discuss sexual topics with their children, they put themselves at an especially great risk for an inability to influence their adolescents' sexual behavior when they compete more with other socialization influences such as peers.

Thorne and Luria's (1986) research suggests additional hypotheses. First, I hypothesize that same-sex peer interactions during childhood help to define what will be sexually arousing during adolescence and adulthood. Furthermore, the fact that these definitions evolve in same-sex, as opposed to cross-sex, interactions contributes to misunderstandings about sexual cues sent or perceived between single males and females, and difficulties in sexual communication in general between partners. Additionally, the same-sex context of this early learning lays the groundwork for future influence by peers in sexual expression. Finally, I believe that the childhood activities described by Thorne and Luria (1986) demonstrate ways in which the development of gender and sexual scripts are strongly intertwined. Engaging in rule breaking among boys and spinning of romantic fantasies among girls with same-sex friends provide concurrent contributions to gender and sexual script rules that help to tie these two scripts together. Thus, defining one's maleness or femaleness in adolescence and young adulthood will be strongly intertwined with definitions of one's sexuality.

Figure 2.1 represents my model that summarizes and expands the hypotheses. The model contains two outcome variables. The first is sexual knowledge. This construct represents children's basic understanding of sexual interactions, related biological processes, and their possible outcomes. It is the basis for the meaning the child will assign to gestures and life experiences that have sexual undertones. This construct is influenced by children's expectations about male and female roles and becomes a part of the sexual self as the child moves toward adolescence. More

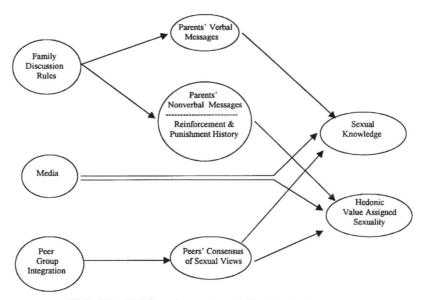

FIG. 2.1. *Childhood sexual socialization influences.*

specifically, it is the seminal foundation of adolescents' understanding of the context and components of their sexual roles.

Children will organize and integrate their sexual knowledge into cognitive schemas. The schemas will fluctuate as new knowledge is obtained and either assimilated into the existing schema or accommodated into a new schema. This does not mean that knowledge in these schemas will be adult like in its logic or clarity. The organization of the knowledge will reflect the stage of cognitive development of the child. Because the ability to examine one's own thinking as a process separate from one's self does not take place until adolescence, younger children will be unable to fully evaluate their knowledge for inconsistencies. Hence, children can, for example, come to the conclusion that conception and fetal development occurs outside a mother's body (Goldman & Goldman, 1982).

Boys' sexual knowledge will be somewhat different from that of girls, the result of differential socialization experiences that have been described. Boys and girls are treated differently from birth by their parents (see Ruble & Martin, 1998, for a review). Additionally, Thorne and Luria's (1986) findings show that male and female preadolescent exposure to sexually influenced knowledge and experiences stand in contrast to one another. These different experiences likely result in gender differences in sexual knowledge that become especially apparent at the end of childhood.

The second outcome variable reflects the hedonic value children assign to their sexual knowledge and experiences. Stated another way, this is the degree of positivity or negativity that children associate with specific sexual issues. The assigned hedonic valence is separate from the content of children's knowledge; instead it captures the emotional quality that flavors their knowledge. For example, when parents are confronted with a preschool son who is touching his genitals, their response about where and if this is appropriate behavior will have content and feeling components. Children will likely internalize the content of the stated rules in this circumstance, as well as the emotional tenor of the message. This latter portion of the parental message additionally becomes a part of the child's sexual self and influences later sexual roles by pairing emotional reactions with particular aspects of role enactments.

Both of these outcomes are hypothesized to be influenced by three sources of socialization. The first source is the children's parents. Three constructs represent the process of parents' socialization attempts. The first is the verbal content of parents' sexual talk to their children. This is a broadly conceptualized variable, capturing both direct references to sexual issues, such as explanations for how a family friend becomes pregnant or why boys and girls are interested in kissing, as well as indirect references to sexuality, such as comments made about nudity in the home. Parents' verbal content directly influences children's sexual knowledge.

Parents' sexual messages, however, also contain nonverbal messages. Parents' affect influences the development of children's social interaction and children are likely to closely monitor the affect of their parents (Radke-Yarrow, Zahn-Waxler, & Chapman, 1983). This means that they will attend not only to what is said, but how it is said or, stated another way, the emotional valence that accompanies the parental message's content. Moreover, parents will often respond to their children's sexual statements and questions with either reinforcement or punishment. Sometimes these will be strong parental reactions, at other times they will be weak. These parental actions are part of the nonverbal behaviors to which children attend, and thus become a part of their sexual hedonic valence.

The type of verbal and nonverbal messages parents send is influenced by the family sexual discussion rules that parents establish (see Fig. 2.1). Thus, there are paths in the model from family discussion rules to both parents' verbal and nonverbal messages. Although families will have discussion rules for the transmission of general information (Kantor & Lehr, 1975), I believe they have special rules for the transmission of sexual information. This is because society assigns a special status to sexuality and suggests that sexual information to children should be restricted. Many parents adopt these societal standards and assume that children should be kept ignorant of sexual issues.

Although I hypothesize that family discussion rules influence parents' verbal and nonverbal messages, I believe that parents will have greater success controlling their verbal messages than they will their nonverbal messages. Unintended nonverbal influences are apt to "leak" from parents. In other words, parents may take pains to filter the content of their sexual messages, but will either not modify their nonverbal behaviors, or will be unsuccessful at completely channeling them in the intended direction. This in turn will influence the development of children's sexual knowledge and hedonic valence. For instance, young children may ask parents if it is permissible to touch the parents' genitals. Parents may attempt to answer such a request in a manner that would be congruent with the sexual discussion rules of the family, but will probably feel uncomfortable with the request no manner how they frame their response. Children will attend not only to the content of what they are told in this interaction, but will also attend to the emotions that accompany the message. Hence, nonverbal behaviors have a path to the hedonic value outcome variable, whereas verbal content has a path to sexual knowledge.

As has been shown, when children interact with other children in schools and in neighborhoods, they encounter another influential socialization group—peers. Thorne and Luria's (1986) study demonstrates that peer groups form consensus about meanings ascribed to different sexual stimuli. This meaning is the interpretation given to what society has deemed sexual cues. Boys' consensus evolves out of a large group process that involves rule breaking and group solidarity. For example, as boys gather in a group to view an illicitly obtained pornographic movie, they are most likely exposed to an unrealistic depiction of gender roles and sexual interaction. Sharing in this experience, and later talking about it with one another, solidifies the sexual messages to which they were exposed. Girls interact in smaller dyads and triads and focus on stories where romance is a major theme and sexual interpretation is a minor chord. Thus, the sexual content focused on by each sex is different. Nonetheless, in these interactions, both boys and girls come to some consensus about the meaning given to sexual interactions and cues, and how they fit into gender and sexual roles. The meaning will contain both sexual content and the hedonic value assigned to the content. Hence, there are direct paths from peer consensus to both constructs.

How well a child is integrated into a peer group will influence the extent to which peers' consensus influences their sexual knowledge and hedonic valence. Children who are highly integrated into a group will be more likely to adopt the views of a group when compared to children who are not as much a part of that group. Integration provides reinforcers and punishments from immediate friends for viewpoints expressed and sexually related behaviors engaged in. This interaction will shape the kinds of influence peers have. Stated more simply, children who are better integrated will be more susceptible to peer influences.

The third socialization force hypothesized to influence the two outcome variables is the media. Children spend a large amount of time viewing television. Estimates indicate that children are exposed to an average of 4 hours of viewing a day by age 4. By the time they graduate from high school, television viewing will capture more hours of their lives than any other activity except sleeping (Singer, 1983). This is not limited to regular children's programming. Many families possess VCRs, thus many children can watch repeatedly favorite movies or shows.

Although links between television viewing and children's sexual knowledge and hedonic value have not been established, investigations have focused on the effects of viewing on children's concepts of gender. The traditional images and role portrayal used by the media, with accompanying emotional scripts, have an effect on children's understanding of gender (Ruble & Martin, 1998). Television viewing has been linked to how children view male and female roles because many of these shows are traditional in their portrayal of how men and women interact. Younger children may be especially susceptible to the effects of this exposure since they often have difficulty differentiating reality from fantasy. Given this large dose of exposure, it is easy to hypothesize that this visual medium affects the sexual knowledge and hedonic value of the sexuality of children. In this way, the media imparts meaning, and organizes behaviors and gestures into larger possible sexual roles.

Eventually, the sexual knowledge of children, paired with the hedonic value assigned to this knowledge, contributes to early adolescent sexual role enactment. At the time of adolescence, the child has experienced more than a decade's exposure to sexual information from parents, peers, and the media. This exposure carries meaning assigned to behaviors and is organized into possible sexual roles for adolescents and adults. The hedonic value assigned to different parts of these roles influences later sexual role enactment in two ways. First, it serves as one influence on the eventual self evaluation adolescents will engage in when enacting sexual roles.

Second, it helps to form emotional responses in later sexual role enact-ment. Sexual roles and scripts will include emotional responses to partic-ular behaviors such as being flirted with, kissed, or caressed. Emotional responses will be influenced by the hedonic value given to a particular sexual behavior. For instance, a prolonged gaze from a potential romantic partner will elicit one type of emotional response, being asked out for a date a different one. Although temporally more proximate forces also influence this role enactment, I posit that the foundation of these roles can be found, in part, in these earlier childhood experiences. The more proxi-mate forces are the focus of the next chapter.

3

The Sexuality
of
Early Adolescence

The previous chapter focused on early and foundational influences on the development of adolescents' sexuality. Different facets of early adolescent lives, however, have stronger effects than these earlier experiences. As is seen here, many of these facets help to shape their developing sexuality. This chapter reviews empirical findings about these forces. Biological changes, an important hallmark of adolescence, are the first source of influence considered. The social influences of family, peers, and dating partners are then reviewed. Finally, I examine different individual characteristics of adolescent. It is important, however, to understand how many adolescents are coitally active to set the stage for investigating these influences. Thus, I first review the scope of adolescent sexual activity.

THE SCOPE OF ADOLESCENT
SEXUAL ACTIVITY

Adolescents engage in a wide range of sexual behaviors that include kissing, fondling, oral–genital contact, and coitus. This section examines how widespread coital behavior is for this age group. Researchers have largely focused on coital rates because of the potential of resulting pregnancies. To this end, national probability surveys have established rates of intercourse among youth in general and different ethnic and gender subgroups in particular. Zelnick and Shah (1983) were among the first to use this approach. In their 1979 survey, they found that 50% of the female teens ages 15 to 19 years, and 70% of the males ages 17 to 21, had experienced sexual intercourse. The average age for first coitus was 16.2 years for girls and 15.7 years for boys. Data collected in 1988 indicated that by age 15, 25% of the females and 33% of the males had experienced coitus (B. Miller & Moore, 1990). By age 19, coital rates were at 80% for females and 86% for males.

There is a popular perception that these rates have continuously and dramatically increased over time. In fact, the late 1960s and early 1970s saw real and sizable increases in the proportion of White and Black teens engaging in sexual intercourse, often referred to as coital rate, although Blacks had higher rates than Whites throughout this period (Hoefferth, Kahn, & Baldwin, 1987).[1] During the 1980s, however, the rate of increase slowed and eventually plateaued, with coital rates for Black teens changing prior to coital rates for White teens (Hoefferth et al., 1987; Sonnerstein, Pleck, & Leighton, 1991). The plateau in coital rates continued throughout the early and mid-1990s (Upchurch, Levy-Storms, Sucoff, & Aneshensel, 1998; Warren et al., 1998) until 1997 when the Centers for Disease Control reported an 11% decrease from 1991 rates in the percentage of adolescents who had experienced coitus (Morbidity & Mortality Weekly Report, 1998). The change was not uniform; decreases occurred among male but not female youth as a group, and among White and Black but not Hispanic adolescents.

A corresponding popular perception that a greater number of teens experience coitus at younger ages is warranted. Hoefferth et al. (1987) reported significant increases across time in the coital rates of young girls ages 12 to 14 years. Similarly, Sonnerstein et al. (1991) found that among adolescent males in 1988, 5% of the 13-year-olds, 11% of the 14-year-olds, and 21% of the 15-year-olds had experienced coitus. Ethnic and racial differences were also evident—Black males were about 2 years ahead of White and Hispanic males in their sexual intercourse experience. A surprising 35% of the Black males age 14 or younger had engaged in

---

[1]This is typically measured by estimating the proportion of adolescents who have engaged in sexual intercourse compared to those who have not.

coitus. Other researchers report parallel results. Day (1992), using 1979 data, found that Black male youth, with an average age of 14.3 years at first intercourse, were younger than Hispanic or White males, and Black, Hispanic, or White females. Additionally, Black females averaged a half-year younger age at first intercourse than White females. Latino males of non-Mexican descent preceded Hispanic males of Mexican descent in their average age of first coitus by a full year, although comparison of females from these two groups showed no differences.

Data from 1990 to 1995 reveal similar patterns (Warren et al., 1998). Black male adolescents' median age for first intercourse ranged from 13 to 13.6 years during this period. This was significantly younger than White (ranged from 16.3 to 16.7 years) and Hispanic (15.6 to 15.9 years) male adolescents. It was also significantly younger than the age reported for Black female adolescents (15.5 to 15.9 years). Similar to patterns from earlier years, there were no differences between Whites and Hispanics in their median age for first coitus.

The higher rates and lower ages for first coitus among Blacks raise the question of whether this may be the result of the disproportionate numbers of this ethnic group living in poverty. Poverty represents a pervasive influence in individuals' lives that is associated with a number of potentially undesirable outcomes. Undoubtedly, analysis by poverty or social class aggregates entire sets of variables that will be teased apart in future research. Nonetheless, such comparisons are telling. The findings from Clark, Zabin, and Hardy's (1984) investigation exemplify this concern. They examined the sexual activity of a nonrandom sample of urban, inner-city Black males who were in Grades 7 to 12. Of these males, 65% reported they first engaged in intercourse at or before age 12, and 23% reported they began their intercourse experience at age 9 or younger. The mean age for first coitus was 11.8 years. Hogan and Kitagawa (1985) similarly found that lower class Black adolescents were much more likely to have engaged in coitus than middle and upper class Black adolescents in a random sample of Black youth from Chicago.

These results suggest that differences between racial and ethnic groups may reflect differences in socioeconomic conditions. Few investigators making ethnic and racial comparisons have controlled for socioeconomic status (SES). Hence, it is difficult to know if younger ages for coital activity are due to different role expectations across ethnic subcultures, disproportionate numbers of minorities living in poverty, or an interaction of these two phenomenons. The work of Furstenberg, Morgan, Moore, and Peterson (1987) represents a singular exception. They made Black–White comparisons of coital transition rates, or the number of individuals first experiencing sexual intercourse, using the 1981 National Survey of Children. Race effects were only slightly affected by family income and mothers' education, and not affected by the employment status of mothers or fathers. The authors concluded that socially disadvantage conditions have a significant, but small effect on racial differences. Even with this conclusion, it is important to emphasize that negative outcomes of teen sexual involvement, such as pregnancy (Jorgensen, 1993), and sexually transmitted diseases (STDs; Aral & Holmes, 1991), are much more prevalent among those who live in poverty compared to those who are from the middle or upper classes.

Once teens engage in sexual intercourse they continue this sexual activity. Sonnerstein et al.'s (1991) report on male coital activity using national probability data is revealing. Respondents averaged five sexual partners since their first coital act, with older males claiming more partners than younger males, and Blacks reporting more partners than Hispanics and Whites. When years since first coitus were controlled, however, racial and ethnic differences in lifetime sexual partners were not significant. A parallel pattern emerged for current sexual activity. For the 12 months prior to the survey, male adolescents averaged close to two sexual partners, with Blacks reporting more partners than Whites. Racial differences disappeared when controlling for years since first coitus and age. Similarly, there were no racial differences in frequency of coitus in the previous month, an average of just under three times, although older males experienced higher frequencies than younger males.

RELATED ISSUES

Early coital activity can result in two, largely unwanted outcomes, pregnancies and STDs. Although neither is the primary focus of this book, a brief overview is in order (see Jorgensen, 1993; Leukefeld & Haverkos, 1993, for in-depth reviews on these topics).

Coital rates for teens in the United States are comparable to other developed Western countries (Hayes, 1987; Jones et al., 1985). Unfortunately, they also earn the distinction of having the highest adolescent pregnancy rate. In 1974, 9.9% of the females between the ages of 15 and 19 became pregnant. This proportion increased to 11% by 1980 and remained fairly steady through 1993 (K. Moore, 1996).

Many of these teens choose to give birth. In 1996, 75.9% of the births (757,038 babies) to girls ages 19 and under were to unmarried teenage girls, with 540,587 births to unwed girls under the age of 17 (Ventura, Martin, Curtin, & Mathews, 1998). The number of unmarried female teens who gave birth increased by 21.1% between 1986 and 1996 (Ventura et al., 1998). It is therefore evident that most of the teens who carry their pregnancies to term do not marry; nor do they offer their child for adoption. Instead, they become single mothers with the accompanying life challenges (Jorgensen, 1993). A significant number of teens choose to abort their pregnancies. In 1991, 38% of all pregnancies to female adolescents ages 15 to 19 ended in abortion (K. Moore, 1996). If these trends continue, an estimated 18% of all teenage girls will experience at least one pregnancy during their adolescent years (Henshaw & Van Vort, 1989).

The statistics for adolescent cases of STDs are equally compelling. Teens accounted for 25% of the 3 million new cases of STDs in 1985 (K. Moore, 1989). Rates vary, however, by specific STD. For example, 29% of the reported cases of gonorrhea in 1990 were among teenages 15 to 19 (Leukefeld & Haverkos, 1993) and current estimates suggest that girls in this age group have the highest rate of diagnosed gonorrheal infection when compared to any other group (Sexually Transmitted Disease Surveillance, 1996). National rates of infection for chlamydia are not recorded by the Centers for Disease Control (CDC), but regional studies suggest that teenage girls have consistently higher rates of infection than do older women. Chlamydia is a particularly insidious disease. It is often asymptotic until the infection is advanced, and it can produce fertility problems that young women will only realize when they attempt to voluntarily conceive later in life. In general, however, STD rates are higher among males and minorities when compared to females and Whites, and are especially prominent among those who live in poverty conditions (Aral & Holmes, 1991; DiClemente, 1993)

Rates of Acquired Immune Deficiency Syndrome (AIDS) are of great concern because infection by the Human Immunodeficiency Virus (HIV) runs the risk of eventually resulting in death. Although the actual number of adolescent AIDS cases is relatively low, figures are misleading. Individuals can be infected with the HIV for upwards of 6 years before showing AIDS symptoms. Furthermore, contrary to other age cohorts, heterosexual transmission is more likely among adolescents (DiClemente, 1993). In 1990, it accounted for 21% of the AIDS cases while homosexual or bisexual contact accounted for only 16% of the cases. Cumulative data

from the CDC indicate that girls ages 13 to 19 years are at a much greater
risk. While only 4% of the male teens with AIDS in this age group have
been the result of heterosexual contact, this was true for a startling 53% of
the female teens with AIDS (HIV–AIDS Surveillance Report, 1997).
Overall, HIV infection patterns among adolescents seem to be following
that of other STDs (Aral & Holmes, 1991).

Conclusions About Early Adolescent Sexual Activity

Taken as a whole, these results suggest that there exist normative role
expectations that teens will engage in coitus and that ethnicity influences
the age at which this will initially occur. Blacks engage in coitus at
younger ages then other groups, and Furstenberg et al.'s (1987) results
suggest that this difference is only partially the result of the disproportionate number of Blacks living in poverty. Subsequent coital activity for adolescent males, nonetheless, is more likely influenced by the age of first
intercourse than by ethnicity. It seems that teens find sexual activity
rewarding and want to repeat their experience. Moreover, teens most certainly experience role expectations connected with their nonvirgin status
that influence them to continue their coital activity. This latter hypothesis
may partially explain why it is that virtually all teens whose first coital
activity involves force still initiate voluntary sexual activity later in their
adolescent years (K. Moore, Nord, & Peterson, 1989).

THE ROLE OF BIOLOGY

Because of the highly visible physiological changes that accompany it,
puberty is one of the most widely recognized signs of adolescence. It is a
stage when adolescents become fully capable of reproduction, the culmi-
nation of a process that began with conception (Dyk, 1993). The first indication that pubertal onset is near is a growth spurt, with girls averaging a
2-year earlier age of onset (normal range of 9.5 to 14.5 years) than boys
(normal range of 10.5 to 16 years). The first outward sign of puberty in
girls is the development of "breast buds," in boys an enlargement of the
testes and scrotum.

   A sequence of external and internal changes follow these initial stages
(Dyk, 1993). External changes in females include increases in breast size,
widening of the hips, and growth of pubertal hair. Male external changes

encompass widening of the shoulders, deepening of the voice, and growth of facial and pubertal hair. Internal changes to the reproductive organs also take place. The most noticeable outcome for females is menarche, or the start of menstrual cycles. Males lack a parallel hallmark, although some researchers use nocturnal emissions, or wet dreams, as a milestone of male development (cf. Zabin, Smith, Hirsch, & Hardy, 1986).

Although the sequence of pubertal stages varies little among adolescents, the age puberty begins, and the length of time it can take to progress through each of the stages, can vary a great deal. The age of menarche, or first menses, can range from 10 to 16.5 years, whereas nocturnal emissions can start between the ages of 12.5 and 16.5 (Dyk, 1993). In sharp contrast to sex differences in the average age of the prepubertal growth spurt, boys' average age of the commencement of pubertal development is only 6 months behind that of girls. The age of onset for menarche has gradually decreased over time; Dyk reported that over the course of 150 years it has dropped from 17 to 12.8 years.

External and internal changes are brought about by increases in the production of hormones 6 months to 1 year prior to the physical changes that accompany sexual development. Testosterone plays a major role in the physical development of adolescent males, as do estrogens in adolescent females. Contrary to popular understanding, however, females also produce testosterone and males also produce estrogens, although there are differences in concentration levels (Dyk, 1993; Udry & Talbert, 1988). For instance, testosterone levels are the same for boys and girls prior to puberty, but after puberty male levels increase by a factor of 10 to 20, whereas female levels merely double (Udry & Talbert, 1988).

Although the noted symbolic interactionist Willard Waller (1951) declared that sexual behavior was biologically driven but socially defined, few scholars have theoretically or empirically considered that these biological changes may influence sexual activity during adolescence. Findings from recent investigations, however, bring to question explanations that fail to incorporate biological influences. Researchers interested in the role of biology in adolescent sexual exploration have taken different approaches.

The first approach centered on the relation between pubertal development and sexual exploration. Some investigators have tested to see if dating and pubertal development are related to one another as most sexual activity takes place in dating. This research does not support a relation between these variables. Gargiulo, Attie, Brooks-Gunn, and Warren (1987) found that menarche status was related to dating behavior in a group of female ballet dancers, but not in a group of female nondancers. Menarche can result in the termination of a ballet career due to the accompanying physical changes, but is unlikely to have a similar effect among nondancers. Thus, they concluded that menarche has social implications but is not related to dating behavior independent of those implications. Similarly, Dornbusch et al. (1981) used a national data set to show that age had a significant, but moderate relation to dating when controlling for pubertal development. The relation between pubertal development and dating was much weaker when controlling for age. They also concluded that there was little association between dating and pubertal development. This line of research can be criticized, however, because it focuses on dating and not sexual activity. Although most sexual activity between adolescents occurs in the context of a dating relationship, not all dating includes sexual activity. Hence, dating is a poor proxy as a measure of sexual involvement.

Examining bivariate relationships has shown a positive association between age at menarche and engaging in coitus for White and Black females using area (Udry, 1979) and nonrandom samples (Zabin et al., 1986). Similarly, early experiences of wet dreams among Black male youth are positively related to early coitus (Zabin et al., 1986). When these same relationships were tested simultaneously against other possible variables using regressions with a national data set, however, an association between age at menarche and coitus was not found for Black, female teens (Leigh, Weddle, & Loewen, 1988).

Some scholars have explored the association between pubertal development and sexual behavior by using a combination of coital status, developmental stage, and age. Age and developmental status were entered into regression models at different steps to capture different aspects of youth's pubertal experience. Udry and Billy (1987) argued that the variance contained in measures of pubertal developmental based on external changes reflects not only physiological development, but also social reactions to that development. For instance, the beginning of breast development in an early female adolescent alerts males, especially older males, to a young girl's changing status. These researchers felt that using age in the analysis would separate social effects from biological effects. They found pubertal development related to the coital activity of White and Black females in the expected direction, but not so for White males. They were unable to test for effects for the Black males because of the small number in their sample. Flannery, Rowe, and Gulley (1993) and Rosenbaum and Kandel (1990) found similar results for the girls in their studies, although they also found age to be positively related to sexual activity for boys. Even with the more consistent findings, this approach can be criticized as age and pubertal status are so intertwined that it may be difficult to artificially separate their effects (Flanner et al., 1993) and may result in collinearity problems (Tabachnick & Fidell, 1996).

Udry and his colleagues (Udry, Billy, Morris, Groff, & Raj, 1985; Udry & Talbert, 1988; Udry, Talbert, & Morris, 1986) have undertaken the most stringent test for biological influences on adolescent sexuality. They drew blood samples from a random sample of White public school students in Grades 8, 9, and 10 students to determine levels for an array of androgens and estrogens. They also assessed different measures of sexuality, including motivation and coital activity. Testosterone had a direct relationship to adolescent males sexual behavior independent of social effects. Testosterone also had a similar direct relationship to adolescent females' sexual motivation, but was not related to their coital activity. Udry and his colleagues concluded that biological influences for females are mediated or filtered by social controls, thereby suggesting that social controls for sexual behavior are stronger for females than males.

Research by Newcomer and Udry (1984) further intimates that heredity may provide an additional, indirect influence on females' youthful sexual activity. They found mothers' reports of their own adolescent sexual activity positively related to their daughters' reports of their sexual activity. Mothers' sexual attitudes, parental control attempts, or sexual communication did not mediate this association with their daughters. They also found a relation between age of pubertal development for biological mothers and daughters, but not for stepmothers, and noted the link between early menarche and early sexual activity for both generations. Because mothers' youthful sexual activity was not associated with the social processes normally thought to be connected with children's sexual socialization, but concurrent links were found between generations for age of menarche and sexual activity, Newcomer and Udry hypothesized that teens' sexual involvement was explained in part by a hereditary component.

Conclusions About Biological Influences

Puberty brings about physiological changes that result in adolescents' ability to reproduce. When such changes bring about noticeable shifts in appearance, they undoubtedly serve as markers for individuals in the adolescent's social environment announcing that the youth has achieved a new maturation level. The recognition of this new status triggers a variety of social–sexual role expectations from peers and parents. Parents may react to the development of hips and breasts in their daughter by establishing new rules for how to interact with boys while those same boys may give the girl attention that has a different quality from the past. In addition to social influences, the work of Udry and his colleagues presents strong evidence for a biological influence on early adolescent sexuality during this developmental period. This directly influences coital activity in the case of males, and is mediated by social controls in the case of females. In other words, increases in testosterone production appears to directly increase the chance of engaging in sexual intercourse among males, but brings about social reactions of parents and peers in girls. The stronger controls for girls may reflect greater consequences that unintended pregnancy has for them and their parents in particular, as well as for society as a whole. Thus, biology plays a role in the developing sexuality of the early adolescent, but is not its sole determinant.

THE ROLE OF FAMILY

Parents serve as the major socialization agents of their children (Gecas & Seff, 1990). However, during childhood, as postulated in chapter 2, parents may not use the same socialization strategy for their child's sexuality as they may in other areas of the child's life. They may limit the amount of sexual information they have given their child and conveyed their discomfort with discussing the topic (White et al., 1995). This potentially results in a deficit in children's sexual knowledge and may link a negative valence to certain aspects of their developing sexuality. In these instances, family discussion rules preclude open discussions of sexual topics during the formative years that build toward adolescence. This earlier socialization process begs the questions of what kind of influence parents have on the sexual activity of their early adolescents. Investigators into this relationship have used two categories of variables to discern the role of parents: family structure and status variables, and family interaction variables.

Family Structure

One of the most consistent findings across cross-sectional studies is that teens from single-parent families are more likely to be coitally active than teens from intact families. This finding has held when controlling for other variables using regional and national probability data sets for Whites, Hispanics, and Blacks (Billy, Brewster, & Grady, 1994; Day, 1992; Forste & Heaton, 1988; Hogan & Kitagawa, 1985; Leigh et al., 1988; B. Miller & Bingham, 1989; Rosenbaum & Kandel, 1990; Upchurch et al., 1998). The single exception has been a finding that having one's father in the home increases the chance of a coital experience for older Black males (Day, 1992). Longitudinal investigations have also rendered findings consistent with the cross-sectional studies for White female adolescents, and, albeit somewhat more weakly for White male adolescents who live with single parents (Thornton & Camburn, 1987; Udry & Billy, 1987) but failed to support a risk for coitus for Black female youth (Udry & Billy, 1987). Children whose mothers remarry are also at greater risk for coitus when compared to children from intact families, but it is not as high as for those who live in single-parent families (Kinnaird & Gerrard, 1986; Thorton & Camburn, 1987; Upchurch et al., 1998).

Scholars have typically explained this finding by hypothesizing that single parents are less able to monitor their children than are two parents, and underscore this point by citing the need of many single parents to work outside of the home. This explanation, nonetheless, has remained largely untested.

Two studies provide possible insight into this finding. Newcomer and Udry's (1987) longitudinal analysis of their White early adolescent sample allowed a comparison between youths who, throughout the course of the study, either lived in a single- or two-parent family, and youths who experienced a parental divorce. They found that more boys who experienced a divorce engaged in coitus than did boys from stable two- or single-parent families. On the other hand, girls from any single-parent situation were more likely to engage in sexual intercourse than girls from two-parent families. Newcomer and Udry speculated that boys who experience parental divorce, and the accompanying disruption, may act out sexually. Alternatively, these authors felt that girls were at higher risk for early coitus just by being in a single-parent household, independent of parental conflict or divorce.

This latter finding may be mediated by a third variable—parental dating. Peterson, Moore, Furstenberg, and Morgan (1985, cited in Strouse & Fabes, 1987) found single mothers who dated had daughters at risk for sexual intercourse, but daughters from nondating single mothers were no more likely to be sexually active at an early age than daughters two-parent families. In a more stringent test of this hypothesis, Whitbeck, Simons, and Kao (1994) used structural equation modeling to demonstrate that the dating habits of single mothers positively and directly influenced their sons' precoital and coital involvement. The effect of their dating on their daughters was indirect—it increased daughters' permissive attitudes which then increased their sexual involvement. These findings suggest that parental modeling, rather than parental monitoring, may be the key variable responsible for previous findings that only asked about family structure.

Family structure includes the presence of siblings. The relationship between their presence and adolescent sexual activity is not completely clear when examining past research. Having a large number of brothers and sisters, or having a sister who has been a teenage mother, increases the chances of coital activity for Black females (Hogan & Kitagawa, 1985). In contrast, the presence of large numbers of siblings was negatively related to coital experience in a White, predominantly Mormon sample (B. Miller, Higginson, McCoy, & Olson, 1987). Similarly, possessing an older sister reduces the chances for early sex for male and female adolescents, as is true of having an older brother for females (Rosenbaum & Kandel, 1990), although other researchers have failed to find similar relationships (B. Miller & Bingham, 1989; Thornton & Camburn, 1987).

Having an unmarried, older adolescent sister who has given birth puts younger sisters at risk for early sexual activity (East, 1996; East, Felice, & Morgan, 1993). Such younger sisters not only hold more accepting attitudes toward premarital sexuality, they also put less emphasis on educational acheivement and career goals, and engaged in more problem behaviors than similarly aged girls with older adolescent sisters who had not born children (East, 1996). As becomes clear in the remainder of this chapter, all of these are risk factors for early coital involvement. It is not surprising, then, that these younger sisters are also more likely to engage in sexual intercourse. The question of whether these findings can be attributable to the effects of the older sibling or to the effects of the family environment, however, is still unanswered.

The inconsistency in findings for sibling influence demonstrates a need for researchers to rethink how siblings effect a young adolescent's sexuality. Stronger and more consistent findings may be gained by focusing on different aspects of the sibling relationships such as closeness, aptness to model a sibling, and seeing a sibling as a potential sexual knowledge source. Nonetheless, East's (1996; East et al., 1993) research on younger sisters who have an older sibling who has given birth suggest that modeling of siblings may also be a factor for some families.

Family Environment

A family's SES can be considered a family environmental variable. Put another way, the socioeconomic conditions in which a family lives establishes a particular context that helps define family interaction. Using a composite SES index shows that Black females who live in poverty are more likely to engage in early coital activity than Black females of higher social class (Hogan & Kitagawa, 1985). Most investigators have not used composite indexes, however, and have relied on single-item indicators of SES. Higher family income is related to the greater likelihood of coitus for Mexican Americans (Aneshensel, Fielder, & Becerra, 1989), but lower likelihood for adolescents in general after controlling for race and ethnic effects (Bingham, Miller, & Adams, 1990). In most investigations, however, income and employment have not been associated with teen coital activity (Leigh et al., 1988; Thornton & Camburn, 1987; Udry & Billy, 1987).

Parental education level is also an indicator of SES. Parental education has a stronger relation to early coital activity than type of employment. The direction of the relation, however, has not always been consistent. Analysis of national probability and smaller randomly generated data sets reveals that parents' education level has a negative effect on their offsprings' sexual behavior, with mothers' education having a stronger relationship than fathers' education (Bingham et al., 1990; Leigh et al., 1988; B. Miller & Bingham, 1989; Thornton & Camburn, 1987). Investigators who found this conjectured that educated parents model and reinforce high educational aspirations in their children, which by themselves are negatively related to early coital exploration. This relation may not be a strong one relative to other variables; some researchers found that the relation of parental education to adolescent coital activity does not hold under more stringent, multivariate tests (Cvetkovich & Grote, 1980; Forste & Heaton, 1988; Mott, Fondell, Hu, Kowaleski-Jones, & Menaghan, 1996; Udry & Billy, 1987; Upchurch et al., 1998), or only has a slight relationship (Thornton & Camburn, 1987).

Additionally, analyses focusing on ethnic and gender subgroups have produced contradictory findings. Similar to other researchers, Day (1992) found maternal or paternal education associated with a lower probability of coital activity for Mexican American females, non-Mexican American Latino males, and White females, as did Leigh et al. (1988) for Black females. Day further reported that maternal or paternal education associated with increases in the probability of coital activity for Mexican

American males and females, Black males, and White males. Even with these contradictions, the overall relation between parental education and teen coital activity in Day's results was weak.

Conclusions About Structural and Environmental Variables

The accumulated evidence on family structure and environmental variables points to a conclusion that these variables are not strongly related to adolescent coital activity, with the possible exception of parental marital status. As demonstrated, even parental marital status is probably mediated by parents' divorce-related conflict, or child-to-parent modeling, variables that are more characteristic of family interaction. The weak and inconsistent findings may reflect the distal relation of these variables to the sexual socialization of youth. Put another way, the sexual activity of teens may be more of a product of their direct interaction with their social environment, mediated by aspects of their personality. Family structure and environmental variables serve as poor indicators of these interactive processes.

Family Interaction

If parents are the primary socialization agents of their children, then it would stand to reason that parental attitudes and norms should be related to their child's sexual activity.[2] Stated another way, parental values should be passed on to adolescents through socialization. As Gecas and Seff (1990) said, "adolescence is a time of testing the effectiveness of childhood socialization" (p. 947). There is support for this conceptualization. Adolescents who believe that their parents would not be upset by their sexual activity, or that their parents approve of teen sexual involvement, are more likely to be coitally active (DiBalasio & Benda, 1990; Hovell et al., 1994; Small & Luster, 1994). Parents' liberal views of premarital sexual activity in general (Cvetkovich & Grote, 1980; Thornton & Camburn, 1987), and specific approval of sexual activity for their children, are further associated with teen coital activity (Baker, Thalberg, & Morrison, 1988). The same is true for general approval of adolescent deviant behav-

---

[2]Although there is theoretical agreement that socialization between parents and children is bi-directional, researchers have focused on parent-to-child effects. This past bias is evident in the review and in the following theoretical chapter.

ior (R. Jessor, Costa, Jessor, & Donovan, 1983). Additionally, there are indications that parents' own premarital experiences may influence their current attitudes. Mothers who experienced premarital pregnancy are more favorably disposed toward premarital sexual activity (Thornton & Camburn, 1987). Finally, teens may see their parents' premarital coital activity, premarital pregnancy, or cohabitation experiences as normative expressions separate from parental stated attitudes—all have positive effects independent of other parental variables (Hovell et al., 1994; Inazu & Fox, 1980; Thornton & Camburn, 1987).

The closeness and supportiveness of the parent–child relationship (Gecas & Seff, 1990; Weinstein & Thornton, 1989) mediate parental norms and values. Teens who feel close to those of their parents have attitudes similar to those of their parents (Taris, Semin, & Bok, 1998), and their sexual behavior is more consistent with their mothers' attitudes than teens who have more distant maternal relationships (Weinstein & Thornton, 1989). Similarly, sons whose parents hold traditional attitudes, and who spend time listening and discussing decisions with them, are less likely to be sexually experienced (K. Moore, Peterson, & Furstenberg, 1986). Daughters who experience support from their mothers are also less apt to engage in coitus (Inazu & Fox, 1980; R. Jessor et al., 1983). Moreover, sons and daughters who abstain from coital activity, or have a single coital partner and are consistent users of contraception, experience greater parental support than offspring who have multiple coital partners or who are inconsistent in their use of contraception (Luster & Small, 1994). Only one study has provided evidence contradictory to these findings and this investigation focused more on precoital than coital behaviors with a Hispanic sample (Christopher, Johnson, & Roosa, 1993).

Parental attempts to control adolescent behavior represent another important quality of parent–child interactions and are connected to teen sexual activity. Greater parental control has been associated with a lower probability of offspring's coital activity (Cvetkovich & Grote, 1980; Hogan & Kitagawa, 1985). Similarly, adolescents' evaluations of parental strictness are negatively related to sexual involvement for White and Hispanic youth (Hovell et al., 1994) and to coital frequency for intercity, Black male youth (Jemmott & Jemmott, 1992). Some researchers have found this to be a curvilinear relationship, with low and high levels of parental control linked to higher adolescent coital rates than moderate levels of parental control (R. Jessor et al., 1983; B. Miller, McCoy, Olson, & Wallace, 1986). As with the previous set of findings, only one study has failed to find a relation between these variables (Inazu & Fox, 1980).

Parental monitoring represents a third family interaction variable related to early adolescent sexual activity. Parental monitoring involves tracking the whereabouts of one's child, knowing and being aware of the friends with whom one's teen associates, and being cognizant of the activities in which one's offspring engages. Parents who monitor closely their early adolescent's daily activities have sons and daughter who are less apt to experience coitus than parents who engage in lower levels of monitoring (Luster & Small, 1994; Small & Luster, 1994). Parental monitoring is additionally associated with lower frequency of coitus and with a lower number of coital partners among Black and Hispanic youth (K. Miller, Forehand, & Kotchick, 1999).

One family interaction variable—parent–child communication—has received more attention than others. White et al. (1995) used canonical correlations to see if different sets of parental, familial, and child characteristics predicted parent–child discussions of specific sexual topics in a rural sample. In the first pattern, discussing a range of sexual topics including sexual values, interactions, fertility, and STDs, was related to parental comfort and willingness to talk about sexual issues, and for mothers, having open communication with their children. Not surprisingly, parents were more likely to discuss these topics as their children got older, began dating, and parents believed they had experienced sexual intercourse. These trends reflect the cultural bias toward restricting children's access to sexual information for as long as possible, as identified in chapter 2. Hence, parents begin to talk to their children about sex only when faced with the increased probability of their offspring becoming sexually active.

The other patterns of association demonstrated the pivotal role of parents' religious beliefs. In one pattern, religious parents who were comfortable with and willing to speak about sexual topics discussed issues of birth, conception, fertility, and abortion in the context of their religious beliefs but were less apt to address controlling sexual behavior, sexual feelings, saying no, birth control, and STDs. These parents held conservative attitudes about premarital sexual interaction. In contrast, nonreligious parents with more liberal premarital sexual attitudes limited their discussions to birth and conception and did not present a religious view of these issues. The final pattern was an interesting one. It involved religious mothers uncomfortable with and unwilling to discuss sexual topics. Their daughters were older and dating. These mothers presented religious teachings about sexuality without specific facts about sexuality. White et al.'s (1995) results hints at the diversity in family approaches to communication about sexual topics. They also demonstrate the influence parental values and standards play in shaping parent–child talks about sexuality.

Other investigations have focused on the relation between family communication and adolescent sexual activity. The public, practitioners, and researchers have continuously hypothesized that good parent–child communication will result in adolescents postponing their coital involvement. Findings, however, have been contradictory. Some evidence exists that parents and teens talk about sexual issues. The poor Black males in Clark et al.'s (1984) sample cited their parents as their major source of information about sexuality and birth control. T. Fisher (1986) found sexual attitude concordance between adolescents and parents who discussed a range of sexual topics. Similarly, Fox (1980), in a review of the early studies in this area, concluded that parent–child communication resulted in postponing coitus. She also found that past sexual communication and the quality of the mother–daughter relationship predicted more recent sexual communication (Fox & Inazu, 1980).

More recent and stringent tests have not always found such a relationship. Early and current parent–child sexual communication have not been associated with coital activity in ethnically diverse samples (Hovell et al., 1994; Inazu & Fox, 1980; Weinstein & Thornton, 1989) or only weakly and inconsistently related (K. Miller et al., 1999). In the same light, open family communication and problems in family communication were not predictive of sexual involvement for poor, Hispanic early adolescents (Christopher et al., 1993); nor was mother–daughter communication related to adolescent contraceptive use among a group of teens who used family planning clinics (Furstenberg, Herceg-Baron, Shea, & Webb, 1984). Work by Treboux and Busch-Rossnagel (1990) provides an exception. They found discussing sex with parents directly and positively predicted precoital sexual involvement for sons who were virgins. Parental discussions indirectly affected virginal daughters' precoital behaviors through the daughters' sexual attitudes.

The lack of consistency in results may be due to a multitude of reasons. First, parent–child communication might interact with parents' attitudes to produce an effect on youth's coital activity. K. Moore et al. (1986) found that reports of parent–child communication were related to lower coital activity for daughters only when parents held traditional premarital sexual attitudes. Certainly White et al.'s (1995) work suggests that parental values shape parents' sexual messages. Conclusions about this effect, however, must be made tentatively, the same parents in K. Moore et al.'s (1986) study had sons who were more apt to engage in sexual intercourse compared to parents who were more accepting of premarital sexual activity. Second, most parents rarely engage in direct communication about sexual matters (Fox, 1980; Goldman & Goldman, 1982) and, as hypothesized in chapter 2, may experience the tension between wanting to impart sexually relevant information while not having family sexual discussion rules that provide the means to do so. Several factors are predictive of their likelihood of talking to their adolescent about sexual issues including comfort level, a desire to talk, religious values, and personal sexual knowledge (Russo, Barnes, & Wright, 1991; White et al., 1995). Moreover, teens may not always be comfortable in discussing these issues with their parents (Fox & Inazu, 1980).

Finally, several methodological issues need to be considered. Findings may be contingent on who is asked about the communication. Newcomer and Udry (1984) found that mothers' reports of communication related to a decreased chance that their daughters were sexually active. This relationship did not hold when daughters were asked about the same communication!

Second, teens and parents do not always agree about the type of sex-related conversations they engaged in (Newcomer & Udry, 1984).

Third, the timing of some investigations of parent–child communication is suspect. Parents may communicate more as their offspring get older, and when they think their adolescent has become sexually active (K. Moore et al., 1986; White et al., 1995). Furthermore, the tenor of these conversations may change from previous ones by becoming more focused on practical matters connected with sexual activity such as how to obtain and use effective birth control (Fox & Inazu, 1980), how to control sexual behavior, or how to deal with sexual feelings (White et al., 1995). Finally, scholars have rarely acknowledged the different facets of communication in their investigations, including the use of nonverbal communication, the bi-directional quality of communication, and have too often relied on single item indicators of a very complicated interpersonal process. Given these problems, it is unclear if there is no relation between these variables or if the relation has yet to be discovered because of methodological limitations in past work.

Conclusions About Family Influences

The only family structure or environmental variable consistently related to early adolescent sexual behavior is parents' marital status. This appears to operate differently for male and female youth. Parallel to other research findings (Jurich & Jones, 1986), it seems male adolescents are more sensitive to the disruption and conflict that occurs between parents during the divorce process and that they may act out sexually during this time. Both adolescent sons and daughters, however, are apt to model their mother's dating and, possibly, sexual activities. Single mothers who date may be confronted with sexual issues that their offspring witness. This may spur different types of parent–child interactions than what occurs for adolescents of single mothers who do not date and for adolescents of two parent families. It is also conceivable that teens with mothers who date see coitus as a way of achieving an adult status similar to their mother.

Not surprisingly, the family interaction variables show a more consistent relationship to early adolescent coital involvement. Parental norms and values have an influence, but that influence seems to be mediated by qualities of the parent–child relationship: closeness, support, monitoring, and conflict. This conceptualization is consistent with empirical findings and theoretical developments in the parent–adolescent literature (see Gecas & Seff, 1990 for a review). The first two of these qualities have different themes. The concept of *closeness* reflects boundary issues between the parent and adolescent and is indicative of the emotional tenor of the relationship. Parental support refers to the degree of unconditional backing or patronage children receive. Support constitutes behaviors parents engage in rather than emotions they feel. Undoubtedly, these two constructs are related.

Parental control attempts, another class of parental behaviors, also play a role. There are different styles of parenting, all of which have a control component (Gecas & Seff, 1990). Unfortunately, the manner in which parental control has been measured does not allow a straightforward conclusion about what types of parenting styles are represented in the curvilinear relation control has to adolescent sexual involvement. It could be hypothesized that low control is characteristic of permissive parents, high control of authoritarian parents, and moderate control of authoritative parents. Similar to the findings reviewed in this chapter, other research points to an authoritative approach, with moderate control, and high closeness and support, as resulting in the greatest number of prosocial outcomes in early adolescents (Gecas & Seff, 1990). This same research points to higher numbers of problem behaviors connected with low or high control paired with low support.

Monitoring by parents influences their adolescents' sexual behaviors. There are three possible, noncompeting explanations for this. First, parents who closely monitor their sons and daughters activities may develop a sense of when it would be appropriate and effective to exert control over their children's behavior. Second, early adolescents whose parents monitor their activities are provided with a believable excuse for not complying with peers suggestions for engaging in questionable behavior: "No way am I going to do that, I'll get caught!" Third, parental monitoring may serve as an external marker of acceptability for behaviors adolescents consider engaging in: "I would get in so much trouble if I did this—and my parents would know!"

Thus, it would appear that parental norms are taken on as personal standards by early adolescents under conditions of parental support and closeness, monitoring, and with moderate levels of control. Communication must be involved in this, but the measures used to date have failed to find a consistent relation, probably because of the simplistic approach taken to measure this variable. Communicating about a range of sexual topics is more apt to occur, however, in families whose communicative environment is open and problem free, especially between mothers and their children (White et al., 1995). This implies that these families develop family sexual communication rules that allow the free flow of information between parents and their children. There may be a need to focus on communication longitudinally, to attempt to access its multiple dimensions, and to see if families develop a particular communication style over time when dealing with sexual issues.

THE ROLE OF PEERS

Peers are one of the other major socialization agents in adolescent's lives. Peer relationships are quite different from family relationships in that they are voluntary, involve equals, and are grounded in friendships (Gecas, 1981). Scholars of adolescence speculate that peers provide reinforcement and support for beliefs, feelings, and actions that parents may not positively sanction (Gecas & Seff, 1990). The question asked here is whether this is true for adolescent sexual development.

Hints about the manner in which peers socialize with one another can be found in Moore's (1995) study of the filtering behavior of young, adolescent girls in malls. M. Moore found that these girls engaged in increased flirting when in a group. Their flirtatious behavior, however, was more apt to be triggered by the flirting of group leaders than by the presence of boys! In other words, modeling of same sex peers was a strong influence on their behavior.

Similar research exists in the area of sexual behavior. There is little doubt that perception of peer sexual activity is positively related to early adolescents' own sexual activity independent of other variables (DiBalasio & Benda, 1990; Gibson & Kempf, 1990; Jessor et al., 1983). Ethnic differences exist in the strength of this association. The relation of perception of friends' sexual activity to early adolescents' sexual activity has especially been true for White (Cvetkovich & Grote, 1980; Jorgensen, King, & Torrey, 1980; Shah & Zelnik, 1981) and Hispanic males and females (Christopher et al., 1993), but not so for Blacks (Cvetkovich & Grote, 1980).

These findings raise the question of whether peers or parents have more influence on the sexual activity of youth. Only a few investigators have included peer and parent measures in their studies. Nonetheless, the findings are remarkably consistent—perception of peer sexual involvement invariably accounts for a greater proportion of the variance in adolescent sexual exploration than parent measures in multivariate analyses (Christopher et al., 1993; Cvetkovich & Grote, 1980; DiBalasio & Benda, 1990; East et al., 1993; P. Miller & Simon, 1974). Treboux and Busch-Rossnagel's (1990) work provides a possible insight into what it is about peers that effect early adolescent's sexual behavior. They found that although both parental and peer approval indirectly affected sexual behavior through adolescents' sexual attitudes, the effect for friends' approval on attitudes was almost three times stronger than the effect for parents for female youth although it was almost equal for male youth. Hence, the perception of peer approval impacts sexual attitudes.

This collection of findings suggests that peers have a more powerful influence than do parents. This conclusion, however, should be tempered. K. Moore et al. (1986), using a national probability data set, found that when parents know all or most of their child's friends, there is a lower chance of these adolescents engaging in coitus. This finding raises the possibility that teens who are close to their parents may be more likely to choose friends whose values and norms are consistent with their upbringing. If true, then parents would have an indirect influence on their offsprings' sexual activity by serving as a standard that would influence adolescents' choice of friends.

These investigations unfortunately suffer from two methodological weaknesses. First, measures of perceived peer sexual activity can serve only as a proxy for actual sexual behavior engaged in by friends. Although some scholars argue that adolescents' perceptions influence behavior, there is a need to evaluate the effects of actual peer behavior to fully understand peer-derived effects. Second, with the exception of Jessor et al. (1983), these studies have been cross-sectional. This leaves unanswered questions of causal direction. Positive association between perceived peer and adolescent sexual behavior could result from adolescents changing their behavior to match friends, or from choosing friends whose behavior matches that of the adolescents. Such cause–effect issues can only be teased apart with a longitudinal design.

Billy and Udry's (1985) 2-year panel study allowed tests of different hypotheses about the relation between early teens first engaging in intercourse and actual versus perceived coital behavior by friends. Furthermore, the design of their study allowed the use of friends' reports of their own coital behavior, instead of perceived behavior, for both White and Black adolescents. They first tested a commonly believed hypothesis that over time adolescents who were virgins, and who had best friends who were sexual experienced, become sexually experienced themselves. This process was true only for White females. They also tested the hypothesis that youth who chose new friends over the 2 years would choose individuals who were similar in their sexual experience. White males and females followed this pattern. Finally, they tested a deselection hypothesis—that individuals dissolved friendships based on their own sexual activity—and found no support within any ethnic and gender subgroup. Their results showed that early adolescents' coital behavior is related to peer coital behavior for White, but not Black adolescents, and that the popularly believed peer influence hypothesis operates only for White females. Instead, White males, and to a lesser extent White females, first experience sexual intercourse, and then choose friends whose sexual experience corresponds to their own.

The ability of friends to influence White females may be moderated by the female's pubertal status. Smith, Udry, and Morris (1985) found that the pubertal development of an individual, and that individual's best friend's actual sexual behavior, were predictive of sexual exploration for White males and females. For the females, but not the males, an interaction between these two variables predicted additional variance. In other words, White females were more susceptible to social influence from their best friends' sexual behavior after they had experienced external and noticeable pubertal changes.

Billy and Udry (1985) findings seem to contradict the fact that 73% of the female teens and 50% of the male teens offer social pressure as the reason why adolescents do not wait for a later age to engage in sexual intercourse (Harris Poll, 1986). This response may reflect a different type of peer pressure than what may be measured by asking about the status of one's best friend's sexual experience. Specifically, early adolescents may experience pressure from the peers they come in contact with in their daily lives. Support for this conceptualization comes from Furstenberg et al.'s (1987) analysis of a national probability data set. To understand their results, it is necessary to remember from the review at the opening of this chapter that proportionately more Blacks than Whites are nonvirgins during early adolescence, and that Blacks experience coitus at earlier ages than Whites. This suggests that Blacks are more accepting of early sexual exploration than Whites (B. Miller & Moore, 1990). If there exists an additional form of peer pressure that originates from teens involved in daily contact, then Blacks attending all-Black schools should differ in their rates of sexual intercourse from Blacks in integrated schools. This is what Furstenberg et al. (1987) found even after controlling for SES differences. Blacks attending all-Black schools were much more likely to have experienced coitus when compared to Blacks enrolled at integrated schools. Furthermore, there were differences in the hypothesized direction between Blacks who were in schools that were 20% integrated, and Blacks who were in schools that were 80% integrated. Day (1992) showed that this same process operates for other groups. He found that the higher percentages of Blacks in schools increased the chances of coitus for Black and White youth of both sexes.

Conclusions About Peer Influences

The findings to date indicate that peer influence may originate from two sources that operate differentially depending on the sex and ethnicity of the group being considered. White females are susceptible to being influenced by the sexual activity of their best friend. This susceptibility is apt to be more pronounced if the teen has progressed in pubertal development to the point that it is noticeable. Concurrently, both White males and females are likely to choose friends with similar sexual experience levels. Hence, White adolescents arrange their peer social environment to receive support for their sexual explorations—support that is unlikely to come from most parents. It is unclear why this is not so for Black adolescents.

An additional source of peer pressure comes from the more generalized peer context that early adolescents encounter on a daily basis. Although research has yet to test the specific mechanisms by which this pressure is felt, two possibilities exist. First, young adolescents often create an imaginary audience that they feel is constantly judging their attitudes, feelings, and actions (Adams & Gullotta, 1983). It may be that this audience is not as imaginary as previously believed in the area of sexual exploration. It may be that peers with whom adolescents come in daily contact create a different type of pressure than what is experienced among close friends. Second, research with young adults has shown that individuals can be placed along a continuum with individuals at one pole representing those who judge the correctness of their behavior by using personal standards, called *low self-monitors,* whereas those at the other pole use social and situational cues and are called *high self-monitors* (Snyder, Simpson, & Gangestad, 1986). Teens who are more characteristic of the latter stance would be more prone to a social pressure than teens who could be described by the former. Further research is needed to see if either of these variables plays a role in the sexual activity of teens.

DATING

Although teens most often engage in sexual intercourse while in a dating relationship, scholars have typically assessed different dimensions of dating by asking only one or two questions. This results in a rather sketchy view about relational influences. This is perplexing as early dating has been associated with early coital activity among White males and females (B. Miller et al., 1986; Thornton, 1990), Black females (Leigh et al., 1988), and in ethnically diverse samples (Small & Luster, 1994). Moreover, likelihood of coital activity in a dating relationship is enhanced when early adolescents see their dating as serious (B. Miller et al., 1986), especially for female adolescents in instances when their dating partner is close in age (Elo, King, & Furstenberg, in press). Early dating is also more characteristic of White teens when compared to Hispanic youth (Aneshensel et al., 1989).

Overall, however, very little is known about dating at this developmental stage. McCabe (1984) theorized that adolescents date simply for its own value. It is not necessarily used to evaluate potential marital partners as might occur at a later age. She sees dating as influenced by three factors. The first, *maturation,* focuses on the role of normal, biological development. *Social influences* from parents, peers, and society are triggered when individuals in the early adolescent's social environment notice the new maturational status of the adolescent. Finally, the *personal meaning* the adolescent gives to dating determines when the youth will begin dating. McCabe viewed this final factor as the outcome of the previous two.

Newcomb, Huba, and Bentler (1986) provided partial support for McCabe's theorizing with an ethnically diverse, random sample of adolescents. They found that dating and sexual involvement were both predicted by the importance teens placed on dating. Furthermore, the importance placed on dating was predicted by experiencing stress that originated, in part, with events within the family.

Sexual involvement that occurs while dating follows a predictable sequence for White and Hispanic early adolescents (Christopher et al., 1993; E. Smith & Udry, 1985). This progression usually begins with kissing, proceeds to touching the female's breasts, first clothed and then directly, advances to touching genitals, and culminates in sexual intercourse. Longitudinal analyses support this pattern of sexual involvement for White adolescents, but not Blacks (E. Smith & Udry, 1985). The only predictable pattern for Blacks is kissing and then coitus; these teens engage in other noncoital behaviors, but fail to follow a discernible pattern. Moreover, with the exception of touching clothed breasts, all other sexual behaviors have a lower frequency than coitus for Black males and females. Given this finding, it is not surprising that Black male adolescents who participated in a focus group tended to equate dating and sexual intercourse (Nix, Pasteur, & Servance, 1988). These males reached a consensus that dating needed to result in coitus after two or three dates or there was no need to continue seeing their dating partner.

Female adolescents are most likely to report that their first act of coitus occurred while in a steady or serious dating relationship, with fewer reporting that the relationship was casual (Faulkenberry, Vincent, James, & Johnson, 1987; Jessor et al., 1983; P. Miller & Simon, 1974; Zelnick & Shah, 1983) especially in instances when they are close in age to their first coital partner (Elo et al., in press). A smaller percentage of male adolescents report that their first act of sexual intercourse occurred while seriously dating, and more report that the dating relationship was casual. Additionally, the first sexual partners for females tend to be 3 years older, whereas partners for males are more apt to be 1 year older.

Only a few researchers have included some measure of relationship dimensions in their investigations. Their findings hint at the role that relationship experiences play in the sexual exploration of early adolescents. The majority of adolescents report that the reason for engaging in coitus is to give or receive love (Jessor et al., 1983). A minority reports that their first experience was in some way negative. Moreover, not only does sexual involvement increase as dating becomes more committed, but there is a concurrent increase in wanting and experiencing emotional intimacy

(McCabe & Collins, 1983). Good sexual communication between dating partners may also be linked to stability in the relationship; Catania et al. (1989) found that poor sexual communication predicted having a number of sexual partners.

There are indications that their male partners may pressure some female adolescents into coitus. A small percentage of teens report that the reason they engaged in sexual intercourse was because of a sense of obligation to their partner or because of being manipulated (Jessor et al., 1983). Cvetkovich and Grote (1980) reported similar findings. They found that when three items in their inventory ("Couldn't say no," "Wanted to please and satisfy my boyfriend," and "Seemed like it was expected of me") were summed, the resulting measure was predictive of coital activity for White and Black females. Jorgensen et al. (1980) also reported that male, but not female, decision making about coitus was predictive of the frequency of sexual intercourse in an adolescent sample. The meaning of these experiences is more fully explored in chapters 7 and 8, which focus on sexual coercion and aggression in dating.

Conclusions About Dating Influences

Conclusions need to be tentative about the role of dating relationship experiences in early adolescent sexuality because of the general paucity of research. The available research findings suggest that increases in commitment and love are positively related to early coital involvement. It is unclear, however, if female adolescents are more prone than males to wait until relationships are serious before engaging in intercourse, or if they are more apt to define a relationship as serious if they engage in intercourse. Longitudinal research, which has yet to be conducted, is needed to explore this cause–effect dynamic. Moreover, good communication about sexual wishes may be related to the stability of the dating relationship. Not all coital experiences are positive. This may be due to the unwanted pressure female teens experience to engage in sexual behavior that they do not want, and for which they may not feel ready.

INDIVIDUAL FACTORS

Researchers have examined a number of individual variables to see if they are associated with early adolescent sexual expression. In these analyses, religiosity, usually measured by how frequently adolescents attend religious services, is consistently and negatively related to teens' sexual expression, even after controlling for the effects of other variables (Forste & Heaton, 1988; Jessor et al., 1983; Mott et al., 1996; Rosenbaum & Kandel, 1990; Taris et al., 1998; Thornton & Camburn, 1989). The association between these two variables exists for White males and females (Aneshensel et al., 1989; Cvetkovich & Grote, 1980; Day, 1992; B. Miller & Olson, 1988), and for Black (Cvetkovich & Grote, 1980; Day, 1992; Leigh et al., 1988) and Hispanic females (Day, 1992). Moreover, regular attendance of services is more strongly related to sexual exploration than being a member of a particular denomination (Thornton & Camburn, 1989). There is evidence, however, that membership in a fundamentalist Christian denomination results in a lower probability of coital activity (Brewster, Cooksey, Guilkey, & Rindfuss, 1998; Leigh et al., 1988; B. Miller & Olson, 1988; Rosenbaum & Kandel, 1990; Thornton & Camburn, 1987).

Thornton and Camburn's (1989) longitudinal study provides insight into which factors relate to adolescent religious participation. Measures over an 18-year period demonstrate that mothers' early religious attendance predicted their later attendance. Additionally, evidence for an intergenerational transmission of religious values can be seen in that this latter religious service attendance by mothers was predictive of their offspring's attendance. Two measures of adolescent sexual exploration—coital participation and number of partners—both had negative reciprocal effects with the adolescent's religious attendance. Finally, adolescents' sexual attitudes had an additional reciprocal relationship with religious attendance. The reciprocal relationships suggest that religious attendance serves as a bulwark against early sexual experience by promoting norms and values that are inconsistent with coital activity. Limiting sexual experience, in turn, helps strengthen attitudes and commitment to the youth's religious practices for those who start out with religious convictions.

Adolescents' attitudes are also consistently found related to their sexual exploration. Nonvirgin teens typically hold more liberal views toward sexual involvement before marriage than do virgin teens (Bingham et al., 1990; DiBalasio & Benda, 1990). Attitudes are predictive of sexual activity, even when considering other variables, for White, Black, and Hispanic males and females (Christopher et al., 1993; Cvetkovich & Grote, 1980; Gibson & Kempf, 1990) and often account for a notable proportion of the variance. Attitudes probably reflect norms that teens hold and adolescents whose norms exhibit an acceptance of early sexual activity most likely exhibit an acceptance of other problem behaviors such as alcohol and illicit drug use. These behaviors, in turn, are also predictive of early coital activity (Dorius, Heaton, & Steffen, 1993; Jessor et al., 1983).

There is a need to be careful about the interpretation of these findings. The correlational nature of the studies make it unwise to make cause–effect conclusions. Although some adolescents may hold liberal attitudes, and these attitudes provide a justification for sexual exploration, others may experience coitus and change their attitudes. Changes may mean that the teen becomes either more accepting or rejecting of premarital sexual involvement. Work by Zabin, Hirsch, Smith, and Hardy (1984) exemplifies this dynamic. Although these reseachers found virgins more likely than nonvirgins to say sex was wrong, 25% of their sample had an inconsistency between their moral evaluation of sex before marriage and their own behavior. Similarly, 50% of the coitally experienced female teens, and 33% of the males, did not think they were old enough to have engaged in sexual intercourse.

There are other cognitive processes that have been hypothesized to be related to early sexual involvement. For instance, it has been posited that teens weigh the potential costs and rewards of possible sexual involvement before engaging in the behavior (Bauman & Udry, 1981; DiBalasio & Benda, 1990). Bauman and Udry called this process subjective expected utility (SEU) and have found that White and Black males hold more positive SEU than White and Black females, and that Black males hold more positive SEU than White males. SEU may have a limited role in coital decisions. Its inclusion in multivariate analyses shows that it is predictive of engaging in coitus for Black female adolescents, and close to being predictive for White females, but is not predictive for White male adolescents. This is not surprising as females suffer stronger negative outcomes for engaging in sexual activity than males. It may also be that friends influence SEU. DiBlasio and Benda's (1990) research suggests that friends may help weigh the costs and benefits of sexual interactions with a partner.

The appraisal of self-worth, or self-esteem, has long been thought to play a critical role in the early sexual behavior of teens by practitioners and public alike. Unfortunately, researchers have reported mixed results. Day (1992) found that self-esteem had a negative relationship to the probability of coitus for Mexican American females and a positive relationship for White and other Latina females in a multivariate analyses. Analysis of this same national probability data set, using a different set of predictor variables and focusing on a range of sexual behaviors, failed to find that self-esteem was related to the sexual activity (Rosenbaum & Kandel, 1990). Similarly, other researchers have failed to find a relationship for Mexican American youth (Christopher et al., 1993).

Miller, Christensen, and Olson's (1987) work shed some light on this inconsistency. They tested the hypothesis that adolescents who conform to personal norms would positively evaluate themselves. They supported this hypothesis by showing that among youth who saw premarital sex as always wrong, virgins had higher self-esteem than nonvirgins. Similarly, among those who saw premarital sex as neither right nor wrong, usually right, or always right, nonvirgins had higher self-esteem than virgins. Even with these results, their conclusion was noteworthy. They found that even given the need to consider adolescents' normative context, self-esteem explained very little variation in either premarital sexual attitudes or coital experience. Thus, self-esteem does not seem to play as strong a role in teen sexual activity as commonly believed.

Locus of control has also received attention. Researchers usually predict that youth who see their lives in their own control (internal locus) are less likely to engage in sexual intercourse than those who see their lives in the control of fate, circumstances, or others (external locus). Although some researchers have failed to find a relation (Christopher et al., 1993), others report that virgins had more of an internal locus than nonvirgins (Jessor et al., 1983) did. Additionally, locus of control has been shown to be related to the probability of coital activity in the predicted direction for Mexican American and other Latino females, and White males and females (Day, 1992). Still others have discovered a curvilinear relationship for youth under the age of 14, and a linear relationship in the predicted direction for those who were between the ages of 15 and 16 (Rosenbaum & Kandel, 1990). Hence, locus of control has a more consistent relation to coital activity than does self-esteem.

Future aspirations are negatively tied to the probability of coital activity for youth. This has typically been assessed by asking about future education or occupation goals, but current academic abilities have been used. With a single exception (Hogan & Kitagawa, 1985), these variables were related in the expected direction (Chilman, 1982; Furstenberg et al., 1987; Gibson & Kempf, 1990; Jessor et al., 1983; Rosenbaum & Kandel, 1990). Multivariate analyses by ethnic and gender subgroups show a relationship for Black male adolescents, and White male and female adolescents (Day, 1992; Udry & Billy, 1987). Longitudinal research with a rural adolescent sample suggests that the association between academic performance and sexual activity may differ when comparing boys and girls. Ohannessian and Crockett (1993) found academic grades to be negatively related to sexual activity 2 years later in life for girls, whereas sexual activity was negatively related to academic activities for boys. Thus, the demands surrounding good academic performance appeared to keep girls from sexual activity. For boys in this study, however, sexual involvement distracted them from performing well academically in school.

Nonetheless, the corpus of the findings in this area suggest that individuals who foresee a future that requires an investment of time and resources may be more motivated to delay coital activity. Possibly, they may see that an unexpected pregnancy can interfere with the accomplishment of occupational and educational goals as so often occurs with peers who have children while still in school (Jorgensen, 1993).

Finally, Jessor and Jessor (1974) proposed that the sexual involvement of early adolescents is indicative of corresponding involvement with other problem behaviors. Specifically, they see teen sexual activity, drinking, and smoking as occurring together, and as deviant only because of age-graded norms. The same behaviors at a later age fail to trigger negative social sanctions because they would not be seen as deviant. P. Miller and Simon (1974) demonstrated early support for these hypotheses by showing that coital transition was associated with delinquent involvement. Similarly, Jessor et al.'s (1983) longitudinal study provides strong support for their earlier postulating. In these analyses, they show that early coital behavior is positively linked to illegal drug use. Mott et al. (1996) reported parallel findings. Coker et al.'s (1994) research provide even broader support for the multiple problem hypothesis. They found risk of early coital involvement for both sexes and all ethnic groups increased if adolescents carried a weapon to school, got into a physical fight, smoked cigarettes, or used alcohol before the age of 13. Undoubtedly, these findings have a social component as perceiving ones' friends as accepting of such problem behavior further contributed to the probability of coital involvement.

In fact, drug use may have a particularly strong relation to early coital involvement. Although drug use affects both male and female adolescent sexual involvement, its overall effect is stronger for female than male teens. Moreover, use of alcohol, marijuana, and other illicit drugs puts White and Hispanic male and female youth at risk for early sexual intercourse (Mott et al., 1996; Rosenbaum & Kandel, 1990). Contrary to popular depictions, only marijuana use is predictive of early coitus for Black males and females (Rosenbaum & Kandel, 1990).

Conclusions About Individual Factors

Two of the findings reviewed in this section likely demonstrate the effects of social institutions on adolescents, with their accompanying socialization experiences. The negative relation of religious attendance to early adolescent's sexual exploration is understandable. Most religions oppose premarital sexual involvement and charge their members to accept this view as a norm in their lives. The consistency of the finding across studies supports this conceptualization. The educational institution is also one that attempts to instill a long-term goal of high school graduation for many, and enrollment in college for others. These goals are apt to be strongly valued by many parents. Sexual involvement, with its subsequent risk of lifelong consequences, would make achieving this goal difficult, if not impossible, for many adolescents. Thus, the negative relation between future aspirations and early sexual intercourse experiences likely reflects that these adolescents have internalized the suggested future goals and are cognitively capable of weighing different outcomes when deciding if certain actions will support or hinder such goals.

Peers involved in deviant behavior may provide a different socialization experience—one that supports early sexual exploration. The cause–effect mechanisms of this are not completely clear. Teens involved in deviant behaviors may seek out teens who engage in analogous actions. The reverse is equally plausible. Nonetheless, once integrated into such a group, group members will provide potent reinforcement for continuing these activities by granting approval and status.

Locus of control may mediate peer effects. Its very conceptualization would suggest this to be true. Furthermore, it may interact with maturational processes. The fact that its effect reverses direction from early adolescence to later adolescence (Day, 1992) supports this hypothesis. Therefore, when individuals experience early adolescence, with its accompanying strong pressures for conformity, youth with an external locus of control would be more open to the general peer pressure written about earlier than would youth with an internal locus of control.

The exact role of SEU (weighing the potential rewards and costs of sexual involvement) is difficult to predict. The number of researchers who have included this variable has been limited. Adolescents, and especially early adolescents, typically see themselves as invulnerable and may hold attitudes that approve of risk taking (Chilman, 1982). Thus, more mature youth are possibly more realistic in how they weigh costs and rewards. This in turn may include a gender effect. The sense of invulnerability felt by early adolescents might lead them to view sexual involvement more favorably, but as they get older, females may realistically see greater potential for negative outcomes than males.

Finally, their attitudes have been more widely investigated with consistent conclusions. Attitudes most likely reflect the values held and norms followed by the adolescents. Given that adolescence is a time of value and identity formation, however, these attitudes are apt to fluctuate. Adolescents may engage in sexual activity that is contrary to their attitudes and the evaluation of this experience may lead to attitude changes, either becoming more liberal or conservative. Thus, it can be hypothesized that it is adolescents' evaluation of their experience that is critical to attitude transformations.

This chapter reviewed the scope of adolescent sexual activity and focused on salient influences on early adolescent sexuality. Unfortunately, scholarly attention on these influences has rarely taken an approach that acknowledges the interconnectedness of the variables involved. Concurrently examining these diverse literatures provides insights into the complex influences on early adolescent sexual expression. At the same time, simply reviewing the empirical findings still provides only a segmented view of these influences thereby demonstrating the weakness of taking an atheoretical approach. Without theory, these variables appear falsely as isolated influences. In the next chapter, theory is used to integrate these findings into a more cohesive view of early adolescent sexuality.

4

A Theoretical Model
of Early
Adolescent Sexuality

The model I propose to integrate the early adolescent sexuality literature can be divided into three components. The first focuses on early adolescents' enactment of their sexuality roles and the relation of these enactments to the different parts of the self-identity of the youth. The second component stresses the influence of parents on their adolescents. The third component integrates influences of peers and dating partners.

THE EARLY ADOLESCENT SEXUALITY
ROLE AND SELF-IDENTITY

With the possible exception of Black youth, young adolescents follow a behavioral pattern of sexual involvement that begins with kissing, is followed by genital fondling, and culminates with sexual intercourse (E. Smith & Udry, 1985). Although young individuals who follow this pattern may halt their sexual involvement at different points in the progression, the progression follows the same overall pattern. Even among Black youth, kissing is a preliminary activity, with similar behaviors following and leading to coitus, although a specific pattern is not discernible.

This pattern of activity does not exist in a vacuum; it represents a behavioral representation of the sexual roles in which adolescents engage. Although researchers have typically focused on the sexual behaviors manifested in these roles, such a narrow focus minimizes what is actually experienced by early adolescents. A critical element is missing, the meaning ascribed by adolescents to their own sexual involvement. For instance, when adolescents kiss, pet, and engage in sexual intercourse they assign symbolic meaning to their experiences as well as enjoying each for its own sake. These meanings can range from sex as romance or love to sex as status or power. Adolescents use meaning to structure their behavior in social settings. Thus, to examine only sexual behaviors precludes a complete view of what constitutes early adolescent sexuality and this limits understanding of what motivates adolescents to engage in this type of involvement (Stryker & Statham, 1985).

Little knowledge exists about what these adolescent sexual roles look like as researchers have yet to investigate them. They are likely to approximate the sexual roles early adolescents see older adolescents and young adults fulfilling. They are also apt to reflect the preadolescent sexual knowledge and hedonic valence that originates in childhood experiences. Hence, roles will include scripts for emotions that may be felt given certain types of dyadic interactions, emotions that will likely intensify with the sexual arousal that can accompany an interaction. They will undoubtedly contain certain cognitions about the meaning of the dyadic behaviors experienced. Additionally, adolescents will assign meaning to nonverbal exchanges that may, or may not, be accurate.

Research findings hint at some of the structural quality of these roles, particularly when coitus is a part of the adolescent's experience. Roles will be experienced in the context of a dyadic relationship, but boys are more likely to define such a relationship as casual, girls as serious. Such discrepancies imply that participants may infer rather than discuss the exact status of the relationship (see also Duck, 1994, for the relevance of this to relationship research). Age differences are liable to be present. Older coital partners may socialize younger, less experienced partners into role dynamics.

When focusing on the roles themselves, several things seem probable. First, early adolescents, and especially male adolescents, are unlikely to possess the skills necessary for keeping a protracted romantic relationship continuing. Moreover, these young adolescents do not have a range of experiences in such roles. Hence, initial role experiences are likely to be of much shorter duration when compared to later adolescence. Role content at this stage is correspondingly going to be much less rich compared to later stages of development. Personal experiences with different partners, and vicarious experiences provided by friends, will eventually change both the duration and role content of the sexuality roles. Both types of experiences will act as feedback to the self as adolescents evaluate their role performance. Later role enactment will be much richer than early experiences. Throughout the experiences of one's role, the meanings assigned to dyadic interactions by the adolescent involved become central to the process of role development.

Meaning partially originates in and becomes a part of the adolescent's self-identity, as it does for adults at different life stages. But the self-identity of adolescents is unique because it is in a state of flux and development. The cognitive abilities of preadolescents prevent them from fully taking the perspective of other individuals (Adams & Gullotta, 1989). As they progress through adolescence, this particular cognitive ability becomes more fully developed. Taking others' perspectives allows young adolescents to do two things. First, they can begin to treat their own identity as a separate cognitive entity. In symbolic interaction terms, this is an important adultlike quality of the self. This allows adolescents to examine the different parts of their identity and to speculate on what would occur if they were to modify their identity in part or in whole.

Second, as the cognitive functioning of adolescents matures toward adult styles of thinking, adolescents can more fully consider and explore potential responses of others to themselves and to their own possible behavior. Some of the "others" who will be considered are important individuals in adolescents' lives—significant others such as parents and close friends. Other individuals will constitute a more diluted group—generalized others such as the overall peer group in a school setting. Adolescent perceptions of the messages sent by both of these groups are likely to play an especially important role in the development of a self-identity (Gecas & Seff, 1990). This examination of self in a social context constitutes the symbolic interaction construct of social self. The construction of a social self by anticipating others' responses is critical to both role taking and role making (Stryker & Statham, 1985).

The process of building a self-identity is one of the central developmental tasks of the period of adolescence (Gecas & Seff, 1990). Given that it is a process, adolescent self-identity often fluctuates and undergoes changes. There are interesting dynamics involved in this process. The developing cognitive abilities allow adolescents to consider a range of potential reactions in others to behaviors they may contemplate engaging in, but adolescents lack the life experiences to accurately and fully evaluate the ramifications of their possible behavior. Hence, adolescents will often think in terms of absolutes rather than in degrees of relativeness. Concurrently, the ability to consider their self as a separate entity, paired with their awareness of others' reactions to their behavior, fosters a form of adolescent egocentricism whereby they see themselves as being "on stage" with their actions under constant scrutiny by others. Moreover, early adolescents value and reward conformity (Steinberg & Silverberg, 1986), and the wish to be an accepted member of a group flavors how adolescents evaluate the acceptability of their behavior in the eyes of their peers. All of these influence the social self created by the adolescent.

The use of the constructs of role, self, and social self in the model is represented in Fig. 4.1. The primary variable that mediates the sexual role enactment is the self as viewed in the present. This construct captures how adolescents see themselves in the role of sexual individual, or their sexual self-identity, and how this relates to their sexual behavior. It is where the person ascribes meaning to sexual behavior. Meaning is reflected, in part, in the sexual values and attitudes of adolescents, and this can explain the close correspondence between many adolescents' sexual attitudes and behavior. But there is a bi-directional influence that operates between the self and the role enactment (Hewitt, 1991). Adolescents do not simply formulate a concept of what their sexual self should be, and then act accordingly. Behaviors are constantly being evaluated, given a positive or negative valance, and assigned meanings that are possibly temporary and subject to revision, appraisals, and comments by others (Duck, 1994). Some of the evaluative process is anticipatory (Stryker & Statham, 1985)—how they see their sexual self as potentially unfolding and in what dyadic context. Some of the evaluative process occurs as the adolescent experiences touches, kisses, and caresses from their partner. Meaning is given to this overall class of symbolic acts as they are experienced. Some of the evaluative process is also retrospective. Because sexual involvement is such a salient experience at this age, it is likely to be cognitively reconstructed several times after it has occurred and examined in minute detail, possibly for some time after the event. Meaning is given to each verbal and nonverbal exchange that took place within an entire interaction during this reconstruction. Additionally, adolescents will assign a positive or negative tone to their interactions as part of this meaning.

If in this evaluative process adolescents find their attitudes and values are congruent with their behavior, attitudes are not likely to change. For example, if limiting sexual behavior is positively valued, and an adoles-

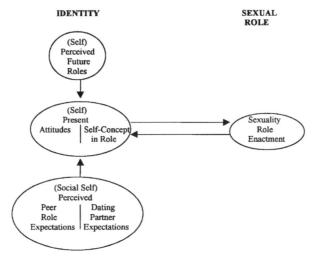

FIG. 4.1. *Early adolescent self and sexuality role enactment.*

cent has limited sexual involvement, then attitudes will not change as a result of this experience. If, however, sexual experiences are incongruent with values and attitudes, then the conceptualization of self will change. For example, if adolescents become more sexually involved than their attitudes say they should, attitudes may change or the adolescents may evaluate their actions as "bad" and develop a self-image as a bad person as related to their sexual role enactment.

There are developmental changes that I hypothesize as occurring in this process as adolescents age and become more experienced. It is unlikely that 12- and and 13-year-olds would have complicated pictures of a sexual role. Their experiences in romantic relationships are very limited, influenced by earlier childhood experiences, and are mostly anticipatory in nature (Thorne & Luria, 1986). Additionally, their cognitive abilities are more limited than those of older adolescents. As adolescents experience dyadic encounters that vary in romantic content, affective environment, and sexual intimacy, it will add to their sexual role content. Moreover, as adolescents move through this developmental period and learn from parents, peers, and dating partners about sexual roles, they will become better socialized to their sexual roles. Much of what will be seen as acceptable or permissible is based on age-graded norms that are a part of this overall social organization. Few parents or adults are likely to condone or support kissing and fondling among 12- and 13-year-olds. They may also discourage dating only one person for a lengthy period of time. Although parents still may not positively sanction these same actions in 17- or 18-year-olds, they may at least better understand their occurrence and presumably would be more accepting of a steady dating relationship. Time, in the form of a social clock that defines appropriateness (Duck, 1994), therefore, is part of the developmental changes that take place in these roles. In the end, older adolescents, when compared to younger adolescents, will have richer and more diverse sexual role experiences and expectations.

There are a number of influences on the developing selves of adolescents. Two of these are relevant to the present discussion of self and are represented in Fig. 4.1. The first is how adolescents perceive themselves in future, adult roles. As adults fill a range of roles (Hewitt, 1991; Stryker & Statham, 1985), adolescents need to consider not only what their future sexual role will be, but also to speculate on their career and marital roles. Researchers have shown that individuals with educational and career aspirations limit their sexual involvement and delay coital involvement until a later age (i.e., Rosenbaum & Kandel, 1990). The reason for this is manifested in this variable. Adolescents who want to pursue careers that require extended and intensive schooling are likely to be focused on their present educational activities, and have less time for becoming sexually involved. Moreover, they may see sexual involvement with its potential lifelong consequences as interfering with the ability to attain their educational and career goals—a possibly common message from their parents. On the other hand, adolescents who see early parenting as a viable adult model, or who have low educational or career goals are likely to construct a sexual role that will accomplish that goal.

The second influential variable that is represented in Fig. 4.1 is adolescents' social self. This is the aspect of the adolescents' self that is influenced by the perceived reactions of peers to their own behaviors, thoughts, and emotions (Gecas & Seff, 1990). Thus, the social self is the receptacle of the perceived expectations of others in the social environment of the adolescent. For the most part, this will represent two social influences. The first is the perceived role expectations of peers about adolescents' own sexual roles. The second of these originate in the perceived role expectations of dating partners. These are not the same as the actual role expectations by self. They are based on the perceived role expectations (Gecas & Seff, 1990). Hence, they are prone to be influenced by the adolescent egocentricism previously discussed and the corresponding need to conform. These variables are discussed further in the following sections.

Parents and Early Adolescent Sexuality Role

Figure 4.2 represents the proposed relationship between parental influences and adolescent sexual role enactment. Parental effects are seen as operating in different ways, but their influence on role enactment is mediated through the hypothesized dimensions of the adolescents' self-identity. Beginning with the top half of the figure, parents bring their own *norms* for sexual behavior, which are grounded in their *values* and *attitudes*, to their relationship with their children. These values and norms represent the meaning parents give to different sexual roles including the sexual roles possible for adolescents and adults. Parental values and norms would encompass, for example, the way parents assign meaning to a neighborhood girl who is premaritally pregnant, the cousin who marries after beginning a promising career, or the school acquaintance who has a reputation for enjoying a range of coital partners. It is also possible that some parents' sexual norms are such that sexual matters are not to be openly discussed between parents and children (Goldman & Goldman, 1982). But in the context of the foregoing examples, it is clear that "sexual matters" encompasses more than talking about specifics of sexual conduct. It extends to the moral discourse surrounding parental treatment of sexuality.

One of the more pervasive influences on these parental norms and values is the family's SES (Gecas, 1979). Social class limits the life opportunities of many individuals, and helps to mold what is acceptable and/or perceived as inevitable role behavior on the part of one's offspring. For instance, Gecas (1979) theorized that working-class parents value conformity and are therefore controlling of their children because the work environment where they will eventually be employed punishes independence and rewards conformity. At the same time, upper and middle-class families have more educational and career opportunities that are available to their children. Parents can then value these opportunities and hold them as an acceptable norm for their children to consider. On the other hand, poverty can be an especially difficult environment for parenting when one considers the sexual roles, with the accompanying behaviors, that are likely to surround and possibly be an important part of the history of families who live in this economic condition (J. Kelley, 1995).

Religiosity also helps to define parental values (Thorton & Camburn, 1987). Participation in religious activities presumably provides a social structure, which reinforces and upholds certain values and attitudes. These values usually stress abstinence from sexual activity until marriage.

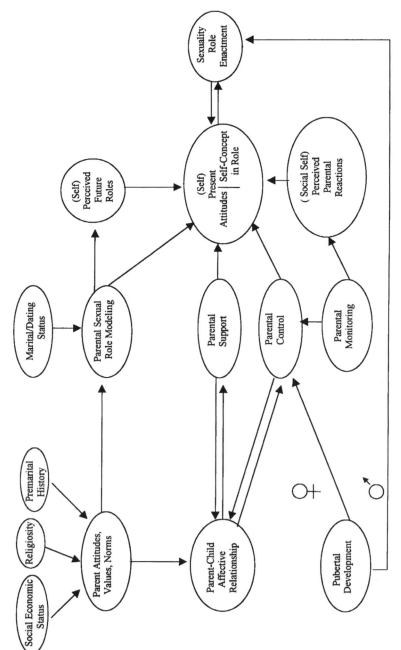

FIG. 4.2. *Parent sexual socialization of early adolescents.*

Religious participation also provides a vehicle for talking about these values within a group setting where taking on particular values as one's own personal standards is rewarded and opposing values are negatively sanctioned (Mott et al., 1996). Consequently, a religious setting provides a particular meaning to sexual activity before and after marriage. Moreover, religious tenets often put sexual values into an overall structure of life values. On the whole, the social organization inherent in religious organizations is hypothesized as contextually supporting parents in assigning role attributes to sexual behavior.

Finally, some of the parents' values and attitudes originate in their own premarital sexual experiences (Fox & Inazu, 1980). The positive relationship between parents' early engagement in coitus and premarital pregnancies, and those of their adolescents, is captured in this variable. Early sexual role experiences by parents are apt to influence what they see as acceptable for or anticipate to be encountered by their own offspring. Some parents may feel that their personal adolescent experiences helped to strengthen their foundation for adulthood and will therefore encourage their child to have similar experiences. Other parents may react strongly to poor adolescent sexual incidents and will strive to ensure that their child will not have parallel experiences. Either will be evident in the values and attitudes parents attempt to pass on to their children through socialization.

Referring back to Fig. 4.2, meanings inherent in parents' discussions of sexual attitudes and values are not enough by themselves to influence the adolescent. These act indirectly through two paths. The first is through the adult sexual role modeling parents provide their adolescents and the second is through the parent–child relationship. Adult sexual role modeling is shown in the model as the sexual role behaviors parents engage in as opposed to the values and attitudes that they talk about. It is captured by parents' marital status, and in the case of single parents their dating status. This differentiation can help explain why single mothers who date have daughters who are more likely to be sexually active at an earlier age than daughters whose single mothers do not date, or than daughters who come from two-parent families (Peterson et al., 1985, cited in Strouse & Fabes, 1987). The single mothers who date provide a different sexual role model when compared to these other parents (Whitbeck et al., 1994). Parents probably also provide information about sexual role modeling through recalling their own adolescent experiences. Family stories about early dating of mothers and fathers provide adolescents with information that they can incorporate into their own cognitive schemas of possible sexual role behaviors specifically and relational learning in general.

Adult sexual role modeling by parents will influence the adolescent in two ways. First, it provides information about future adult roles and will therefore influence that dimension of the adolescent's self. If parents model sexual activity within a marital relationship, this, for instance, will provide one potential future role model for the adolescent to consider adopting. Second, parental statements of values and attitudes, mediated by the role behaviors that parents provide, will have an effect on adolescents' self-conceptualization of their own sexual roles. It is important to emphasize that this is only one influence of several on the adolescent self. Competing peer and dating influences are also present and are explored later in the chapter.

As I have reviewed, researchers have found that different qualities of parent–child relationships are also related to the sexual role enactment of adolescents. These are represented in the bottom half of Fig. 4.2. This portion of the model separates the affective tenor of family interaction, the parent–child relationship, from the parental behaviors of support, control attempts, and monitoring. The relation between the affective variable and the two first behavioral variables are bi-directional. The manner in which these variables are hypothesized as operating on adolescents' self spells out one avenue of socialization that has received strong support in other areas of adolescent development (Gecas & Seff, 1990; cf. Peterson, 1995), a process important to symbolic interaction theory (Hewitt, 1991; Stryker & Statham, 1985). It is through socialization that adolescents learn what constitutes acceptable role behavior for their present and later adult life.

Parental values and attitudes are proposed as influencing the affective environment of the parent–child relationship. If parents value the role of authority and expect immediate adolescent conformity to parental demands, they are likely to have a distant relationship with their child (Gecas & Seff, 1990). In contrast, parents who are authoritative in that they explain decision making and encourage independence in their adolescent are likely to have parent–child relationships characterized by closeness and positive feelings.

Parents who are close to their children are, in turn, likely to be supportive of them. Support is demonstrated in listening and discussing adolescents' thoughts and feelings, and in helping adolescents in their endeavors (Gecas & Seff, 1990). Parents who engage in these behaviors foster a positive relationship with their offspring, thus the bi-directional influence between these two variables (Peterson, 1995). Additionally, parental support results in a number of relevant positive attributes in adolescents including identifying with parents, moral internalization, autonomy, and voluntary compliance with parental wishes (Peterson, 1995). Parents who are less close to their adolescents, however, are less likely to be supportive of them. Low levels of support will correspondingly result in less closeness.

Parental control attempts are independent from support (Gecas & Seff, 1990), but are hypothesized as also influencing the type of emotional climate that characterizes the parent–child relationship. Close relationships are commonly identified with a moderate amount of parental control (Peterson, 1995). In these cases, adolescents are aware that parents will rationally enforce rules, but parental rules are not so pervasive that control is a constant factor in adolescents' lives. Nor are close relationships apt to be identified with a lack of control attempts on the part of the parent. Moderate control is likely to be characterized by the use of induction—explaining reasons behind parental decisions. This use of a rational process promotes mutual respect as well as individuality for the adolescent (Peterson, 1995). Again, control behaviors in which parents engage are likely to influence the affective environment of the parent–child relationship.

Parental monitoring additionally influences adolescents' sexual role enactments. As is seen in Fig. 4.2, its influence is indirect. Parents who monitor their early adolescents' activities know their child's friends, know where their child is going, and know what their child is doing. This knowledge will prove useful when parents make decisions about when to exert control. In other words, parents will use the information they gather from their monitoring in deciding whether and how to intervene in their offspring's activities. This, however, is not the only path of influence for parental monitoring. Adolescents are cognizant of their parents' monitoring. This awareness cues adolescents that they need to evaluate the acceptability of their sexual role behaviors from their parents' perspective. Thus, from a symbolic interaction perspective, parental monitoring leads early adolescents to consider parental reactions to possible sexual role enactments in their social self.

Figure 4.2 reflects the research findings that parental support influences adolescent sexual activity (Jessor et al., 1983; Weinstein & Thorton, 1989). The model hypothesizes that this support acts through the self-identity of the early adolescent. Support influences the adolescent to be more likely to choose the parents' attitudes and values as one's own. In this process, adolescents identify with a parent and see the parent as someone whom they want to please. This identification, then, becomes evident in adolescents adopting parental norms as their own. Put another way, parental use of support helps foster an environment that allows parents to pass on to their children one set of meanings connected with the sexual roles. The emotional environment thus nourishes the identification with parental values. This represents, therefore, one path by which parental socialization takes place.

Socialization also takes place through parental control attempts and monitoring. Similar to findings in other areas of adolescents' lives, research has shown that the relation between parental control and sexual involvement is curvilinear (Gecas & Seff, 1990). As can be seen in Fig. 4.2, this curvilinear relation is hypothesized to act through the adolescent's self. Again, parental monitoring, coupled with moderate control attempts, allow the adolescent to cognitively explore different sexual role behaviors, and consider the potential range of parental responses. This operates in conjunction with the effect of parental support. Thus, if adolescents identify with their parents and want to please them, they will choose a sexual role that will be within the parameters allowed by parental control attempts.

The final endogenous variable in Fig. 4.2 is pubertal development. Pubertal development works differently for males and females. Initially, let us consider female adolescents. Udry and his colleagues' work suggest that the effect of female adolescents' pubertal development is mediated by social influences (Udry et al., 1986). Parents represent one of the more important classes of social influences who would be concerned with controlling female adolescents' sexual behavior. Thus, the model hypothesizes that the advent of puberty in female adolescents increases parental control attempts in their daughters' sexual roles. The primary triggers for this will be the appearance of secondary sex characteristics. However, parents who are aware of earlier signs of approaching puberty, such as the prepubertal growth spurt, may begin control attempts even earlier. As Fox and Innazu (1980) revealed, parents, and more specifically mothers, become concerned with future sexual explorations in their adolescents and attempt to prepare their children for future sexual encounters. Work by Udry and his colleagues (1986) further shows that these same social controls are not as strong an influence on male adolescent sexuality. Their findings indicate that there is a direct path from male pubertal development to sexual role enactment. This is also reflected in Fig. 4.2.

Peers, Dating Partners, and Early
Adolescent Sexual Role Enactment

Peers represent another socializing force in the lives of adolescents, one that is potentially stronger than parents when considering sexual experiences. Dating partners are another group of conceivably potent socializing agents. These two groups of significant and generalized others help adolescents define the diverse sexual roles that they and others in their social group will fill. Peers and dating partners help to establish the symbolic meaning attached to role behaviors, as well as what constitutes acceptable role expectations and behaviors. These may parallel the meanings and expectations of parents, or they may clash with them. When adolescents' experience contradictory demands from parents and peers, they are apt to experience role conflict over what constitutes normative behavior for themselves (Peterson, 1986).

Figure 4.3 shows the final part of the model that uses symbolic interaction to inform the corpus of the early adolescent sexuality findings. Parents are hypothesized to act on peer influences indirectly by influencing friend choice. This is hypothesized to be a function of the closeness of the parent–child relationships. Adolescents who experience close relationships with their parents will more likely choose friends whom their parents approve (Fletcher, Darling, Steinberg, & Dornbusch, 1995; Steinberg, Lamborn, Dornbusch, & Darling, 1992). Friend choice, in turn, is conceptualized as influencing two of the endogenous variables in the model.

The first of these is peer attitudes, norms, and role expectations. Who adolescents choose as friends will greatly influence the sexual attitudes and role expectations to which they are exposed. Peers differentially reward and punish certain activities. Adolescents experience these peer consequences either directly as a result of their behavior or indirectly through the vicarious experiences of friends. As adolescents discuss what role behaviors and different roles symbolize, they socially construct the meaning behind the diversity of sexual behaviors that can occur. This meaning likely extends to the dyadic contexts of the sexual behavior. Thus, this variable represents one starting point for imparting various sets of meanings in adolescents' lives.

The peer norms and role expectations variable represents two types of peer influences. The primary peer influence comes from the group of individuals with whom an adolescent identifies close friends, or in symbolic interaction terms significant others. These are peers in the true sense of the

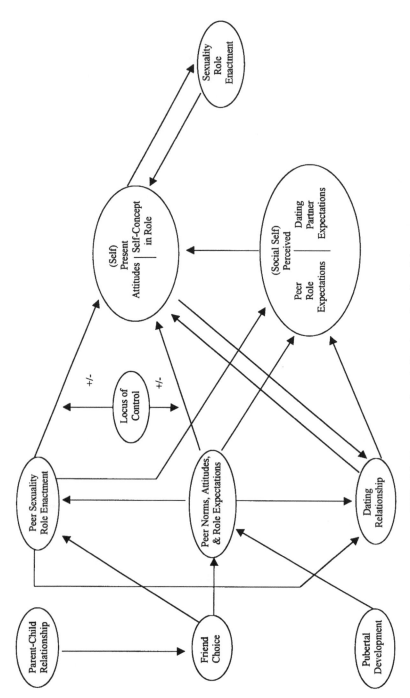

FIG. 4.3. *Peer sexual socialization of early adolescents.*

70

word. They are individuals who are considered friends, who are important to the adolescent, and who can provide rewards, such as status or praise, or punishments, such as scorn or isolation, that will shape the adolescent's self. These are voluntary relationships that are entered into predominately among equals. The second peer influence comes from generalized others in the early adolescent's social environment. These are the source of role expectations that originate in the larger peer milieu. These role expectations possibly allow for the social status ranking of individuals, and the peer groups with which they associate, in the overall social organization in which adolescents find themselves. This type of influence is represented in reports by adolescents that social pressure is the main reason why many young teens fail to delay engaging in intercourse (Harris Poll, 1986).

It needs to be emphasized that the norms and role expectations of this age group will not always be logical nor realistic for many of the same reasons outlined when discussing the sexual roles of this group. Early adolescents are limited by developing cognitive abilities, lack of experience, and inaccurate conceptions held over from childhood. One source of the inaccuracies is the gender-based, differential peer socialization that occurred in preadolescence, as reviewed in chapter 2. Much of the peer socialization prior to this occurred within same sex groups. The cross sex peer groups that will become characteristic of later adolescents begin to emerge at this developmental stage (Adams & Gullotta, 1990). Hence, sex differences will exist in sexual role expectations and in the understanding of the dynamics of role interactions.

Peer norms and role expectations are likely to be influenced by pubertal development (see Fig. 4.3). The appearance of secondary sex characteristics among individuals within a social environment will become a focal point for group discussions. At times, it may be members of an immediate social group who experience physical changes. The ramifications and meaning of these changes then become the target of discussion. For instance, boys who dance close to girls at this age easily experience erections and may ask their male friends about similar episodes. In these discussions, meaning is imparted to the experience, to the role of female partners in the experience, and to possible future interactions with the same partners. In a similar vein, the noticed pubertal changes may involve someone outside of the immediate group. These same boys will then discuss the meanings behind changes in breast size among the female adolescents they encounter daily. For example, a particular girl who previously went unnoticed may become an object of fantasy as her body becomes more adultlike.

As can be seen in Fig. 4.3, peer attitudes, norms, and role expectations are central to peer socialization. Their influence operates on the remaining two peer variables, as well as having direct paths to an adolescent's self and social self. The path to peer sexuality role enactment is considered first. It is expected that the role expectations of the peer group corresponds to actual role behavior. Expectations and enactment do not, however, match perfectly. For one thing, opportunities may not always correspond with the wishes of the adolescents. Those who wish to find readily available sexual partners may not always have their wishes fulfilled, although the finding of some researchers that the average age of first coital acts are as low as 12 and 13 in some locations questions if this will always be true (Erickson & Rapkin, 1991). More importantly, however, the misconceptions and limited experiences and abilities of early adolescents will result in awkward interactive dynamics that will keep these youth from realizing some of their role expectations. Nonetheless, peer norms and role expectations are one of the important forces guiding the development of peer sexual role behavior.

Both peer role expectations and role enactment influence the dating relationships of adolescents. Influence of the peer role expectations comes in the form of contributing to the meaning of a given adolescent's dyadic behaviors, as well as giving status to an adolescent for having dated a particular individual. Romantic interests are likely to be the target of discussion with peer groups. Discussions of these interests allow adolescents to consider each part of a role, interpret its meaning, and decide on its acceptability. Peers also model sexual role behavior, a potentially powerful socialization process for this age group (Gecas & Seff, 1990). Modeling occurs in part through direct observation and in part vicariously through peers sharing their experiences. This modeling also influences the dating relationship experiences of adolescents.

There are certain qualities of the dating relationship that could increase the likelihood of progression toward coitus. Agreements of monogamy and statements of love and affection would be examples of these qualities (Elo et al., in press; Jessor et al., 1983). Feelings of closeness and exclusivity would also make contributions. The fact that many of these feelings and experiences are new and fresh for the early adolescent will add to their experiences of uniqueness.

The variables of peer norms and role expectations, peer sexuality role enactment, and dating relationship experiences are hypothesized to effect adolescents' social selves. Recall, the social self is how one views one self in relation to those involved in one's social environment—what symbolic interactionists call "the looking glass self." Although adolescents consider different possible roles via role taking, they concurrently consider their peers' reactions to these roles within their social selves. Thus, the path between these three variables and social self highlights the importance of perceived expectations of peers and dating partners. The emphasis here is on perception rather than actual expectations as perceptions are the substance of the social self (Gecas & Seff, 1990). The perception carries the meaning that the adolescent attributes to peers' and dating partners' attitudes, expectations, and behaviors. These become central to how adolescents see themselves relating to their social sphere. The social selves of adolescents have an impact on the adolescents' own sexual self-identities influencing attitudes, values, norms, and self concept.

I hypothesize that the peer variables of peer norms and role expectations, peer sexuality role enactment, and dating relationship experiences have direct effects on the adolescent's self. The demonstrated association between peers' sexual attitudes and adolescents' own attitudes (Zelnick & Shah, 1983), and between peer and adolescent sexual behaviors (Billy & Udry, 1985) evidence the viability of this path. These effects are moderated by locus of control. Locus of control is related to the sexual behavior of early adolescents (cf. Rosenbaum & Kandel, 1990). Thus, it is hypothesized to moderate the effect of both peer role expectations and peer sexual role behavior. Stated another way, adolescents will vary on whether they see important events in their lives to be in their own control, reflecting an internal locus of control, or in the control of others or fate, showing an external locus of control. Peer sexual role expectations and enactment will have a greater effect on adolescent's self among those adolescents who have an external locus of control. They will be more susceptible to peer influences.

I propose that dating relationship experiences are different from other peer influences in how they are associated with the self. As seen in Fig. 4.3, the perception of one's dating partner's expectations are a part of the social self. These expectations are linked to how an adolescent see's him or herself in a sexual role. This, in turn, influences the actual sexual role enactment of the adolescent. Performance in the sexual role is then evaluated and this evaluation becomes a part of the adolescent's sexual self-identity. Self-identity is also likely to respond to relationship conditions. Hence, there is also a path between dating relationship and the self that will also affect sexual role enactment. However, how the adolescent defines him or herself in the relationship is also likely to effect one's relationship experience. The path between dating relationship and adolescent self, therefore, is bi-directional.

It is highly probable that sexual roles and dating roles will be closely intertwined for many adolescents. In many instances, certain dating role conditions will be necessary for sexual involvement to occur. This may not, however, be the case for all adolescents. Sexual roles may be a part of a deviant self-identity for example (Coker et al., 1994; Jessor et al., 1983). In this case, sexual role enactment is a part of an identity that allows for a range of behaviors that go against social norms. These behaviors may include the use of alcohol and other illicit drugs, the use of weapons, or engaging in physical violence. Thus, there is a need to separate these two types of roles from one another.

The proposed model accounts for the effects of the majority of the variables that were reviewed in the previous chapter. Two variables—religiosity and ethnicity—have not been adequately treated and deserve special mention. Although the effects of religion were considered in the section on parents, it is important to examine how adolescent religiosity influences sexual expression. The work of Thornton and Camburn (1989) is especially important here. These researchers found that the influence of religion begins with the parents, and specifically the mother in childhood. The mother prompts childhood participation in a religious environment, participation that fosters adolescent religious involvement. The model reflects these experiences in the effect of parents' religion on their own attitudes, values, and norms, and through parents' socialization (see Fig. 4.2). It is also apt to have an effect through parental influence on friend choice. Adolescents who participate frequently in religious service (the typical manner in which this variable is operationalized) are hypothesized to be predisposed to choose friends with attitudes and role expectations that are consistent with their religious environment. Peer norms, in turn, will be evident in these same peers' sexual role enactment (Mott et al., 1996). Moreover, adolescents probably choose dating partners from this same group of individuals, dating partners who possess common expectations about role enactment. The peer variables will then act on the different parts of the adolescent's self. Hence, religious effects can be accounted for in the socialization processes inherent in the model.

Ethnicity operates in a similar fashion. Parental attitudes, values, and norms will reflect parents' ethnic backgrounds. Similarly, many of the adolescents' peers are likely to be of the same ethnic group, thus their role expectations and enactments will be molded by the ethnicity present in their lives. Specific sexual behaviors may have different meaning across ethnic groups. Blacks, with their younger and greater participation in coitus and their lack of a discernible pattern of sexual interactions, will have a different set of meanings ascribed to sexual involvement than will Hispanics and Whites. Additionally, differences in early adolescent sexual role interpretations and expectations may exist within ethnic groups. Day's (1992) findings points to the fact that Hispanics from a Mexican subculture may differ in their sexuality when compared to Hispanics from other Spanish-speaking countries.

Ethnic differences will correspondingly be evident in the self-identity of adolescents (Bell-Scott & McKenry, 1986; Mirandé, 1986). Adolescents of color develop self-identities that reflect how they relate to the majority culture, as well as how they relate to their own ethnic group. This potentially involves minority adolescents recognizing that there exists different meanings to sexual behaviors depending on whether they are relating to a peer of their own or different ethnic group. Racial homogamy in dating may operate in part because the meaning of a partner's behavior is easier to understand with a member of one's own ethnic group.

This model attempts to explain early adolescent sexual expression. The next two chapters explore sexuality for the next developmental stage—late adolescence and young adulthood. As is seen, the sexuality of individuals at this later stage is richer, reflecting more life experiences and more developed cognitive abilities. Chapter 5 reviews researchers' findings; chapter 6 integrates this literature using symbolic interaction concepts similar to those used in this chapter.

5

Older Adolescent
and
Young Adult Sexuality

Our culture lacks a specific rite of passage that establishes when individuals achieve adulthood. Graduation from high school may serve as one proxy for such a rite. At a minimum, high school graduation serves as a marker that an individual has achieved a higher developmental status. Although the majority of adolescents graduate from high school, what occurs after graduation differs across individuals. Some seek full-time employment, others pursue training in a trade, and still others further their education. Concurrently, although there are those who marry directly after high school (considering heterosexuals only at this point), most wait until their early or mid-20s before settling down. In fact, the mean age at marriage has increased in recent years (Mare, 1991). This means that heterosexual individuals of this developmental period are spending more time exploring interpersonal relationships with individuals of the opposite sex through dating—and this exploration often includes sexual involvement (*Sexually Transmitted Disease Surveillance,* 1996).

This period of life, therefore, is marked with new developmental tasks. Choices about employment versus education underscore a degree of personal freedom and responsibility characteristic of adult status. Parents and family are still important, but older adolescents need to develop a sense of individuation separate from their family of origin. Hence, peers and romantic partners become an important source of socialization as the transition to young adult is sought and experienced. Furthermore, individuals need to develop and become integrated into a social network of peers. The development of personal freedom that permeates other areas of older adolescents/young adults' lives is also an important thematic attribute of the sexual expression of this developmental period. It is not surprising that age-graded norms allow greater freedom to explore one's sexuality (T. Smith, 1994).

What constitutes normative sexual behavior for this age group has changed over the past several decades. Ehrman's (1959a, 1959b) pioneering efforts from the 1940s and 1950s indicated that although males reported a higher incidence of sexual intercourse before marriage than females, coitus was relatively rare before marriage for dating couples. Comparisons of the 1950s and 1960s show an almost twofold increase in the number of singles who experienced intercourse while casually and steadily dating (Bell & Chaskes, 1970). Subsequent contrasts of male and female college students of the 1960s and 1970s revealed a further relaxing of the social strictures against engaging in coitus (Bauman & Wilson, 1974; Bell & Coughey, 1980; King, Balswick, & Robinson, 1977). Similar to the national probability studies reviewed in chapter 3, comparisons for the next decade suggested that the number of individuals in this developmental group who were engaging in premarital intercourse reached a plateau in the 1980s (Robinson, Ziss, Ganza, Katz, & Robinson 1991). More recent analyses of late 1980s and early 1990s national data sets reveal that 80% of single women in their 20s (Tanfer & Cubbins, 1992) and 88% of single men in their 20s and 30s (Billy, Tanfer, Grady, & Klepinger, 1993) were coitally experienced. Moreover, many of these individuals had multiple coital partners. One of the best designed and most recent national probability studies asked young, single adults how many coital partners they experienced in the previous 12 months. Although 56% of women ages 18 to 29 experienced a single intercourse partner, 24% had between two and four coital partners, and 6% experienced more (Laumann, Gagnon, Michael, & Michaels, 1994). Reports from men in the same age group for the previous 12 months similarly showed that although the majority, 41%, had a single coital partner, proportionately more men than women experienced between two and four partners, 30% of the men in the sample, or more than four partners, 14% of the men in the sample (Laumann et al., 1994).

Several trends are noteworthy in these studies. Not only are there more older adolescents and young adults engaging in sexual intercourse today, many are doing so with a greater number of premarital partners, and often with less interpersonal commitment (Lauman et al., 1994). Although Ehrman (1959a) found that if coitus occurred it was most likely to be during engagement, more recent research indicates that simply having a monogamous dating commitment, without future plans, is a sufficient condition for sexual intercourse for many young people (Carroll, Volk, & Hyde, 1985; Christopher & Cate, 1985b; Peplau, Rubin, & Hill, 1977; Roche & Ramsbey, 1993). There is also a convergence in the sexual behavior of males and females (Oliver & Hyde, 1993). Not only are their coital rates becoming markedly similar, there is only a small difference in the average number of lifetime sexual partners they have had (Herold & Mewhinney, 1993; Oliver & Hyde, 1993). Finally, the overall magnitude of change has been much more marked for females than males over the past decades (Earle & Perricone, 1986).

MALE AND FEMALE SEXUALITY

As DeLamater (1987) stated, the fact that young male and female's adult coital rates are converging should not be taken as a sign that there is a corresponding convergence in their sexuality. In fact, it seems far from the truth. Research has uncovered a number of differences that point to divergence in the sexuality of the genders for single individuals at this developmental stage.

Dating is an appropriate place to begin comparisons as dating serves as the most common vehicle used to gain sexual access. Not surprisingly, male and female older adolescents and young adults approach dating differently. Women are more likely than men to evaluate potential dating partners on their career potential, companionship, emotional support, and similarity of religious values (Asmussen & Shehan, 1992). Men worry more than women about how to encourage sexual intimacy; women correspondingly worry more than men about how to discourage sexual intimacy. These worries are probably based in gender differences in sexual expectations. Men want more sexual involvement after fewer dates, and with less emotional commitment, when compared to women (Cohen & Shotland, 1996; Knox & Wilson, 1981; Roche, 1986; Roche & Ramsbey, 1993). Moreover, men and women are aware of their discrepant expectations (Cohen & Shotland, 1996; Knox & Wilson, 1981). Thus, it is not surprising that single male and female worries about sexual interaction form mirror images of one another.

Male and female older adolescents differ in their sexual attitudes and values. Males are more permissive than women are towards sexuality in general, and premarital sexuality specifically (Cohen & Shotland, 1996; Gfellner, 1988; Hendrick & Hendrick, 1995; Hendrick, Hendrick, Slapion-Foote, & Foote, 1985; Herold & Mewhinney, 1993). Moreover, men are more apt than women to approach dyadic interaction with personal standards supportive of engaging in casual sex (Herold, Matika-Tyndale, & Mewhinney, 1998; Maticka-Tyndale, Herold & Mewhinney, 1998). Although both men and women of this stage of development are equally likely to see sex as one of the closest forms of communication that can additionally be used as an instrument of pleasure, they differ in that women are more sexually responsible and conventional than men (Gfellner, 1988; Hendrick et al., 1985), and men are more pleasure-oriented (Hendrick & Hendrick, 1995).

The divergence in attitudes may be linked to gender differences in perceptions of cross-sex, interpersonal interactions. Although both men and women are capable of differentiating sexually interested behavior from friendly behavior, males see more sexual cues in male–female interactions (Shotland & Craig, 1988) even when females are not attempting to send sexual cues (Abbey & Melby, 1986). This has led some researchers to postulate that males have a lower sexual perception threshold—they are more likely to search for and perceive sexual interest in dating partners, even when these partners have no sexual intentions.

Given the differences in attitudes and perceptions, it is not surprising that males and females are dissimilar in their motives for engaging in sexual intercourse. Males identify being horny, seeking pleasure, and needing sex as reasons for coitus more often than women do (Carroll et al., 1985). Men are also more apt to engage in coitus to relieve stress or because they find it arousing to have their partners sexually assert themselves (Hill & Preston, 1996). Women offer a need for emotional involvement to explain their coital interactions (Carroll et al., 1985; Hill & Preseton, 1996). Differences also exist for restraining sexual urges. Women cite not enough love, not knowing a potential partner well enough (Carroll et al., 1985), or moral convictions for not engaging in sexual intercourse, whereas men are more apt to choose the disapproval of others as a restraining reason (Jedlicka & Robinson, 1987). It is especially telling, however, that 46% of the men in Carroll et al.'s sample felt they should never neglect an opportunity for sexual intercourse if one presented itself, that there were no reasons to restrain sexual urges.

Differences also can be found between men and women of this age in what they report is pleasurable and arousing. Compared to men, women enjoy foreplay and afterplay more than sexual intercourse, and prefer to spend more time in these stages of sexual involvement (Denney, Field, & Quadagno, 1984). The reason for this may be linked to differences in what is experienced as arousing. Even in early adolescence (see chapters 3 and 4), sexual interactions tend to follow a progression that begins with kissing, progress through different forms of fondling, may include oral–genital contact, and culminate in intercourse. Later adolescents and young adults continue to follow this scripted progression. Males, however, generally find their arousal level increasing at each of these steps except for oral contact with female genitals (Geer & Broussard, 1990). The same is not true for women. Women's arousal is not additive as they progress through the sequence of sexual interaction and they find some stages of the progression more arousing than others. For example, women report experiencing similar levels of arousal from having their genitals touched or kissed, typically precoital behaviors, as they do from intercourse. Geer and Broussard (1990) suggested this means that male arousal is a stronger influence on the progression of sexual involvement than female arousal. It may additionally mean that male sexuality may be less complex than female sexuality. Male sexuality may be tied to certain behaviors and their accompanying stimulation from sights and sounds (Buss, 1989; Franzoi & Herzog, 1987), whereas women's sexuality may be linked to different parts of their social psychological self.

Evidence exists that female sexuality is more integrated into different dimensions of their personality. Mercer and Kohn (1979) factor analyzed a range of sexual and personality measures for males and females. For males, behavioral measures of sexual expression formed a single factor separate from a second personality factor. Females were different; the factor structure of their responses was such that the measures of sexual expression loaded on different factors that concurrently included personality measures. Hence, male sexuality appears to be unidimensional, female sexuality to be multidimensional.

Further evidence of this is revealed in the work of Cryanowski and Anderson (1998). Their work reveals that women posses two sexual schemas, a positive schema and a negative schema, that are a part of their sexual self and act as cognitive filters that direct sexual behavior. The two schemas are independent of one another and both exist along a continuum. Women with a high positive schema have more sexual experience, a higher sexual desire, and are lower in anxiety than women with a low positive schema. Women with a high negative schema are less sexually experienced, more sexually avoidant, and have lower sexual self-esteem than women with a low negative schema. Cryanowski and Anderson's work is not the only indication that female sexuality is composed of a number of independent dimensions. Myers, Kilmann, Wanlass, and Stout (1983) factor analyzed an array of sexual indicators for a female sample. The first factor reflected an overall level of current and past heterosexual activity. The second captured noncoital, heterosexual interaction that resulted in orgasms. These particular findings provide convergent validity for Geer and Brousard's (1990) finding that female arousal fails to follow the usual progression taken by most couples. Other factors focused on responsiveness to different coital positions, comfort with heterosexual contact, latency to orgasm, gratification from masturbation, and sexual precocity. That these factors were either unrelated, or had a low magnitude of association, shows the complexity of female sexuality. Unfortunately, a similar analysis has not been performed for males of this developmental period.

These findings have two implications. First, they illuminate the ways that older adolescents' and young adults' male and female sexuality contrast with one another. Differences exist in sexual attitudes, values, perceptions, motivations, and what is experienced as arousing. These differences are most likely the result of divergent sexual socialization experiences and differences in socially prescribed and sanctioned sexual role expectations. Second, the majority of researchers whose work is reviewed in this chapter took a similar approach, one focused on either coital status, or the interactional sequence of sexual behaviors that culminates in intercourse. This approach takes the male, rather than the female, experience as the standard. It potentially leaves important dimensions of female sexual experience underrepresented and unexplored.

DATING RELATIONSHIPS AND SEXUALITY

Attempts here to identify the connections between early adolescents' dating relationships and their sexual role enactments were constrained by a paucity of research findings in the previous two chapters. Although I hypothesized that certain qualities of these early dating experiences could increase the chance of coitus, these assertions focused almost solely on commitment, love, and closeness. Knowledge of dating for older adolescents and young adults is much richer. Hence, there is a clearer picture of how dating experiences are interrelated to the sexuality of individuals of this older developmental stage. Dating relationships are the vehicle used by older adolescents and young adults to explore their sexuality. As dating is concurrently the vehicle used to establish and explore romantic relationships, many relationship dimensions and properties become tied to and associated with sexual expression. Sprecher and McKinney (1993) speculated about where sex fits into close relationships and see sexual behavior as serving a number of possible functions. They postulate that sex can be used as an act of intimacy, a sign of affection or love, a form of self-disclosure, a part of interdependence, a way to maintain a relationship, or as an act of exchange. As I show here, their conceptualizations are strongly supported by research findings.

Dating Roles

Dating, and any subsequent sexual interaction, is largely shaped by gender-based role expectations. Even though women's, and to a lesser extent men's, roles have been modified in the areas of education, employment, and family life, dating roles have been more resistant to change (Lloyd, 1991). For instance, although older adolescent and young adult women feel it is acceptable to directly ask a man for a date, and to pay for the date as well, they rarely do so regularly (Asmussen & Shehan, 1992). Additionally, women who ask men on dates must cope with men who have increased expectations for sexual involvement, expectations that are rarely met (Mongeau & Johnson, 1995). Moreover, when women ask men for dates, the budding relationship seems to have a decreased chance of becoming permanent; it is likely to end by three dates (K. Kelley, Pilchowicz, & Byrne, 1981). Instead, women strongly rely on nonverbal behavior to capture men's attention and communicate their interest in them, thereby availing themselves of indirect rather than direct influence attempts.

M. Moore (1985) identified several of these communicative behaviors through an ethnological study conducted in a varied set of interpersonal contexts. She found smiling one of the most frequent nonverbal signals of interest women use, often accompanied by either a brief or prolonged glance directed at the male. Gestures such as hair flipping, tipping one's head to bare one's neck, and strategic touching or caressing of inanimate objects provide other cues of interest. Women also employ certain body postures to convey their receptiveness. They at times lean toward males, may brush their breasts against them, or engage in prolonged contact with their knees, thighs, or feet. These are effective cues; women who displayed them with a high frequency were approached an average of four times an hour, as compared with .5 average approaches for women who were low in frequency, regardless of the interpersonal context.

These traditional roles extend to the sexual realm. Women, more than men, assign males the role of sexual initiators while concurrently being concerned about how to limit sexual involvement (Asmussen & Shehan, 1992). Men comply with this role assignment by initiating sexual intimacy more frequently than women (O'Sullivan & Byers, 1992). This role fulfillment has its rewards; men and women both find their sexual interaction more pleasurable when men initiate the interaction than when women initiate it. Hence, Ehrman's (1959b) early finding that men initiate sexual contact while women limit how much occurs seemingly applies just as much today as it did over four decades in the past. Moreover, initiating activity, and the responses to initiations, are predicted by whether the dating relationship is casual or steady, but not by an individual's gender-role ideology, emotional responses to sexual cues, or level of sexual experience (O'Sullivan & Byers, 1992). This suggests that sexual initiation behavior is apt to be driven by socially prescribed role expectations related to dating stage rather than by individual variables.

Relationship Properties

Researchers have taken a variety of approaches in their attempts to uncover the interpersonal chemistry that leads to dating couples engaging in sexual intercourse. This interaction may also be socially scripted into different role expectations. One way to test for role expectations would be to ask virgins what they perceive will influence their first act of intercourse, and compare their responses to what nonvirgins report actually influenced them. Christopher and Cate (1984, 1985a) provided such a comparison. Virgins in their study anticipated that their initial act of coitus would be influenced by three factors. In the first, virgins expected that they and their partners would be physically aroused and receptive to each other's advances. The second suggested that their first act of coitus would take place in a loving and committed relationship where there was a possibility of a future with the partner. Female virgins felt this factor would be more important to them than male virgins. Finally, virgins felt that circumstances, such as alcohol or drug use, and how romantic or special the date would be, would play a role in their coital decision.

These factors had a high correspondence to what nonvirgins report actually influenced them in their first act of intercourse in their latest relationship (Christopher & Cate, 1984). These same three factors emerged as influences with only two differences. First, the relationship factor was more important in sexual decision making than what nonvirgins anticipated. Second, a fourth factor emerged as an influence—feelings of pressure and obligation that originated in part from the dyadic interaction, and in part from how coitally experienced one's peers were. Males found this fourth factor a stronger influence than females. The correspondence between the virgins and nonvirgins responses suggest that not only is sexual behavior scripted, but the dyadic events and personal experiences that surround the sequence may be scripted as well.

It would appear that one of the stronger parts of this role prescription emphasizes the importance of emotional closeness in sexual and coital decisions. The earliest investigations into dating sexuality by Ehrman (1959b) and Kirkendall (1961) showed that intimacy and love were associated with sexual involvement, and that this was a stronger association for women than men. Their early findings were confirmed by a number of analyses undertaken during the 1970s (Curran, Neff, & Lippold, 1973; Davidson & Leslie, 1977; Lewis & Burr, 1975). The consistency of the findings led one research team to include love in their path model. DeLamater and MacCorquodale's (1979) extensive investigation of correlates of sexual involvement revealed a direct path between love and sexual involvement.

These earlier findings have been replicated in more recent works. Christopher (1993) also tested a path model that predicted sexual involvement and included love. He found love operated indirectly on sexual involvement through expressions of emotional intimacy and caring. Similarly, Cate, Long, Angera, and Draper's (1993) work revealed that dating relationships improve when the emotional tenor of the relationship plays a role in the initial coital decision of dating individuals. Thus, it is evident that feelings of love and intimacy are strongly and positively tied to sexual involvement while dating. This may help explain their effect even among early adolescents.

Not all scholars agree about the causal direction of the relation between love and sexual involvement. Aron and Aron (1991) suggested that research that ties these variables together can be arranged along a continuum. One extreme represents those who believe that love can be ignored, or that love is the result of sexuality—sociobiologists typically fall into this category (i.e., Buss, 1989, 1998). Those at the other extreme believe that sexuality can be ignored, or that sexuality is the result of love—the position of certain philosophers, existentialists, and object relations theorists. The middle position represents a popular one among those who subscribe to a social psychological explanation of relationships and sexuality. In this position, sexuality and love are equally important when explaining close relationship phenomena.

Dyadic commitment has an equivalent strong role in sexual involvement. Early researchers noted that sexual involvement increased as commitment increased, and that coital involvement was much more probable when couples made a monogamous commitment (Bell & Chaskes, 1970; Herold & Goodwin, 1981). Two research teams, using different methodologies, later showed that commitment plays different roles for different couples. Peplau et al. (1977) conducted a 2-year longitudinal study of the sexual interactions of dating couples. Christopher and Cate (1985b) asked dating couples to retrospectively recreate their dating relationship while focusing on their relationship experiences at different developmental stages. The findings of the two studies provide convergent validity for the different roles commitment can play.

Both research teams revealed that some couples choose not to engage in coitus, and limit their sexual interactions to noncoital behavior. Peplau et al. (1977) called these couples *sexually traditional couples,* whereas Christopher and Cate (1985a) called them *low involvement couples.* Individuals in this type of relationship believe that love by itself fails to justify sexual intercourse; coitus is to be saved for marriage (Peplau et al., 1977). Not surprisingly, these individuals hold conservative sexual attitudes, and have limited lifetime sexual experience (Christopher & Cate, 1985b).

At the other end of the continuum are couples who engaged in coitus with very little commitment, often on the first date. Peplau et al. (1977) found these *sexually liberated couples* to be interested in eroticism. They believe that sex with love is desirable, but sex without love is acceptable. Christopher and Cate's (1985b) *rapid involvement couples* were very similar. Their initial coital decision was influenced by feelings of physical arousal, and they held liberal sexual attitudes.

The two research teams diverged on how many remaining couple types existed. Peplau et al. reported that there was one other couple type, *sexually moderate couples.* These couples wait at least 1 month before engaging in coitus. They require love but not long-term commitment for this level of sexual involvement, and were inclined to have a romantic view of both love and sexual interaction.

Christopher and Cate (1985b) found two other couple types. *Gradual involvement couples* engage in coitus concurrent to considering becoming a couple. They hold liberal sexual attitudes, and even though their initial act of coitus is influenced by the quality of their emotional relationship, their decision to engage in intercourse is intertwined with their decision to become monogamously committed to one another. *Delayed involvement couples* are very different. The quality of their emotional relationship also plays an important role in their coital decision making. They, however, hold conservative sexual attitudes. This may explain the pattern of their sexual interaction. They resolutely limit their sexual involvement until making a monogamous dating commitment. This level of commitment serves as a sexual watershed once reached, allowing them to explore their sexual involvement as fully as the other coitally experienced couples.

The consequence of first coitus for dating individuals' relationship development depends on what influenced their decision to engage in intercourse with their partner. Dating relationships improve for young adult men and women when their initial coital decisions are tied to judgments about the current quality of the relationship (Cate et al., 1993). Specifically, when emotional closeness plays a role in deciding to first engage in coitus with a partner, young adults are sexually satisfied with their coital experiences and perceive their relationships as getting better as a consequence of more becoming sexually involved.

Other relationship experiences play an important role in the sexual expression of dating individuals. Individuals who balance the costs and rewards they receive from their relationships, relative to the perceived rewards and costs of their partners, have been conceptualized as having equitable relationships. When one dyad member receives a disproportionate number of rewards, that person is overbenefited. Underbenefited individuals receive a disproportionate number of the relationship costs. Comparisons of these three types of relationships show that individuals in fairly equitable relationships are more sexually intimate than the other two. Moreover, they are likely to engage in coitus because both partners want that level of sexual intimacy (Walster, Walster, & Traupmann, 1978).

The effects of rewards, costs, and equity appear to also operate when focusing purely on the sexual role interactions of dating individuals (Byers & Demmons, 1999; Byers, Demmons, & Lawrence, 1998; Lawrence & Byers, 1995). After controlling for the effects of satisfaction with the dating relationship as a whole, young men and women are most satisfied with the sexual interactions with their partner when sexual rewards exceed sexual costs, when sexual reward levels exceed the rewards they expected, when sexual costs are lower than the costs they expected, and when they judge there is equality in the sexual rewards and costs their partners receive.

Relational conflict is another relationship experience linked to sexual involvement. Each of Christopher and Cate's (1985b) couple types experienced high levels of such conflict at the dating stage where they either engaged in sexual intercourse, or came close to engaging in it in the case of low involvement couples. Analyses of all the individuals in the study as a group paints an interesting picture. Relational conflict was the strongest predictor of sexual involvement for first date and casually dating, and was only surpassed by love for the stage of considering becoming a couple (Christopher & Cate, 1988). Moreover, this was a positive association, but given the correlational nature of the study it is difficult to establish a cause–effect relation between these variables. One possible explanation, differences in the sexual expectations of males and females lead to increases in conflict that may be resolved, in part, by becoming more sexual involved. Another possibility, couples engage in intercourse without discussing its ramifications. When faced with this highly symbolic interaction, conflict ensues as the couple decides what meaning to ascribe to their actions, and what parameters to assign to their relationship.

Couples may also experience conflict over their sexual role enactments (Long, Cate, Fehsenfeld, & Williams, 1996). Differences may arise over the type, frequency, and whether to engage in particular sexual behaviors. Sexual conflict covaries with other relational qualities including increases in general relational conflict, and decreases in relational and sexual satisfaction. Moreover, sexual conflict appears to influence relationship development. Long et al.'s longitudinal investigation found that increases in sexual conflict measured at the beginning of their study predicted relationship dissatisfaction 4 months later for both young men and women with a stronger effect for women.

Christopher and Cate's (1988) analysis showed that two additional relationship experiences are related to the sexual involvement that occurs on first dates and while casually dating. The first involves a set of relationship maintenance behaviors that are used to increase intimacy at these early dating stages. These include intimate self-disclosure, changing one's behaviors to meet the needs of a partner, and talking about the meaning of the relationship. It is not surprising that engaging in these acts is positively associated with sexual involvement as they promote intimacy. The second experience is ambivalence about a relationship's future, which has a positive relationship with sexual involvement. As with conflict, the correlational nature of the data makes it important to be cautious about cause–effect conclusions. It is conceivable that engaging in certain sexual behaviors could lead one to have questions about a relationship's future. It is also conceivable that ambivalence about making a commitment could be resolved by increasing sexual involvement if the predicted rewards outweighed the predicted costs.

Communication

In his landmark study of sexual behavior before dating, Kirkendall (1961), compared the tenor of six types of relationships where sexual intercourse had taken place. These relationships ranged from having sex with a prostitute to having sex with a fiancée. He noted that the type of sexual communication varied as relationships progressed from a client–provider relationship to one characterized by marriage plans. He found that couples' capacity for sexual communication grew with the emotional intensity of the relationship. Moreover, the amount of argumentative and persuasive communication decreased sharply once coitus was experienced. The experience of intercourse itself, however, failed to facilitate dyadic communication.

Research since Kirkendall's (1961) investigation provides additional insight into how older adolescents and young adults' communication is related to their sexual activity. The type of sexual vocabulary used by persons of this age is largely dictated by the interpersonal context of the verbal exchange (Simkins & Rinck, 1982). When in mixed-sex company, males and females use formal or clinical terms for genitals and acts of sexual intercourse. When with one's lover, differences emerge. Males and females both prefer using formal terms for female genitals in this context. Females similarly prefer formal terms for male genitals, whereas males are more prone to use colloquialisms or slang. For the act of intercourse, however, both males and females switch to using euphemistic statements referring to it as "making love" or "rolling in the hay" although males at times also favor slang. Differences in vocabulary choice additionally exist in same-sex conversations and discussions with one's parents. This demonstrates that one's choice of sexual vocabulary is symbolic of the interpersonal context and further illustrates how social role prescriptions influence dyadic interaction.

Context, however, is not the only determinant of when and how dating partners speak with one another. Herold and Way (1988) examined different predictors of sexual self-disclosure in a group of single females. Virgins were most likely to self-disclose about sexual matters if they felt their partner would be comfortable talking about sexual issues, if they were committed in their dating relationship, and if sex was not that important to them in their life. These variables were also predictive of nonvirgins' sexual self-disclosure to their partners with the addition of sex guilt.

It is likely that such self-disclosure will contribute to couples developing similar or shared interpretations of sexual phenomenon as their relationships develop. Work by Lally and Maddock (1994) demonstrates, however, that the development of shared sexual meanings among engaged couples is somewhat dependent on social context. They found that couples who attended church, were from the same religious denomination, and had higher levels of education were more similar in the meaning they assigned to sexual events than were couples who did not posses these characteristics. As religion and education can be viewed as socializing agents, Lally and Maddock's findings suggest that participating in these social institutions either results in assigning similar meanings to sexual events, or prompts couples to talk and come to some level of agreement about how sexual phenomenon should be perceived.

These studies should not be interpreted to mean that most sexual communication between dating partners is verbal. Males and females at this stage of development are much more likely to rely on nonverbal cues to initiate sexual interactions and some do not use any verbal cues in these instances (O'Sullivan & Byers, 1992). Snuggling, kissing, and allowing one's hands to wander are preferred over dropping verbal hints or simply asking (Jessor, 1978). Even when verbal initiation cues are used, they are more likely to be ambiguous than direct (O'Sullivan & Byers, 1992). Nonverbal cues are effective—they are apt to be followed by some form of satisfying and pleasurable sexual activity.

The reliance on nonverbal cues, as opposed to direct verbal queries, probably reflects a strategic choice by dyad members. As Cupach and Metts (1991) stated:

> For the partner seeking sexual compliance, indirectness and ambiguity facilitate the accomplishment of two sequentially ordered goals: to gain sexual access and to avoid rejection. Although these goals may appear to be logical alternatives, they are not. Gaining sexual access is a task accomplishment, and avoiding rejection is a self-image or face-maintenance goal. Indirect strategies accomplish both goals. (pp. 97–98)

Cupach and Metts also stated that nonverbal cues can be successful and O'Sullivan and Byer's (1992) research show this to be true in most cases. Thus, the failure of a partner to respond to nonverbal initiation cues does not have to be interpreted by the individual as a personal rejection because an explicit overture for sexual involvement was not made. Hence, the person saves face (see also Denzin, 1970; Tracy, Craig, Smith, & Spisak, 1984, for further discussion of these issues).

Choosing to use nonverbal over verbal messages opens the door to miscommunication because of the potential ambiguity in interpreting this type of cue. Unfortunately, nonverbal miscommunication has yet to be the focus of research, but verbal miscommunication has been investigated. Two forms have been examined. The first involves saying no to sexual intercourse when in fact individuals would really like to engage in coitus. Males and females who engage in this behavior have been conceptualized as offering token resistance to sex (Muehlenhard & Hollabaugh, 1988). Older adolescent and young adult males in our society are more likely than females to have engaged in token resistance at least once (Muehlenhard & Rodgers, 1998; Sprecher, Hatfield, Cortese, Potapova, & Levitskaya, 1994). Token resistance is most likely to occur after partners have dated a number of times and are romantically interested in one another (O'Sullivan & Allgeier, 1994).

When women are asked why they engaged in this form of miscommunication, their reasons fall into one of three categories (Muehlenhard & Hollabaugh, 1988). The first group of reasons are practical—women fear appearing promiscuous, are uncertain of a partner's feelings, do not want to be taken for granted, or are concerned about pregnancy or STDs. The second group focus on feeling inhibited—the women experienced emotional, religious, or moral concerns; are uncomfortable with sex; or are self-conscious about their bodies. The final group of reasons are manipulative in nature—women have a desire to be in control or exert power, are angry with a partner, or want to engage in game playing. Women who offer manipulative reasons are apt to have engaged in coitus with their partner on a previous occasion (Shotland & Hunter, 1995). When men are asked the reasons they offered token resistance, the pattern of responses are similar. Emotional and relational concerns are at the forefront (O'Sullivan & Allgeier, 1994). These are followed by being worried about practical issues and social image. Game playing and control attempts are the least offered reasons.

Practical reasons may be particularly compelling ones for women to use token resistance. Muehlenhard and McCoy (1991) found that women were more likely to say no to coitus when they want to engage in it with a new dating partner because they believed that their partner held a double standard. Hence, these women believed that by saying no they would be judged as "respectable" and not as "easy." As these researchers point out, the double standard puts women in a double bind when it comes to sexual communication. Such findings may explain why token resistance often reflects women's ambivalence abut whether to become coitally involved with a dating partner (Shotland & Hunter, 1995).

The other type of miscommunication mirrors token resistance, saying yes when meaning no or, as some have coined it, *feigning sexual desire* (O'Sullivan & Gaines, 1998). The small number of studies in this area limits insights into this phenomenon. O'Sullivan and Gaines reported that men and women most often engage in sexual acts because of emotional intimacy conerns. Similarly, Sprecher et al. (1994) revealed that males and females who offered token resistance, or who engaged in unwanted sex, were more likely to see love as characterized by game playing. They also saw love as erotic, romantic, and passionate, and less likely to involve friendship. These research findings suggest that older adolescents and young adults' conceptualization of dating and sexual roles shape the way they attempt to influence their dating partner. Such findings may explain why token resistance often reflects women's ambivalence about whether to become coitally involved with a partner (Shotland & Hunter, 1995).

Influencing A Partner

Using nonverbal cues is only one way to sexually influence a dating partner. Once one partner wants to engage in sex, that individual must influence the other partner to comply with his or her wishes. If the partner does not want to be involved in sexual activity, he or she must conceive of some way for limiting sexual involvement. This type of interaction involves the use of influence or behavioral attempts to change a partner's behavior.

Early research into this area asked individuals to write essays about how they would either influence a partner to engage in or avoid coitus with an imaginary dating partner. McCormick (1979) found that although seduction was identified as increasing the chances of sexual intercourse, the use of rewards, coercion, logic, information, manipulation, body language, deception, moralizing, and relationship conceptualization were additionally perceived as either increasing or decreasing coital chances. Perper and Weis (1987) similarly found that talking, using environmental and situational signaling, touching, and kissing were seen as making coitus more likely, whereas avoiding and ignoring cues were commonly viewed as ways to reject advances. LaPlante, McCormick, and Brannigan (1980) asked individuals to report on their own dating experience. In their findings, males used both indirect and direct techniques in attempts to engage in coitus and females used both indirect and direct techniques in attempts to avoid coitus.

Christopher and Frandsen (1990) built on this early work by positing that older adolescents and young adults do not use one influence technique at a time, but rather use a number of them in concert as an overall sexual influence strategy. They tested this assumption by factor analyzing responses to an array of influence techniques garnered from previous research. Four influence strategies resulted. One they called the *emotional and physical closeness strategy,* which included making liking and loving statements, physically touching, acting seductively, and communicating with one's hands, and was positively related to sexual involvement. Another they called a *logic and reason strategy,* which entailed the use of authority, logic, insistence, and compromise. It was negatively related to sexual involvement, and was used more by individuals who wished for less sexual activity suggesting that the goal of this influence strategy was to limit sexual interaction. The final two influence strategies, *antisocial acts* and *pressure and manipulation*, involved using sexual aggression and are discussed in chapters 7 and 8.

Conclusions

The conclusion that can best be reached from this literature review is that relationship phenomena play an important role in the sexual experiences of older adolescents and young adults. Probably because relationship development so often transpires at the same time that sexual involvement ensues, these phenomena become strongly intertwined. Hence, the role behavior that occurs in dating relationships concurrently influences the evolution of sexual involvement, especially in the initial stages of dating. Socially learned role prescriptions are initially relied on because dating partners have little knowledge of each other, and have failed to develop a relationship history that includes the emergence of shared meanings for symbolic gestures (Duck, 1994). This is especially true of the highly symbolic gesture of sexual interaction.

The common importance placed on intimacy, love, and commitment shows the importance these relationship experiences play in scripted sexual interaction. Other relationship experiences, such as relational conflict, sexual conflict, sexual rewards, sexual costs, equity, maintenance behaviors, and ambivalence are additional influences, albeit not as important as those previous ones. Communication is also a salient part of a sexual role enactment. Certain nonverbal cues must have socially recognized meaning if they are to be effective at initiating both cross-gender romantic interaction and subsequent sexual activity. The fact that much of the communication is nonverbal may be related to past experiences in families where sexual vocabularies are limited if not nonexistent (see chapter 2). It may additionally be related to the fact that sexual interaction itself is a form of nonverbal communication. Finally, use of nonverbal cues allows one to save face when partners are not responsive.

Power and influence attempts are a part of any close relationship (Huston, 1979). That some individuals purposefully engage in sexual miscommunication reflects attempts to influence dating partners and represents how these individuals conceptualize relationship and sexual roles. Such influence attempts are linked with other techniques to form overall influence strategies that either increase or limit sexual involvement.

PARENTS AND PEERS

The theoretical model of early adolescent sexuality I proposed in the previous chapter identified parents as a strong socializing force in these young people's lives. Although parents may still influence sexual role enactments in these later developmental stages, the tenor of their influence changes. One of the developmental tasks of older adolescence and young adulthood is to become independent of one's parents while still maintaining a positive, emotional relationship. At the same time, older adolescents and young adults need to become integrated into a peer or friendship network that reinforces their forays into the world of adults. Peers can provide reinforcement for behaviors that parents would not, such as with sexual involvement. Although these developmental tasks do not necessarily clash with one another, there is at least a possibility that they might.

The existence of these two tasks led early sexuality researchers to use reference group theory to guide their investigations into peer and parental influences (Lewis, 1973; Mirande, 1968; Teevan, 1972). In brief, this theory postulates that males and females of this age will choose individuals, or *referents*, with whom they identify. Referents are used to judge the correctness of one's behavior. These early scholars speculated that choosing one's parents rather than peers as referents results in a lower level of sexual involvement. This hypothesis was largely supported for both pre-marital sexual attitudes and behaviors, but was stronger for daughters than sons (Lewis, 1973; Teevan, 1972; Walsh, Ferrell, & Tolone, 1976). There are indications that choosing parents as referents may be a function of different dimensions of the parent–child relationship. Individuals of this age who cite their parents as their primary source of sexual know-ledge are less likely to be coitally experienced than those who cite peers as their primary source (Lewis, 1973; Spanier, 1977). Moreover, parental attitudes about premarital sex are positively associated with the attitudes of their older adolescent and young adult offspring (DeLamater & Mac-Corquodale, 1977a; Herold & Goodwin, 1981) and with family sexual communication (G. Fisher, 1986). Parental influence may be mediated by the quality of the parent–child relationship. Feeling close to one's par-ents, and seeing one's parents as understanding and affectionate, are related to lower levels of sexual involvement (DeLamater & Mac-Corquodale, 1977), and feeling that a parent is comfortable with dis-cussing sexual matters is related to daughters' sexual self-disclosure to parents (Herold & Way, 1988). The association of these parent–child relationship variables to sexual activity is consistent across different pop-ulations, although it is only moderate in size and, again, is stronger for females than males.

Peers are most often chosen as referents if parents are not. Whether this results in sexual activity on the part of the older adolescent or young adult depends on the referent peers. If youths perceive their friends as limiting their sexual activity, they are also apt to limit their own sexual involve-ment (Mirande, 1968; Teevan, 1972). If, however, referent peers are seen as sexually active, individuals are more likely to be sexually active them-selves (Davidson & Leslie, 1977; Herold & Godwin, 1981; Walsh et al., 1976). This is a strong, direct relationship and holds even when tested in multivariate models (DeLamater & MacCorquodale, 1977; Reed & Wein-berg, 1984; B. Schultz, Bohrnstedt, Borgatta, & Evans, 1977). This social effect appears to generalize to sexual intentions. If friends are perceived as supportive of engaging in casual sex, such perceptions increase young individuals' intentions to engage in casual sex (Herold et al., 1998). It is important to note that this research does not necessarily suggest that older adolescents and young adults attempt to match their friends' level of sex-ual involvement, typically they see their friends as more sexually permis-sive and active then themselves (Cohen & Shotland, 1996; Ehrman, 1959b; Roche, 1986). Nonetheless, the perception of peer sexual activity provides a source of modeling and vicarious reinforcement for young adults' own sexual socialization.

Although the perception of peers' sexual behavior affects the sexual activity of both males and females at this stage of development, the role peers play for males and females may be different. Males, more than females, experience pressure to engage in coitus in part because they see their friends as sexually involved (Christopher & Cate, 1984) and report that their friends exert pressure on them to become sexually experienced (Muehlenhard & Cook, 1988). Males are also quicker to tell friends about their coital activity and tell more friends than females (Carns, 1973). Moreover, males' friends are more likely to approve of their activity than are females' friends. Thus, although both males and females model their friends' sexual activity, males appear to additionally gain peer status and social reinforcement for engaging in coitus.

Although parents and peers are specific and potentially significant social influences on the sexuality of older adolescents and young adults, the larger culture also exerts an influence. In recent times, the most telling example of this is the way the media and others have continually raised the specter of AIDS. This attention poses the question of whether this more distant social environment factor is associated with changes in sexual behavior. General worries about contracting STDs are low for this group (Asmussen & Shehan, 1992; Davidson & Moore, 1994), although many discuss AIDS in some capacity in their relationships (Sprecher, 1990). Individuals currently, however, are making few changes in their sexual behavior, and very few report regular use of condoms (L. Carroll, 1988; Davidson & Moore, 1994; Herold & Mewhinney, 1993; Sprecher, 1990).

The most frequent behavioral changes that have occurred in response to AIDS awareness attempts are that individuals report being more selective in their choice of partners by asking about potential partners' sexual histories, and getting to know them better before engaging in intercourse (Davidson & Moore, 1994; Herold & Mewhinney, 1993; Sprecher, 1990). Young women are more likely than young men to use these techniques. Unfortunately, sharing sexual histories has little association with condom use (Kellar-Guenther & Christopher, 1997). Precautions against AIDS additionally appear to be linked to the level of relationship involvement. Individuals who are in a steady relationship indicate that AIDS concerns have no effect on their sexual activity, whereas uninvolved individuals, and especially males, report that they are more selective in choosing sexual partners (Carroll, 1988; Davidson & Moore, 1994). There is evidence that condom use is more frequent with coitus in casually dating relationships as compared to monogamous relationships (Kellar-Guenther & Christopher, 1998; S. Moore & Barling, 1991). Relying on a dating partner's promise of sexual fidelity as means of protection does not always decrease risk of exposure. Ample evidence exists that a surprisingly high number of single individuals violate such promises (Forste & Tanfer, 1996; Sheppard, Nelson, & Andreoli-Mathie, 1995; Stebleton & Rothenberger, 1993). Some individuals indicate that they have become not only more selective, but engage in less frequent sexual activity (Carroll, 1988). A close examination of the characteristics of these individuals questions whether they would be sexually active even without the threat of AIDS.

Conclusions

Although parents continue to exert an influence on the sexual behavior of older adolescents and young adults, this influence is mediated by the quality of the parent–child relationship and is only moderate in strength when compared to their potential influence during early adolescence. Perception of peer sexual behavior plays a much more salient role in the sexual involvement of individuals of this age. Furthermore, although these perceptions serve as a model for sexual behavior for both males and females, males who "kiss" (or do more) and "tell" are additionally motivated to engage in coitus by the social rewards and peer status gains that can be achieved from their sexual exploration. Finally, it appears that the proximal social environment is more influential on sexual expression than the distal social environment.

INDIVIDUAL INFLUENCES

It is apparent that dyadic and social influences play a part in the sexual activity of older adolescents and young adults. Researchers of sexuality at this stage have also demonstrated that individual factors are related to sexual exploration. As is shown here, these range from the influence of biology, to the impact of one's dating and sexual history.

Biology Revisited

Sociobiologists interested in dating see it as the means by which individuals choose mates who facilitate the survival of their genes in their offspring. Explaining the survival of genes is a central interest to scholars in this field. Because choosing such partners involves sexuality, sociobiological views are important. One such sociobioligist, Buss (1989), examined how males and females attract potential mates. He postulated that mate selection involves competition and the wishes of the opposite sex determines what type of courtship displays men and women will value. In a series of studies, he demonstrated that men, more than women, display their "marketable" resources by bragging about their strength, athleticism, and sexual prowess. Women were more apt then men to display cues such as wearing makeup, altering their appearance, wearing stylish clothes and jewelry, and acting nice. He believes that the goal of these female practices is to appear young and healthy, thereby emphasizing their reproductive ability. When newlyweds were asked what they did to attract their mates, parallel results were obtained. Moreover, the same tactics were identified as effective means of attracting the attention of someone of the opposite sex in yet a third study. Buss concluded that utilizing such intrapersonal resources are effective strategies for increasing and marketing one's reproductive fitness.

Simpson and Gangestad (1991) were similarly concerned with reproduction strategies. They identified a number of personality traits that, by their interpretation of the personality literature, are related to one another, suggesting the existence of a core personality construct. These traits include extroversion–introversion, self-monitoring (discussed shortly), dominance, lack of constraint, and disinhibition. Simpson and Gangestad constructed a measure to tap into this core personality construct, called *Scale Zeta*, and administered it to both identical and fraternal twins. They found that the scores from the identical twins were highly correlated with one another (intraclass $r = .76$), whereas the scores from the fraternal twins were only nominally related to one another ($r = .16$). Simpson and Gangestad concluded from this test that *Scale Zeta* represents a genetically determined personality construct because identical twins were so similar in their scores, whereas fraternal twins were not.

Simpson and Gangestad (1991) also showed that *Scale Zeta* is highly related to one's sociosexual orientation, the second construct they use. They proposed that individuals either possess a restricted or an unrestricted sociosexual orientation. Those with a restricted orientation pair their sexual involvements with emotional closeness and commitment, have fewer sex partners, rarely, if ever, engage in one night stands, and have sexual fantasies only about their current partner. Individuals with an unrestricted orientation have a greater number of sex partners, are more likely to have experienced one-night stands, often fantasize about partners other than their current dating partner, and require less commitment before engaging in sex. Simpson and Gangestad proposed that because they provided evidence that their *Scale Zeta* has a genetic component, and because *Scale Zeta* is strongly related to one's sociosexual orientation, that one's sociosexual orientation is also likely to be genetically determined. In other words, they hypothesized that individuals are either sexually restrictive or unrestrictive in their dating relationships because of their genetic makeup.

One criticism that can be levied against the sociobiological approach is that it fails to identify the linkages between genes and behavior. The path between these two variables is not likely to be direct and probably involves yet-to-be identified factors. Thus, although biology may play a role in the sexuality of older adolescents and young adults, the specifics of that role are not completely clear at this time.

Attitudes, Values, and Norms

Researchers in the 1970s (Clayton, 1972; King, Abernathey, Robinson, & Balswick, 1976), the 1980s (Carroll, 1988; Herold & Goodwin, 1981; Earle & Perricone, 1986), and the 1990s (Tanfer & Schoorl, 1992) consistently reported that having a permissive premarital sexual attitude is positively associated with sexual activity in dating or the intention to engage in sex (Herold et al., 1998). Premarital sexual attitudes, however, have changed over the course of these investigations (Oliver & Hyde, 1993; T. Smith, 1994). Given that the number of coitally active individuals has increased, it is not surprising that attitudes toward premarital sexual activity have similarly become more liberal over the past several decades (T. Smith, 1994), with females experiencing a more dramatic shift in attitudes than males (King et al., 1977; Robinson et al., 1991; Sherwin & Corbett, 1985).

I speculated in the previous chapter that sexual attitudes of adolescents become more complex as they mature, a speculation supported by research. Premarital sexual attitudes held by older adolescents and young adults are multidimensional. Reiss (1964), in an early, seminal contribution, proposed that premarital sexual permissiveness could be measured. His original proposition has been well supported even in more current research (cf. Sprecher, McKinney, Walsh, & Anderson, 1988). Yet, Hendrick et al. (1985) showed that although permissiveness constitutes one of the more important sexual attitudes, it is not the only premarital sexual attitude. Older adolescents and young adults also hold beliefs about sexual responsibility, communion, instrumentality, conventionality, and power.

Attitudes reflect one's standards or values. Reiss (1960), in another of his important works, proposed that standards influenced sexual decisions by individuals. He proposed that most individuals commonly held four standards. The *double standard* allowed males to explore their sexuality in and out of marriage, while demanding that women restrict coital activity to marriage. Those who hold a standard of *permissiveness without affection* focused on pursuing pleasure and engaging in body-centered coitus without worrying about commitment. In contrast, the standard of *permissiveness with affection* required partners to be emotionally involved with one another, and judged engaging in intercourse for other reasons as unacceptable. Finally, there are those who value *abstinence*, where coitus is seen as too valuable and intimate to be engaged in without the sanctity of marriage.

Tests by Reiss (1960, 1967) of his proposed standards upheld their existence. Later work demonstrated that the prevailing norm for individuals at this stage of development was permissiveness with affection (cf. DeLamater, 1987) and suggested a need for an additional standard, *nonexploitive permissiveness without affection* (Jurich & Jurich, 1974). Additionally, although it was clear that the double standard existed in the 1950s (Ehrman, 1959b) and the 1960s (Kaats & Davis, 1970), research findings that demonstrated a convergence of male and female coital rates, and similarities in sexual decision-making processes, led some researchers to question whether the double standard still existed (Christopher & Cate, 1984; DeLamater & MacCorquodale, 1979). Later experimental investigations show that it is still alive and functioning, restricts sexual activity for present day women to committed relationships, and has become subtler. In these investigations, subjects give their impressions about a person who, they think, is real. In fact, the person is fictitious and has been assigned certain characteristics such as gender, level of sexual experience, and age by the investigators to see if these manipulations results in different responses. The results clearly show that the double standard is used to judge the correctness of others' behavior by many contemporary youths (Jacoby & Williams, 1985; Mark & Miller, 1986; Sprecher, McKinney, & Orbuch, 1987, 1991).

Reiss (1960) is not the only scholar to propose a typology of premarital sexual standards or values. D'Augelli and D'Augelli (1977) offered an alternative typology based on the moral, relationship, and sexual reasoning of older adolescents and young adults. Their typology contains three groups of virgins. The first group had dated very little and were sexually inexperienced. The second group adamantly believed that intercourse should be saved for marriage, but that other forms of sexual activity were acceptable if love and commitment were present. The third group had not experienced intercourse, but would be willing provided the right partner and the correct relationship conditions. Nonvirgins stood in equal contrast to one another. Some engaged in intercourse because of their emotional involvement and relationship commitment. Others were not as concerned with commitment as they were with reaching a clear, mutual understanding about the meaning of their actions with a potential coital partner. Finally, there were nonvirgins who were confused about where sexual intercourse fit into their lives. These individuals often engaged in coitus early in dating relationships, but found it difficult to explain their actions.

Gfellner (1988) offered a third typology of standards. Her typology is based on individuals' cognitive understanding of their sexual behavior and contains four levels. At the *hedonistic* level, individuals view sexual activity as something to be enjoyed or rejected with little concern for the consequences of their actions. Individuals at the *conventional* level use their immediate social group to define their sexual experiences. They see sex as a way of showing affection, and attaining security and love. The *interpersonal* level is an advancement on the other two as it is more dyadic than external in its reasoning. Individuals at this level think in terms of their own needs and emotions, but realize the reciprocal nature of sexual involvement. The highest level, *interdependence*, is an extension of the previous one in that it shows an understanding of how sexual interaction and relationships evolve and change over time.

The three personal values or standards typologies appear to have common threads. Each can be arranged along a continuum. At one end are individuals with a value stance that focuses on sex as a means of pleasuring oneself. At the opposite end are those whose sexuality is deeply integrated into their conceptualizations about relationships. Additionally, common to these typologies is the view that relationship-centered standards represent a higher moral reasoning level than individually centered standards.

Religiosity

From the mid-1960s to the 1990s, older adolescents and young adults were substantially less likely to feel that engaging in sexual intercourse was immoral (Robinson et al., 1991; T. Smith, 1994). Even with this shift

in values, investigations into the relation of religiosity to sexual involvement have consistently shown that religious service attendance is negatively related to sexual activity in general, and coital engagement
specifically (Earle & Perricone, 1986). This has been true of research conducted in the 1950s and 1960s (Ehrman, 1959b; Kirkendall, 1967), the
1970s (Bell & Chaskes, 1970; Curran et al., 1973; Jackson & Potkay,
1973; Spanier, 1976), the 1980s (Roche, 1986), and the 1990s (Roche &
Ramsbey, 1993; Tanfer & Cubbins, 1992; Tanfer & Schoorl, 1992). Thus,
the relation of religiosity to sexual behavior is robust. Moreover, not only
religious service attendance, but different measures of one's religiosity are
related to efforts to limit sexual involvement with dating partners (Clayton, 1969, 1972; Mahoney, 1980). This relation is independent of other
factors shown to be salient predictors of sexually involvement at this stage
of development (J. Kelley, 1978; Reed & Weinberg, 1984; Schultz et al.,
1977; Tanfer & Cubbins, 1992).

The specific mechanisms behind this relation suggest that religiosity
operates indirectly through other variables. Schultz et al. (1977) found
that religiosity operated indirectly on sexual involvement through perceived peer behavior. DeLamater and MacCorquodale's (1977) analysis
revealed that religiosity's effect was mediated by one's personal standards. Herold and Goodwin (1981) similarly found that adamant virgins,
potential nonvirgins, and nonvirgins differed in how religious they were.
These findings suggest that older adolescents and young adults who are
integrated into a religious peer group do two things. First, they use peers
from their religious group as referents. Second, they are influenced by
religious doctrine to develop a set of sexually conservative personal standards that influence other factors associated with sexual activity and eventually act to inhibit sexual exploration (DeLamater & MacCorquodale,
1977; T. Smith, 1994).

Personality and Personal History Factors

There are a number of personality factors that have been investigated by
sex researchers to see if they are related to sexual activity in dating. For
instance, Mosher (1966, 1968) developed a measure of *sex guilt* that he
later showed was negatively related to sexual involvement (Mosher &
Cross, 1971). Older adolescents and young adults who are high in sex
guilt have been found to hold less permissive sexual standards, to be more
likely to feel that sexual involvement before marriage is morally wrong
(Mosher & Cross, 1971), to believe in more sexual myths, and are more

likely to be virgins than those who are low in sex guilt (D'Augelli & Cross, 1975; Mosher & Cross, 1971). Moreover, the moral reasoning of individuals with elevated levels of sexual guilt is characterized by the law-and order-stage of moral development (D'Augelli & Cross, 1975; Propper & Brown, 1986). In other words, these individuals believe in the sanctity of rules and that social rules should be upheld for their own sake.

Gender differences have been found to exist. Older adolescent girls and young women typically possess more sex guilt than similarly aged males (Daughtery & Burger, 1984; Lewis, Gibbons, & Gerrard, 1986; Mosher, 1979). Moreover, women's sex guilt is more closely associated to their sexual attitudes and sexual satisfaction than is true of men (Cate et al., 1993). This may reflect differences in socialization processes and society's greater concern with finding means for controlling single female sexual expression (DeLamater, 1987; MacCorquodale, 1989). The consistency of this finding has led some researchers to investigate women who possess high levels of sexual guilt. Interestingly, not all of these women restrict their sexual involvement (Lewis et al., 1986), although they may have fewer coital partners than women low in sex guilt (Davidson & Darling, 1993). Women who are high in sex guilt and are sexually experienced have difficulty processing sexual information. Surprisingly, when presented with sexual vignettes, these women are more likely to remember reasons the individuals in the vignettes gave for engaging in coitus than reasons for not engaging in coitus. Lewis et al. postulated that these women may be looking for reasons that their own sexual behavior is discrepant with their sexual values. These reasons may keep them from feeling guilty. Their moral dilemma, paired with a disposition to seek positive reasons for engaging in coitus, could put them at risk for exploitation by dating partners who can provide such reasoning, and for pregnancy because their guilt leads them to believe coitus is unlikely to occur so they are less likely to use contraception (Lewis et al., 1986).

Self-monitoring is an additional personality construct that has been shown to be associated with sexual behavior at this stage of development (Snyder et al., 1986). Self-monitoring refers to a process by which individuals base their behavior either on their own attitudes and dispositions (low self-monitors), or on social and interpersonal cues of situational appropriateness (high self-monitors; Snyder et al., 1986). These two types of individuals differ in their sexual activity. Low self-monitors are more prone to developing close, committed dating relationships (Snyder & Simpson, 1984), explaining why they have fewer sexual partners, fewer one-night stands, and are less accepting of casual sex than high self-monitors.

Other researchers have been interested in personal motivations behind not engaging in coitus. Fear of pregnancy is a restraining factor for both males and females (Driscoll & Davis, 1971; Jedlicka & Robinson, 1987). Both also cite not being in love as a reason, although females are more likely to experience this than males (Driscoll & Davis, 1971; Sprecher & Regan, 1996). A similar pattern holds for personal beliefs against engaging in premarital coitus. Although both virginal men and women cite this as a reason, women cite it more frequently (Sprecher & Regan, 1996). An additional category of reasons focuses on feelings of personal inadequacy and insecurity. Surprisingly, fear of contracting an STD does not seem to play a role in the sexual decision making of these youths (Jedlicka & Robinson, 1987).

Finally, the sexual and dating history of young adolescents and older adults have an effect on their present sexual behavior. Current sexual involvement for individuals of this age has been positively related to early dating, more frequent dating, and a greater number of monogamous dating commitments (Caroll, 1988; Ehrman, 1959b; Lewis, 1973; Reed & Weinberg, 1984; B. Schultz et al., 1977; Spanier, 1976). These youthful influences are probably related to one another and are triggered by early dating. Physical attractiveness is also related to each of the dating factors, which may explain why it is concurrently and positively related to sexual expression (Curran et al., 1973; Kaats & Davis, 1970). Alternatively, the role of physical attraction in sexuality may be socially scripted. Investigators have presented dating vignettes of men and women who vary in their attractiveness and have asked respondents to rate how sexually active they perceive these individuals to be (Garcia & Kushnier, 1987). Highly attractive females are linked to correspondingly high levels of sexual activity suggesting links between physical attraction and sexual involvement in social scripts.

Youthful engagement in coitus and lifetime sexual experience have similarly positive relation to present sexual activity (DeLamater & MacCorquodale, 1979; B. Miller & Moore, 1990; Tanfer & Schoorl, 1992). The timing of first coitus has additionally been linked to other aspects of older adolescents and young adults' sexuality. Koch (1988) examined its impact on later sexual functioning. She found that women who report initial experiences of pressure, negativity, or engaging in first intercourse with someone they did not know well, later indicate that they may be repulsed by sexual contact, lack sexual interest, and/or have problems attaining orgasms. Men have parallel experiences, although they are not as strongly effected. Men who felt pressured into their first coital act later report a lower level of sexual interest than men who had first coitus for other reasons. Men who reacted negatively to their loss of virginity had more ejaculation problems than men who had positive experiences. Finally, age at first sexual intercourse has been tied to the time when individuals marry and experience childbirth (B. Miller & Heaton, 1991). Those who engage in coitus early in their life are slow to marry and have children.

Tying It All Together: Path Models

A few researchers have proposed and tested path models in attempts to show how variables from these different domains are related to sexual behavior in dating relationships. B. Schultz et al. (1977) conducted separate tests of their model for men and women who were either in a committed dating relationship or were casually dating. Perceived sexual behavior of friends had a strong direct effect on sexual involvement for both sexes and in both types of relationships. Religiosity had a negative direct relation to sexual activity and a negative relation to perceived peer behavior under all conditions except for women who were casually dating. For men and women who were casually dating, dating frequency also had a direct, positive relation to their sexual behavior, and a concurrent, positive relation with perceived friend behavior.

DeLamater and MacCorquodale (1977) conducted a more extensive analysis using both college students and individuals who were of the same age, but who were not students. Perceived peer behavior, lifetime sexual behavior, and the intimacy of the current relationships all had direct effects on present sexual behavior with intimacy having the strongest association. Intimacy was predicted by the individual's sexual standards, which had an additional, reciprocal relationship with lifetime sexual behavior. Lifetime sexual behavior was further predicted by peer standards. Finally, one's sexual standards originated in part in one's parents' standards and in part in one's own religiosity.

Christopher (1993) took a different approach by focusing more on how relationship experiences are related to sexual interaction. Similar to DeLamater and MacCorquodale (1977), he found that lifetime sexual behavior directly related to current sexual behavior. He also found a positive, strong, and direct relation between the use of an emotional and physical closeness sexual influence strategy and current sexual behavior. This strategy, in turn was positively predicted by both intimacy and conflict. Intimacy experiences was singularly predicted by empathy in his model.

Conflict, however, had a number of predictors. Intimacy was a positive predictor, as was self-monitoring, and possessing beliefs that dating relationships between men and women are inherently adversarial. Finally, empathy, understandably, was negatively related to conflict.

Conclusions

Several conclusions can be reached from the literature reviewed in this section. Biology may exert an influence on the sexual behavior of older adolescents and young adults but the specific mechanisms are not clear at this time. Simpson and Gangestad's (1991) work suggests that its effect is indirect, operating through one's personality. It is also evident that one's attitudes, values, and norms are an additional influence on sexual involvement. Norms provide one source of meaning for sexual activity and can be arranged along a continuum. At one end are those who define their sexual activity in terms of its capability of giving one's self pleasure. At the other end are those who define their sexual involvement by seeing it integrated into their relationship scripts. Religion provides one possible origin for norms. Attendance at religious services can concurrently provide potential peer referents who, in turn, influence one's sexual involvement. Because religiosity also influences early adolescent coital involvement (see chapters 3 and 4), it is possible that religion represents a long-standing influence in the lives of some youths.

Certain personal factors also play a role. Sex guilt typically inhibits sexual activity for most individuals. High self-monitors are influenced more by their peers. Finally, lifetime experience in dating and sexual behavior results in a greater likelihood of experiencing coital activity in one's present dating relationship.

The corpus of the older adolescent and young adult sexuality literature illuminates the increased complexity of sexual expression at this age compared to early adolescent sexuality. These youths experience a multitude of influences. Similar to earlier developmental periods, parents often continue to attempt to exert a socializing force. Yet, if parents are not viewed as referents, their ability to socialize is limited. Peers play an even more prominent role. They continue to influence individuals' attitudes and provide ideas about how sexual roles can be enacted. One of the more notable developmental changes, however, occurs in the tenor of dating relationships. Dating relationships are more complex and thereby richer in their experience. Chapter 6 demonstrates how this complexity and richness evidence itself in sexual role enactment.

6

A Theoretical Model
of Older Adolescent
and Young Adult Sexuality

The model I use to integrate the body of literature for older adolescents and young adult sexuality is similar to the previous, early adolescent model, but reflects developmental changes. Parental influence diminishes as adolescents mature and become young adults. This is a normal developmental experience as young adults need to establish their independence from parents while maintaining emotional closeness. Concurrently, integration into a peer network becomes increasingly important. Peers provide vital support for ventures into adult roles through emotional support, modeling, and vicarious experiences. Even more important are the dating experiences of the developing individual. Dating allows adolescents and young adults to practice relationship skills that will be important in the development of close relationships and later in marriage. Dating experiences are richer and fuller at this developmental stage than they were during early adolescence. More is also known about how sexual roles are enacted. The model reflects each of these changes.

Determination of what roles to enact also reflects the developmental changes that characterize individuals of this age. Role enactment is likely to be more strongly a function of the self and less a function of the social

environment of older adolescents and young adults. Although these significant others still have an impact on the roles in which an individual
engages, their influence is more in offering choices about roles and suggesting meaning that can be assigned to behaviors. Influences on sexual
role enactment shifts more to the individual and dating partners. Dating
partners are likely to become more influential on sexual role enactments
as relationships develop. Final choices about how to behave in sexual
roles, however, ultimately lie within the individual.

The Sexual Self of Older Adolescents and Young Adults

Central to the model are two previously used symbolic interactionist constructs, the self and the social self (see Fig. 6.1). Their use here reflects
developmental changes proposed to have taken place. The self is still
hypothesized to be composed of two parts. The first reflects the sexual
attitudes, values, and norms the individual holds. As Hendrick et al.'s
(1985) findings show, however, the sexual attitudes of individuals at this
developmental stage are not singularly focused on permissiveness but are
more complex. They additionally include beliefs about sexual responsibility, communion, instrumentality, conventionality, and power. This diversity in attitudes demonstrates the increasingly greater cognitive abilities of
older adolescents and young adults as they mature and gain in experience
that in turn reflects a stronger sense of self. With time and experience,
these individuals can cognitively examine their selves as a separate entity.
In this process, older youths recognize that sexuality involves more than
just decisions about whether to engage in coitus. Sexuality is seen as a
multidimensional phenomenon and research would indicate that females
of this age see greater complexity in their sexuality than males (Myers et
al., 1983). Cognitively examining these different dimensions results in
more complicated attitude structures. Complexity is also the result of
related cognitive developments that allow individuals to consider others'
viewpoints separate from one's own. This role-taking process results in a
more fully developed social self, which is the part of the individual that
considers the viewpoints of others, and which in turn influences an individual's sexual self-concept (see Fig. 6.1).

Different attitude stances are organized by the deeper values held by
youth, and values and attitudes become the base for premarital sexual
standards or role norms of youths. Central to these norms is the individual's orientation toward premarital sexual permissiveness. I have posited

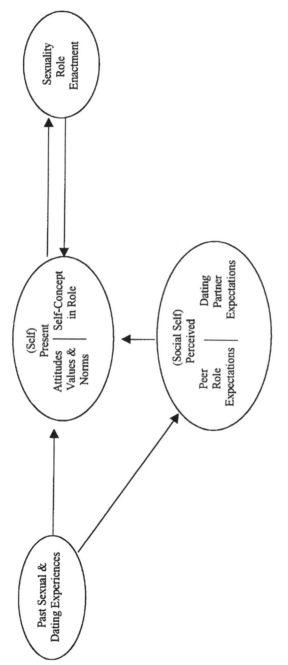

FIG. 6.1. *Older adolescent and young adult self.*

that the different norms or standards of permissiveness that have been proposed and researched can be arranged along a continuum. At one end are the norms that value and allow body-focused, pleasure-oriented, sexual involvement with little concern for interpersonal consequences such as the feelings of one's sexual partner. At the other end of the continuum are norms that fully integrate sexual involvement with relationship experiences. Norms that consider and value a relationship perspective may be the outcome of more advanced social and cognitive development. The ability to take another's viewpoint, combined with concern about that person's feelings, show greater moral maturity than being focused on self-pleasure.

These normative role orientations represent the different meaning structures youth ascribed to sexual behavior. Sexual behavior symbolizes something different in each normative stance. In one case, it stands for the love and commitment experienced by the individual. In another, it may represent the primacy of one's self-gratification, possible conquest, and a sense of interpersonal power without concern for sexual responsibility.

The other part of older adolescents' and young adults' self is their perceptions of their own enactment of a sexual role (see Fig. 6.1). I explore different premarital sexual roles later in this chapter; it is sufficient at this time to state that these youths cognitively examine their sexual role performance in great detail. This does not mean they solely evaluate the adequacy of their sexual performance, but that they carefully scrutinize other role-related phenomenon including the meaning of verbal and nonverbal communication, the manner of their own and their partner's dress, and the dyadic decisions and interactions that occurred. Meaning is ascribed to these interactional nuances during this process. The source of the assigned meanings comes, in part, from the attitudes, values, and norms that the individual holds. There exits, however, a number of other potential sources of meaning that youths may consider when they construct their own meaning system. These are the focus of later sections of this chapter.

There is a dynamic tension between the two parts of the self that form one's sexual self-concept. Role enactment is measured against one's values and norms. If there is a reasonable match between the behaviors engaged in and the values held, then one's sexual self-concept will be positive. When one's behavior is inconsistent with values and norms, then one's self-concept will be negative. This process is the source of sexual guilt. Sexual guilt is the result of having sexual values and norms that are so restrictive that engaging in sexual behaviors results in feelings of guilt. At times, a youth's norms are restrictive enough that even imagining one's self in a potential sexual role results in a poor self-image. This explains why virgins have higher levels of sexual guilt than nonvirgins (D'Augelli & Cross, 1975; Mosher, 1979). In these instances, the sexual guilt, in combination with the restricted norms, has a prohibitory effect on sexual exploration.

The construction of self by a youth of this age is influenced by a number of different variables. One is the youth's actual *sexual role enactment*. There is a bi-directional, dynamic relation between these two variables. The role behavior of older adolescents and young adults in part originates in how they picture themselves behaving in that role (Stryker & Statham, 1985), but actual experiences may not match their cognitive role rehearsals. In these cases, the actual role experiences can lead to changes in the cognitive representation of that role. Thus, there is a bi-directional path between these variables in Fig. 6.1. The second variable that influences the construction of one's self is one's *past dating and sexual experiences*. Past sexual experiences are likely to lead to current sexual involvement (cf. Christopher, 1993; DeLamater & MacCorquodale, 1979). Earlier dating and sexual experiences become a part of one's self-definition and help form one's present norms and standards. The direction of these influences depends upon the type of experience. Positive past experiences will serve to bolster values and role choices. Hurtful or negative experiences will cause youths to dissect their experiences and revisit their attitudes, norms, and choices to see if changes would protect against similar experiences in the future.

The final variable that influences the sexual self-identity of later adolescents and young adults is their *social selves*. The use of this construct in this instance parallels its previous use (see chapter 4). This part of the self considers the reactions of significant individuals in the lives of older adolescents and young adults. The most influential of these individuals are peers and dating partners. Because of the increased cognitive abilities already described, the social self is richer at this stage. Youths are better able to take others' perspectives and have experienced a wider range of cross-gender interactions. Considering these different perspectives allows older adolescents and young adults a fuller understanding of their own role norms and behaviors.

Parents and Older Adolescent–Young Adult Sexuality Roles

Parental influences on these youths' sexual role enactment parallel, but do not completely replicate, those hypothesized to exist for younger adolescents (see Fig. 6.2). Research has shown that the quality of the parent–adolescent relationship plays a significant part in determining whether parents have an influence on the sexual role behavior of older adolescents and young adults (cf. DeLamater & MacCorquodale, 1979). This is first represented in the model by the *present parent–child relationship*. Similar to its use for early adolescents, this variable represents the emotional tenor of the parent-child relationship. It captures the closeness of parents to their offspring. This closeness manifests itself behaviorally in *parental support*. This type of support includes acts of helping, bolstering, and advocating. The relation between these two variables is bi-directional (Peterson, 1995). Support by parents will foster emotional closeness and out of closeness comes emotional support.

The present parent–child relationship is influenced by two variables. The first is *parents' attitudes, values, and norms*. This variable reflects in part how parents react to the developmental changes taking place within their child. Parents may see increased independence of thought and action as being an important step toward adulthood and will value fostering these changes. Alternatively, parents may not judge their child ready for taking on adult responsibilities and may act to slow their adolescent's development toward this coming status. This variable also captures parental orientations toward the increased awareness of sexuality inherit in older adolescence and young adulthood. Parental norms may validate or deny these changes. Moreover, parental beliefs about the sexuality of individuals of this age in general, and their orientation toward the developmental changes in their offspring in particular, will influence the emotional tenor of the parent–child relationship. When parents' values and norms nurture a close relationship with their child, with concurrent parental support, it will increase the likelihood of the adolescent adopting the meanings parents offer for the different sexual role enactments of youth. Two other variables, however, influence this socialization process.

The present parent–child relationship is likely influenced by the quality of the *past parent–child relationship*. Historical influences play a role in all relationships, including parent–child relationships. Older adolescents prepare to move from one developmental status to a new one and the stage of adolescence is marked by large changes in these individuals' lives. If the parent–child relationship during early adolescence was of high quality, it is liable to foster a similar experience during the latter part of this developmental stage. Similarly, if later adolescence is characterized by a good relationship, it will provide a solid foundation for the parent–child relationship of young adulthood. Earlier positive relationship experiences should not, however, be considered a guarantee of similar experiences in

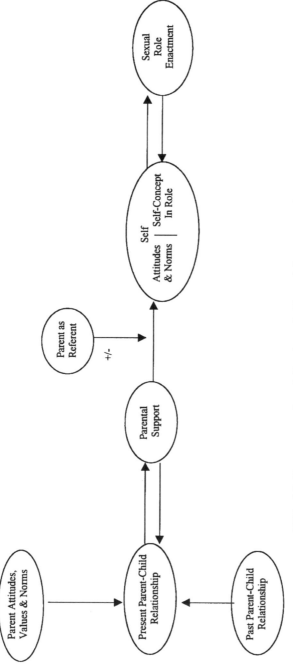

FIG. 6.2. *Parent sexual socialization of older adolescents and young adults.*

113

the present. Parental role expectations for each new developmental stage may not coincide with the expectations of their children. Such intergenerational role conflict may diminish the quality of the present parent–child relationship. Comparisons between past and present relationship experiences provide one indicator of how well parents and adolescents are adapting to the adolescent's changing developmental status.

As Fig. 6.2 indicates, the variables of parental values and norms, and the quality of past parent–child relationship, operate on the present parent–child relationship, which in turn operates indirectly on the adolescent's self-identity through parental support behaviors. This represents the socialization process by which parents pass on the meaning they assign to different aspects of adolescent sexual role enactment. Research would indicate that another variable is critical and moderates the actual degree of parental influence, whether adolescents or young adults perceive their *parents as referents* (Lewis, 1973; Spanier, 1977). When individuals of this age identify with their parents, they consider how their parents would judge a potential sexual role enactment. If they see their parents as accepting a particular role, they likely enter into that role. This process involves using parents as a referent to judge the moral correctness of a particular set of role behaviors. Parents are more likely used as referents when they are supportive and a close parent–child relationship exists. They are less likely to serve as referents when there is an absence of support and the tenor of the parent–child relationship is characterized by tension and hard feelings.

Comparisons of the parent socialization model for this stage with the early adolescent parent model show one other significant change. Parental control attempts are not a part of this model. Although parents continue to have a controlling influence in other areas of their offspring's lives at this stage (Gecas & Seff, 1990), research would indicate that parental ability to influence offsprings' sexual behaviors decrease as adolescents get older and move into young adulthood. Hence, although parental control attempts may have an influence during the time adolescents move into the later part of this stage, their ability to change behavior through control decreases markedly by the time their children become young adults. Hence, parental control is not a part of this model.

Peers and Older Adolescent–Young Adult Sexuality Roles

Peers become increasingly important in youths' lives as they approach adulthood. They provide reinforcement and status for trying out adult roles. They are asked for advice for a range of life events (Gecas & Seff, 1990). Peers also become referents for friends, thus the perceived moral standards of peers can become the base for decisions by other youths (cf. Herold & Goodwin, 1981). When peer interactions focus on sexuality, meaning is assigned to the different parts of the sexual roles that are scrutinized. Peers, therefore, constitute another important prominent socializing force in older adolescents and young adults lives.

Figure 6.3 depicts the model used for peer socialization influences at this stage of development. Most of the variables and paths in this model again parallel those used in the early adolescent model. The first of these is the *peer's attitudes, norms, and role expectations*. Peers at this stage spend time discussing different viewpoints about life experiences and sexual interaction will be accorded a special status in these discussions because of its salience for this age. Two things occur in these discussions. First, possible sexual roles will be socially constructed. Dyadic and individual acts, emotions, motivations, and norms will be integrated into role complements. In this manner, different peers help to process and organize their own and vicarious experiences. Take, for example, a peer discussion about what a woman wears on a first date and her date's reaction. Peers may decide that wearing a revealing dress on a first date means that a young woman is sending a message to her date that she is sexually available and willing to engage in coitus. The young woman may be labeled as sleazy and in control of the level of sexual involvement. The young man may be viewed as being surprised and happy at this turn of events, and may be labeled a willing sexual partner. The young man may not be judged as pejoratively; men may be viewed as likely to engage in coitus whenever the opportunity arises. In this example of constructing male and female sexual roles, motivations (e.g., sexual desire) behaviors (e.g., choice of dress) communication (e.g., the nonverbal meaning of the dress) commitment status (it was the first date), and emotions (e.g., surprise), are melded together to form a coherent entity. In this social construction, roles revolve around particular positions, such as willing man or sexually available women, with specific differential, male and female role expectations.

In the second event that occurs in peer discussions, meaning is assigned to the various aspects of the roles as different sexual roles are constructed. Consider the example again. Special meaning is assigned to the young woman's dress given the relationship status of the couple—it was a first date. If the same dress was worn in an established relationship a different meaning may be assigned. It may be viewed positively as the female partner trying to be sexy for her partner. The behavior is the same in both

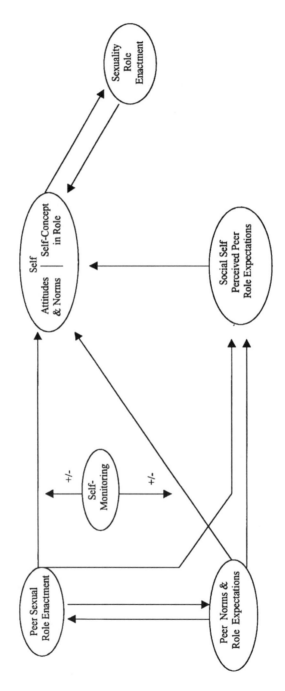

FIG. 6.3. *Peer sexual socialization of older adolescents and young adults.*

examples, but given a different meaning because of the interpersonal, or role position, context. In the first instance, a negative connotation is assigned, in the second a positive one. Hence, meaning often includes a reinforcement or punishment dimension (Duck, 1994). Some behaviors will be judged appropriate and correct, whereas others will be seen as inappropriate and unsuitable. These group consensuses become important for establishing peer role norms and expectations. It should be noted, however, that accurate interpretations of motivations and affect may not always be made. Discussions may take place in same-gender peer groups and lack insight into the opposite gender's motivations, expectations, and experiences. This may be especially true of male groups considering that males have a lower and possibly more inaccurate threshold for perceiving sexual cues in cross-gender interactions (Abbey & Melby, 1986; Shotland & Craig, 1988).

Peers' actual sexual role enactments are influenced by their group's norms and role expectations. Individuals use peer-derived role expectations as guidelines for how they should act in their sexual roles. Peer norms and expectations also help in interpreting the actions of one's dating partner. Actual experiences are taken back to the peer groups to be examined, often in minute detail, and assigned meaning. The attitudes, norms, and role expectations of peers may change with this input from actual experiences. Hence, there is a bi-directional path between these variables in Fig. 6.3.

Both of these variables will act directly on the social self of the youth. Here, individuals weigh how peers will view the sexual role enactment they are considering, or have enacted. Based on peer-stated norms and role expectations, they examine the meaning they think peers will give to a set of interactions that form a role. Certain acts likely gain them rewards, such as recognition or elevated peer status, whereas other acts may result in punishments, such as disapproval or lowered status. Peer role enactments also serve as models for particular sexual roles. When peers engage in a sexual role, and receive reinforcement either from a dating partner or from peers, they provide vicarious learning experiences for the individual. As young adults and older adolescents picture themselves in similar circumstances, they cognitively treat themselves as a separate entity while concurrently considering how peers would react to them in these circumstances. Focusing on themselves in this peer context constitutes important processes that occur in the social self (Stryker & Statham, 1985).

Peer norms and role expectations, and their role enactments, are hypothesized to influence also the developing sexual selves of older adolescents and young adults. The development of one's own norms and values are influenced by what one's peers accept and how they behave (cf. DeLameter & MacCorquodale, 1979; Herold et al., 1998). But this relationship is hypothesized to be moderated by an individual factor, how much self-monitoring an individual engages in (see Fig. 6.3). Recall that self-monitoring is a process by which individuals base their behavior either on their own attitudes and dispositions (low self-monitors) or on social and interpersonal cues (high self-monitors; Snyder et al., 1986). High self-monitors attend to peer behavior and use this as a standard for guiding their own actions. High self-monitors will therefore be more susceptible to being influenced by their peers than low self-monitors. Their norms and choices in premarital sexual roles are apt to be based on peer modeling and social approval. This accounts for the early research findings that when peers are chosen for referents, they influence individual sexual behavior (Mirande, 1968). In the present model, this is true only if youths are high self-monitors. Low self-monitors focus more on their own individual belief systems when choosing which sexual roles to enact.

Before leaving peer influences, one related issue needs addressing. Different findings in the literature suggest that same-gender peer influences are stronger for male youth than they are for female youth. Males at this age are more likely to engage in coitus because of social pressures (Christopher & Cate, 1984; Muehlenhard & Cook, 1988) and males are more likely to tell friends of their sexual experiences (Carns, 1973), suggesting there are peer-related rewards that can be gained for coital experiences (see chapter 5). These findings intimate that male peer groups may be different from female peer groups, and/or that males find same-gender social interactions a potent source of reinforcement. It could be speculated that this is the result of the early learning about sexual matters that occurs in preadolescent groups. The large, amorphous groups where males interact simultaneously provide meaning to what constitutes being sexy and what it takes to be a male (Thorne & Luria, 1986). Peers at this earlier age provide strong reinforcement for particular behaviors that may have lasting effects into later developmental stages. It may result in a special status for same-gender peer groups among males that does not have a parallel among females as they are more focused on dyadic and triadic interactions at this early age.

Dating Relationships and Older
Adolescent–Young Adult Sexuality Roles

It may be helpful to review how roles are conceptualized before examining the qualities of the sexual roles of older adolescents and young adults. When individuals enter into interpersonal interactions, they focus on who is involved, cognitively organize their interaction, and reach conclusions about how they should behave (Hewitt, 1991). Identifying who is present involves assigning persons *positions*, such as parent, best friend, or dating partner. Positions reflect the roles that these people fill. Roles are "an organized set of ideas or principles that people employ in order to know how to behave" (Hewitt, 1991,p. 94). Roles do not simply revolve around a set of behaviors that must be engaged in, but rather are "a *perspective* from which conduct is constructed" (p. 95). As described later, individuals are not passive recipients of social prescriptions in this process, but actively make choices about their positions and the corresponding roles with social prescriptions offering one set of potential choices. Thus, for the purposes of my model, individuals are conceptualized as using their knowledge of different positions to (a) assign meaning to the different parts of their interactions with a dating partner, (b) suggest guidelines for how they and their partner should act, and (c) make choices about how they should behave within a given role. Stryker and Statham (1985) take this concept one step further and hypothesize that perspectives on how to interact also include an affective component. In other words, role perspectives provide additional cues for how individuals should feel when they encounter certain types of interactions. This line of thinking is consistent with investigators of emotions who propose that emotion consists of physical arousal and a cognitive appraisal of the circumstances accompanying that arousal (cf. Berscheid, 1983). Arousal and cognitive appraisal have a bi-directional relationship. Hence, the cognitive appraisals associated with role enactments can be seen as easily eliciting a particular set of prescribed emotions.

The sexual roles of individuals are therefore integrated into their dating roles. It is beyond the scope of this book to examine the structure of dating roles; sexual roles are examined only with reference to specific dating experiences. Most of the sexual role enactments of older adolescents and young adults, however, take place in dating relationships and there are different dating partner positions. These range from a partner to fill an evening's time without concern for a future, to someone who is considered as a possible relationship partner, to a fiancee. Each of these positions has accompanying roles. The sexual roles that are a part of these positions will differ depending on how well individuals know their dating partners. During first dates and while casually dating, partners have little knowledge of each other, so they rely on the role perspectives offered by parents, peers, and past dating partners, as well as their own evaluations of previous dating and sexual experiences to guide and interpret their interactions. These different socializing agents have offered a range of role perspectives that include potential behaviors and meanings. The individual takes these different possibilities and cognitively structures them into meaningful role complements within him or herself. These complements are then used as an individual interacts with a dating partner. If the relationship is longstanding, however, partners will have developed more individuated rules for interaction and their own set of symbols used to assign meaning to each other's behaviors. Thus, in either casual dating or established relationships, the essence of dating and sexual roles revolve around the choices made in the interaction of the two dating partners. It is through interaction that a couple organizes, structures, and gives meaning to the time they spend with one another.

Figure 6.4 attempts to capture the interactive dynamics that are a vital part of the sexual role enactment of older adolescents and young adults. The left side of the figure, under the heading of self, represents what one person experiences, the right side represents what the partner experiences, the middle represents the dating and sexual role enactment of the couple. Causal paths mirror one another when considering perspectives of the two partners. This simplifies the dyadic interaction that occurs in real life. The model should not be interpreted as saying that interactive role experiences are completely synchronic, or that partners always focus on the same part of the role. In fact, especially in the early and casual phases of dating, dating partners may experience a certain awkwardness in orchestrating behaviors and may assign very different meanings to the same interaction. Time and investment are needed before joint dyadic symbols develop. Either or both partners may not be willing to make these investments, choosing instead to follow socially accepted role prescriptions to guide their dating interactions. The *intraindividual* processes depicted in the model, however, are the same for both partners, although how either partner sees her or himself within their corresponding roles may differ considerably.

For either partner, one's sexual role begins with the self. The self is central to the role enactment process. In the self, meaning is assigned, deci-

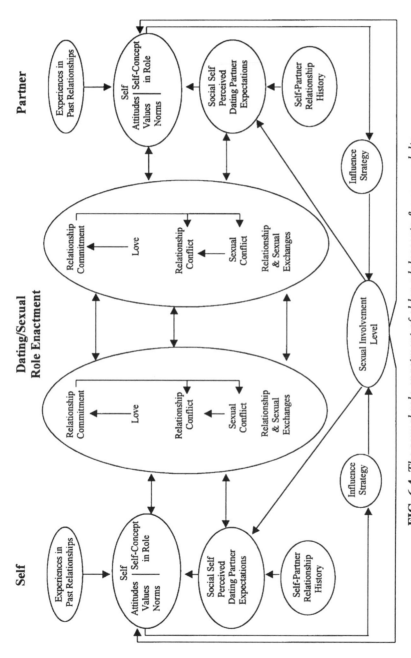

FIG. 6.4. *The sexual role enactment of older adolescents & young adults.*
(*Note: To make the figure easier to read, two-headed arrows are used to indicate bi-directional influences*)

sions about engaging in role behaviors are made, and role performance is evaluated using one's values and norms. The self considers the role perspectives offered by the different socializing agents and, through active choices, melds these into a set of role norms and expectations. This role making includes possible behaviors, interpretations of dyadic interactions, and emotions that may be felt if certain behaviors occur or messages are communicated. Individuals then consider which expectations to apply to their own and their partners' role positions. These expectations guide the dating relationship experiences with their partners.

Scholars have identified different relationship experiences that are salient to sexual involvement. These become important when examining possible role enactments and are represented in the model in the center of Fig. 6.4. Personal commitment to a relationship is the first of these. It is often a central part of the sexual role (Christopher & Cate, 1985a; Peplau et al., 1977). Although research indicates that not all youths need commitment to engage in coitus, high levels of commitment increase the chances it will occur. In fact, there appears to be a shared norm among most individuals of this age that sexual intercourse is expected when a monogamous commitment has been made (Robinson et al., 1991; T. Smith, 1994). In some cases, however, it may be the absence of commitment that makes engaging in sexual interaction attractive. Consider the male who holds a double standard. He may not see a future relationship as a possibility with his present dating partner, so he feels unencumbered about engaging in coitus with her. Even in this scenario, the level of commitment plays an important role in sexual role decisions.

Commitment increases when individuals experience rewards in a relationship (Rusbult, 1980) and love easily can be seen as a reward. Thus, commitment is related to how much love one experiences. This is depicted in Fig. 6.4 by a path from love to commitment. Moreover, love is another key element in sexual role enactment. Researchers have consistently shown the importanance of love in sexual decision making (cf. Cate et al., 1993; Christopher, 1993; DeLamater & MacCorquodale, 1977) and there appears to be a shared norm among individuals of this age that being in love is a sufficient (but not necessary) experience to justify engaging in coitus (Caroll et al., 1985). This is especially true for women, although love is positively related to sexual involvement for both genders.

Increases in commitment results in increases in relational conflict in dating relationships (Braiker & Kelley, 1979). As a couple's relationship becomes more involved, role conflict will inevitably emerge because of differences over issues such as dyadic goals, use of time, how to spend money, and whose friends will become the "couple's" friends. The additional finding that relational conflict and sexual involvement are positively related (Christopher & Cate, 1985a) suggests that dyadic conflict must be a part of Fig. 6.4. There are different possible explanations for this relationship. For some, conflict may occur because of differences in male–female sexual role expectations. For others, engaging in sexual intercourse before defining what it means for the couple may result in conflict over what the sexual encounter symbolizes. In established dating relationships, conflict may cause dating partners to question their relationship commitment and spur discussions about what their relationship means. Such conflict may be particularly frightening for the couple as they have few structural commitment mechanisms to keep them together when compared to married individuals. Couples may then engage in sexual involvement as a symbol of their redefined commitment.

Sexual conflict also often ensues as couples increase their emotional and sexual involvement with one another (Long et al., 1996). This type of conflict represents another form of intradyadic role conflict for the couple. They must negotiate their sexual roles by coming to an agreement over such sexual issues as what kinds of sexual behaviors they will engage in, how well their sexual expectations will match, and how both partners will reach sexual fulfillment, to name but a few. Conflict over these issues will undoubtedly effect the social selves of the individuals involved as they come to a better understanding of the sexual expectations of the partner. Moreover, resolution of this conflict will additionally effect individuals' relationship role self-concept and is associated with more general relational conflict. Recall that Long et al. (1996) found sexual conflict positively related to both relationship satisfaction, an evaluation of one's dating role enactment, and relationship conflict. Moreover, their longitudinal tests demonstrated that sexual conflict uniquely effects relational satisfaction across time for dating couples.

Finally, a number of relational and sexual exchanges are related to sexual involvement and I therefore included them in the model. Equity is one example (Walster et al., 1978). Equity's exact role in dating relationships has been questioned (Cate, Lloyd, Henton, & Larson, 1982). Some scholars have concluded that equity is not as important as the overall reward level in ongoing relationships. According to these investigators, equity may become important only as a sign of relationship deterioration. Equity is therefore not shown as being related to the other relationship dimensions as its association with them is unclear at this time.

More specific to individuals' sexual role enactment, sexual rewards, sexual costs, their expectations for both sexual rewards and costs, and sexual equality are related to sexual satisfaction (Byers & Demmons, 1999; Byers, et al., 1998; Lawrence & Byers, 1995). Concluding that one has received a sexual reward or cost is the product of evaluating one's sexual involvement as either positive or negative and likely reflects the meaning for a particular sexual act. For instance, engaging in coitus on a first date may be valued by a young adult man but perceived as less than ideal by a young woman. Evaluating whether one's sexual expectations are being met takes place in the self where sexual interactions are compared to one's sexual role expectations. Moreover, such expectations are based in the sexual standard that are also part of individuals' sexual self.

There are bidirectional paths between self and partner for each of these relationship experiences in Fig. 6.4. These paths depict the interactive quality of sexual and dating roles. Undoubtedly, the commitment, love, relational conflict, sexual conflict, and dyadic exchanges of one partner influence the corresponding relationship experiences of the other. Other paths that cross relationship dimensions may exist, however, researchers have not teased apart these dynamics and symbolic interaction theory is not clear as to what these paths should be. Hence, I take a simpler approach by showing a correspondence across partners' relationship dimensions. It is through this interaction that the relationship is built, and that joint meanings are assigned to gestures, behaviors, words, and nonessential things that become part of the couple's dating and sexual role enactment. The longer a couple is together, the more individuated their roles become when compared to the social role prescriptions offered by significant others.

Relationship experiences have two intraindividual impacts. First, as reflected in the bi-directionality of the paths from the relationship experiences and the self, these experiences are compared to the individual's sexual role expectations. In other words, one's experience with commitment, love, conflict, and dyadic exchanges are compared to what one expects from one's preferred sexual role. Evaluations of congruency between one's role expectations and one's role experiences will likely result in continuing the same line of behavior. Incongruencies will prompt either changes in role expectations, or behavioral changes with a partner so as to meet one's goals for the relationship. This comparative process is dynamic and ongoing, but is especially influential during the initial stages of dating, and at developmental milestones that result in changes in commitment level.

Second, relationship experiences provide information about one's dating partner's role expectations. Some of this comes direct from the partner via verbal communication. Much of it is likely to be inferred from the nonverbal interactions that take place. These messages become that part of the social self that considers the expectations of one's dating partner when making sexual role choices, a process that involves role taking. The more information one has about a specific partner, the more accurate one's judgment of that person's expectations will be. There is an additional historic influence that also comes to bear on the social self in Fig. 6.4. This additional variable shows the influence of past relationship experiences with a particular partner. These all coalesce to allow a more accurate reading of a partner's expectations. If a couple lacks a history, individuals are more likely to base expectations on the role prescriptions that they have constructed based in part on the influence of significant others, and in part from past dating relationships' experiences (see Fig. 6.4).

These dyadic influences may bring changes to or reaffirm existing sets of sexual norms and role expectations. In fact, rewarding relationship experiences in this very potent crucible of interaction can provide a strong impetus for changing one's norms to resolve conflicting role expectations between one's self and one's partner. Partners are capable of providing powerful reinforcements for compiling with or punishments for the resistance of their wishes, especially in established relationships. Moreover, given their proximal position in an individual's life, and their special positional status assigned by society, romantic partners may have the greatest influence on an individual when it comes to shaping sexual norms when compared to other social influences.

As individuals make decisions about how sexually involved they would like to be, they utilize influence strategies to let their partner know how receptive they are to becoming sexually involved. Receptive strategies are predominately nonverbal in nature (O'Sullivan & Byers, 1992). Certain nonverbal cues are likely to have been given meaning by social role prescriptions. Successful use of these will result in the nonverbal gestures becoming symbolic of sexual wishes in more established dating relationships. In fact, some couples may never use verbal cues if nonverbal cues work—rejection of an initiation can then be seen as a misunderstanding and not a rejection of the person (Cupach & Metts, 1991). Nonreceptive strategies are more likely to be verbal (cf. Christopher & Frandsen, 1990) thereby taking the ambiguity out of the rejection message.

The end result of mutually acceptable receptive strategies is sexual involvement. The level of sexual involvement depends on the norms and role expectations of the self and partner. It will carry its own symbolic meaning, as influenced by the processes already described. In addition, sexual involvement, in turn, influences both the self and the social self (see Fig. 6.4). The evaluative function of the self will be applied to sexual interactions in a manner that parallels what occurs for other dyadic inter-actions. Moreover, sexual interactions provide insights into a partner's sexual wishes, wishes considered in one's social self. These feedback mechanisms again demonstrate the interactive quality of sexual role enactments.

So what do actual sexual role enactments look like? The research of Peplau et al. (1977) and Christopher and Cate (1985a) provide examples. Some couples experience sexual intercourse while casually dating with low levels of love and commitment, but elevated conflict. These individu-als have permissible premarital sexual standards that, according to the model, guide them in this particular role enactment. Other couples with more permissible standards seem to use sexuality as a means of testing the waters when deciding if they should make a commitment to one another, even though they experience more moderate levels of love and conflict. Some couples, or the female partner, delay sexual intercourse until they are monogamously committed and in love with one another even though they also experience higher levels of conflict. These couples have less per-missive sexual standards. Still other, less permissive couples have high commitment and love, but limit themselves to precoital involvement.

Undoubtedly other sexual role enactments are possible. Certainly work in the area of personal sexual standards suggests that there are more sexual role prescriptions than the four just outlined. For example, some couples may not engage in any sexual involvement, or may engage in coitus only as a means of self-pleasure and gratification (D'Augelli & D'Augelli, 1977). What my model hopefully reflects is that in all of these possible role enactments there is a mix between dyadic interaction and intraindividual processes that shape and become a part of the sexual role enactment.

Gender Differences

There are qualitative differences in the sexual role enactments of single men and women. Both are aware of the traditional male and female role prescriptions that originate in the socialization processes already described (Cohen & Shotland, 1996; Knox & Wilson, 1981; Roche, 1986; Roche & Ramsbey, 1993). These are taught by parents and peers through stories about others, and evaluations of different individuals' dating and sexual experiences. The media also provides an almost continuous flow of examples of traditional gender dating and sexual role enactments. In this discourse, males and females are accorded their own particular motivations, cognitions, emotions, and behaviors as part of their respective sexual roles. Individuals who do not follow these prescripted roles are likely to be viewed negatively. At the same time, individuals who follow prescripted role expectations will be viewed positively.

Although there are indications that traditional roles have changed, as evidenced in the greater acceptance of sexual intercourse for unmarried women (Oliver & Hyde, 1993), there are also indications that these changes reflect more subtle judgments about women's sexual expression. Evidence of this subtlety can be found in Sprecher et al.'s (1988, 1991) studies on the acceptance of the double standard, and in Muelenhard and McCoy's (1991) finding that while some women openly express sexual interest in a new dating partner, not all do even when they are interested. Even considering these changes, many of the traditional tasks in dating are easily followed by many of the individuals who are involved. Although women can and do ask men out for dates, this is still something of an unusual occurrence (Mongeau, 1995). Moreover, women are still, for the most part the "sexual gatekeepers" of the dyadic interaction. Traditional roles call for women to link their sexual decision making to their relationship experiences. Hence, men's and women's roles have evidenced some change, but changes are slow in taking place.

Individuals are first exposed to traditional gender-specific sexual roles during childhood and early adolescence. The exposure during early adolescence may be particularly formative because conformity is valued and highly rewarded at this age. This exposure provides a potent vicarious learning experience. It occurs at the same time as early learning about one's sexual role. Thus, how single men and women should behave in a dating relationship becomes intertwined with how one should act in one's gender role.

More proximal social forces also support traditional gender-linked sexual role enactments. Concerns about a dating partner's expected reactions to nontraditional role behavior can shape an individual's role behavior. Muehlenhard and McCoy (1991) found that apprehension about a partner's beliefs in a double sexual standard effectively stopped some women from letting their partners know they were feeling sexually receptive toward them. They worried that the dating partner may devalue them, assigning them the position of "loose" or "easy" women. These women instead followed traditional gender role prescriptions in their sexual role enactment. They hid their sexual feelings from their partners rather than communicating and acting on them.

It is unlikely that many youths will vary far from these gender dating roles, especially in the early stages of dating. Traditional roles provide guidance for how to behave in a situation filled with unknowns. Moreover, they do so for individuals whose lives are filled with uncertainties. Young adults are just beginning to create a meaningful and lasting life structure. Much of what they face in life is uncertain, but the decisions they make often can have long-term consequences. Many of these individuals are apt to find comfort in having role prescriptions to guide them in one of the more important parts of their lives—the romantic and erotic interactions with a member of the opposite gender. Scripted reactions can be considered as likely outcomes when one does not know how a partner will actually react to a particular action of one's own.

Moreover, there are certain structural qualities to traditional gender dating roles that make changes in them take place at a slower rate than other gender-related roles. Dating roles for most individuals are transitory, they eventually lead to marriage and are therefore not lifelong. They are also experienced by individuals who have limited power that can result in large-scale societal changes. Traditional gender role expectations, therefore, are not likely to quickly change in the immediate future.

By this point in the book, I have described the salient factors related to sexuality during childhood, early adolescence, and older adolescence–young adulthood. Moreover, I have offered theoretical models for how these variables are interrelated to one another. These writings reflect an assumption that both members of the dyad jointly agreed with or successfully negotiated their sexual involvement. In some cases, however, one member of the dating couple ignores the partner's sexual wishes to limit sexual involvement and forces his or her sexual desires on the partner. Such instances of sexual aggression are the focus of the next two chapters.

7

Sexual Aggression in Dating

Dating couples do not always agree on how sexually intimate they should be. Men, when compared to women, typically want greater sexual involvement with fewer dates (Cohen & Shotland, 1996; Knox & Wilson, 1981). Many times, women, in contrast, make sexual intimacy contingent on increases in emotional intimacy. As highlighted in the previous chapter, this discrepancy in sexual wishes translates into dating couples having to negotiate an acceptable level of sexual involvement. Characteristically, these disagreements happen between romantically interested partners who have dated for a while and have engaged in prior mutually consented-to sexual behaviors (Byers & Lewis, 1988). Strife between couples often focuses on whether to engage in sexual intercourse.

In many of these instances, the women send verbal and nonverbal cues that they are unwilling to engage in the contended sexual behavior (Byers & Lewis, 1988; Koss, Dinero, Seibel, & Cox, 1988). Most men will stop their advances and may even apologize for their actions (Byers & Lewis, 1988). Unfortunately, this is not always the case, as at other times one member of the dyad ignores the partner's rebuffs and coerces him or her into unwanted sexual behaviors. The frequency and correlates of such sexual aggression in dating are the focus of this chapter.

The Frequency of Sexual Aggression in Dating

It is difficult to estimate the frequency of sexual aggression among singles as no researchers to date have used a national probability sample in their studies. Moreover, sexual aggression has been operationalized in different ways by researchers, thereby yielding contrasting estimates across studies. This makes it very difficult to gauge how many victims of sexual aggression exist.

Koss and her colleagues report the best estimates to date. Using a national sample of more than 3,000 college women, she found that 53.7% had experienced some form of sexual victimization since they were age 14 (Koss, Gidycz, & Wisneiwski, 1987). Many of these women were victims of rape (15.4%) or attempted rape (12.1%). Others were sexually coerced—overwhelmed by men who pressured them, presented continual arguments, or made use of their position of authority (12.1%). Still others experienced unwanted sexual contact such as fondling, kissing, or petting (14.4%).

Koss further divided her sample by focusing exclusively on women who had been raped and examined the type of relationship that existed between the female victims and the male aggressors (Koss et al., 1988). Comparatively few of these women were raped by strangers (11.1%) or family members (which included husbands—9.4%). More of the rapists were nonromantic acquaintances (26.1%), but even a greater number, slightly more than 50%, were dating partners. Casually dating partners constituted 22% of the rapists, seriously dating partners 31.4%.

These figures must be viewed cautiously. Koss additionally sampled close to 3,000 college men and their reports of their own aggressive behavior differed markedly from the women's reports of victimization (Koss et al., 1987). Few of the men admitted raping (4.4%) or attempting to rape a woman (3.3%). Although the number of men who acknowledge sexually coercing a woman (7.2%) or engaging in unwanted sexual contact (10.2%) was closer to the number reported by women, the figures were still discrepant. Some underreporting would be expected given the punitive social sanctions that can accompany engaging in these acts. Still, it is noteworthy that many of the women raped by dating partners (sexual interactions that fit the legal standards for rape) failed to view their victimization as a crime—73% of those casually dating and 71.2% of those seriously dating fell into this category (Koss et al., 1988).

Other researchers, using smaller college-based samples, have produced a wide range of estimates of sexual aggression. When single women have been asked about experiencing any unwanted sexual contact, investigators have sometimes found high rates of sexual aggression experiences, such as 95.3% (Christopher, 1988), 83% (Copenhaver & Grauerholz, 1991), just over 75% (Garrett-Gooding & Senter, 1987; Muehlenhard & Linton, 1987), and 59% (Abbey, Ross, McDuffie, & McAuslan, 1996), and sometimes found low rates of experiences, such as 37.4% (Berger, Searles, Salen, & Pierce, 1988) and 34% (Ward, Chapman, Cohen, White, & Williams, 1991). These estimates are usually calculated by considering any form of sexual aggression for any sexual behavior. Estimates decrease markedly when specific forms of aggression are considered. For example, when single women are queried about their experiencing the use of threats or force for any sexual behavior, rates of between 21% and 29% emerged (Berger et al., 1988; Kirkpatrick & Kanin, 1957). Men's reports of using such assaultive means result in rates of between 2.3% and 31% (Lisak & Roth, 1988; Wilson, Faison, & Britton, 1983). Women have also been asked about incidents involving pressure, manipulation, continual arguments, lying, and nonthreatening physical persuasion (Christopher, 1988; Copenhaver & Grauerholz, 1991). Their reports of encountering these forms of influence more closely approximate males reports of using these techniques—both fall between 20% and 27% (Berger et al., 1988; Lisak & Roth, 1988; Ward et al., 1991; Wilson et al., 1983).

Researchers have examined rates of sexual aggression among early adolescents, although studies of unwanted sexual activity in this population are comparatively rare. K. Moore, Nord, and Peterson (1989) used a single question from the 1987 National Survey of Children to measure incidence of forced sex or rape. By the age of 14, White females (5%) had lower rates than Black females (11.9%). It is likely, however, that this study tapped into all forms of sexual aggression, including incidents of incest and stranger assaults. Erickson and Rapkin (1991), using a middle and high school sample, analyzed different types of unwanted sexual experiences. Of the youth in their study, 15% had encountered unwanted sexual contact. Of these adolescents, they estimated that 31% of the females experienced coitus because of force separate from incidents involving familial sexual abuse. Moreover, 35% of the cases of unwanted coitus did not involve threats or physical coercion; many of these adolescents engaged in coitus simply to please their dating partners. Similarly, Small and Kerns (1993) found that 36% of girls in Grades 7, 9, and 11 in their sample experienced unwanted coitus with another teen. Comparable rates existed for the girls at each grade. Boyfriends (31%) were the most frequent perpetrators followed by friends (22%), and first date partners (18%), although there were instances of perpetrators among acquaintances (14%) and second date partners (7%) as well. Other investigators (Poitras & Lavoie, 1995) reported similar rates. Taken as a whole, these initial investigations demonstrate that many adolescents experience sexual coercion in their relationships with dating partners.

As can be seen, the majority of researchers in this area have concentrated primarily on the victimization of single women. However, single men may also be victimized by their female dating partners. Across two studies, Struckman-Johnson and Struckman-Johnson (Struckman-Johnson, 1988; Struckman-Johnson & Struckman-Johnson, 1994) found that between 16% and 22% of the men in their samples engaged in unwanted vaginal, oral, or anal intercourse while dating. Most of these men experienced psychological pressure (between 42% and 52%) from a dating partner, or their partners attempted to get them intoxicated (43%) or did both (41%), although some men experienced physical force (10%), or a combination of physical and psychological pressure (28%). Waldner-Haugrud and Magruder (1995) reported comparable rates of young men's experiencing dating partners who coerced them by applying pressure through the use of intoxication or a combination of intoxication and psychological pressure. Muehlenhard and Cook (1988) similarly found that 22.7% of the men in their sample engaged in unwanted sexual activity largely because their dating partner used nonviolent coercion.

Although the findings of these studies make it clear that the use sexual coercion is not limited to men, this conclusion must be tempered by the realization that single women experience more overall sexual coercion in their dating relationships than men (Christopher, Madura, & Weaver, 1998; Christopher, Owens, & Stecker, 1993a; Muehlenhard & Cook, 1988). Additionally, men are more adept at ending unwanted sexual advances at lower levels of sexual intimacy, such as kissing or fondling, whereas women more frequently experience unwanted coitus (Waldner-Haugrud & Magruder, 1995). Moreover, women suffer more grievous and long-term consequences because of their victimization experiences (Struckman-Johnson, 1988; O'Sullivan, Byers, & Finkelman, 1998).

Forms of Sexual Aggression

The findings of these and other studies suggest the existence of two broad forms of sexual aggression. How researchers have measured and categorized responses when investigating sexual aggression provides one form of support for this conclusion. Koss grouped aggressive men and victimized women according to the type of sexual aggression that took place (cf. Koss, Leonard, Beezley, & Oros, 1985). One group, involving sexually assaultive men, used harm, physical force, or both to attain oral, anal, or vaginal intercourse. A second group, sexually abusive men, forced or threatened force to gain sexual contact of some sort, but not penetration. Sexually coercive men, a third group, achieved coitus through verbal pressure, but did not threaten or use force. Other researchers have used similar categorization schemas (Lisak & Roth, 1988; Wilson et al., 1983).

Comparison of the men from the three groups revealed that those who threatened or used force were similar to one another in their attitudes and beliefs about rape, and in believing it normal to associate aggression with sexuality (Koss et al., 1985). Verbally coercive men were different from those in the other two groups in that they were less likely to see women as sexually free. These findings suggest that there is one form of aggression that involves the use force or threats of force and a second form that characteristically involves nonforceful verbal coercion.

A second indication that two forms of sexual aggression exist comes from the work of Christopher and Frandsen (1990). As previously reviewed (see chapter 5), these researchers asked participants to report on how they influenced their dating partners in their most recent sexual interaction. Factor analysis of the responses resulted in their proposing that at least four influence strategies exist, two of which involved sexual aggression. The first, termed an *antisocial acts strategy,* included influence techniques such as threatening force, using force, ridiculing and insulting a partner, and getting angry. The second, called *pressure and manipulating,* included the influence techniques of pressure, ignoring a partner's actions, using persuasion, manipulating a partner's mood, being persistent, and talking fast and telling lies. The two factors were correlated with one another ($r = .64$), intimating that some individuals who use one strategy also use the other.

A third indicator that there are two broad forms of sexual aggression comes from a study by Koss and Oros (1980). They conducted in-depth interviews with women whose descriptions of their sexual aggression experience met the legal definition of rape. They divided these women into those who labeled their experience as rape and those who did not. Comparisons of the two showed that those who perceived their experience as rape reported more threats of bodily harm, incidents of physically being hit or beaten, and threats with a weapon. In addition, they were more apt to see their aggressor as violent, and to react by screaming, crying, and making it clear they did not desire coitus. Women who did not label their experience as rape more often saw their aggressor as attractive, gentle, sexy, emotionally strong, and understanding. Thus, women's experience with the more violent form of aggression was used to define their experiences as rape whereas being coerced into coitus by nonforceful means did not lead to the same perceptions in the women.

The corpus of this literature leads to the hypothesis that there are two forms of sexual aggression, *sexual assault* and *sexual coercion*. *Sexual assault* involves threats of or engaging in force and/or bodily harm. This is socially recognized and labeled as sexual aggression even if it does not culminate in rape. It involves a direct power assertion on the part of one dating partner against a partner's sexual wishes. The divergence between single women's reports on this type of aggression in in Koss et al.'s (1987) survey, and men's willingness to admit to this form of aggression, exemplifies the strength of the punitive social sanctions for engaging in this form of aggression as well as possibly how rare it may be.

Sexual coercion involves verbal and psychological coercion, pressure, and manipulation, but does not include threats or actual use of physical force or harm. Although this is still aggression in that one dating partner asserts his or her sexual wishes over the wishes of the other dating partner, it is not as widely labeled socially as aggression. The lack of an aggressive label is evidenced in the convergence in male and female reports of its occurrence in Koss et al.'s (1987) work, suggesting that males who admit using this do not expect negative sanctions. It may additionally account for some women's unwillingness to acknowledge that their partner raped them (Koss & Oros, 1980; Lloyd & Emery, 1999). This lack of an aggressive definition is not limited to dating partners. There is corresponding evidence that without a clear use of force by a single male on a date, others in this age cohort may not perceive sexual coercion as rape (Shotland & Goodstein, 1983). Hence, individuals who use this influence strategy are not as likely to experience negative sanctions and, in some cases, may even be rewarded for their actions by their peers (Boeringer, Shehan, & Akers, 1991).

FACTORS ASSOCIATED WITH SEXUAL
ASSAULT AND COERCION

Gender-Based Dating Roles

In the early stages of dating, single individuals spend time in private settings with partners while typically having very little personal knowledge about them. Furthermore, although being on a date is often a positive experience, it is full of unknowns (Burkhart & Stanton, 1988). As discussed in the preceding chapter, deciding how to behave in this social situation is made easier by commonly held role expectations about how single men and women should act on a date. These role expectations serve to eliminate some of the ambiguity that is so often experienced by both parties. Traditional, socially scripted dating role expectations for men require them to be responsible for a number of tasks. Men are to approach a woman for a first date, to call for follow-up dates if previous dates were enjoyable, and to suggest a monogamous commitment when he feels the time is right. In the sexual realm, men are to initiate sexual activity, and to spur the couple toward greater sexual intimacy (Peplau et el., 1977; Poppen & Segal, 1988). Women, on the other hand, are to attract a date and hold his attention using indirect influence techniques. Moreover, women are sexual gatekeepers—the ones who decide the sexual limits. Scholars theorize that some of the elements of these normal dating role expectations contribute to acts of sexual aggression.

Lloyd and Emery (Lloyd, 1991; Lloyd & Emery, 1999) theorized these normal role expectations result in a male dating theme of being in control of the progression of the relationship, and a female theme of dependence on the partner and the relationship. Women's theme of dependence is accompanied by feelings that women are responsible for maintaining the dating relationship once it is established. Lloyd and Emery continued by pointing out that single individuals often hope and expect that their dates will be punctuated by a theme of romanticism. Partners are expected to structure their dates to heighten feelings of romanticism, and romantic experiences help define the quality of the relationship. Furthermore, romanticism is positively valued and apt to be rewarded by both dating partners, as well as by friends and family members who listen with delight to accounts of dates characterized by a romantic theme.

Lloyd and Emery (Lloyd, 1991; Lloyd & Emery, 1999) posited ways in which these three dating role qualities, men's theme of control, women's theme of dependence, and the role of romanticism, relate to sexual aggression. They proposed that men's control of the sexual interaction leads them to believe that they are responsible for not only their own sexuality but the sexuality of their female partners as well. Hence, women's sexual wishes may not be valued and/or considered by their partners. They additionally speculate that beliefs in romanticism encourage couples to stay together even when one partner exploits the other. Romanticism may cause aggressive behavior to be redefined as nonexploitive by the parties involved. This can result in the sexual aggression being overlooked, excused, or forgiven. Women's role expectations of dependency and as relationship caretaker make them especially prone toward utilizing these maintenance strategies to institute relationship repair after acts of sexual assault or coercion take place. Recall Koss et al.'s (1987) findings that slightly more than 70% of the dating women who were legally raped did not view their experience as a crime. Lloyd and Emery (1999) reported similar results. On realizing that their dating partner raped them, the women in their qualitative study often defined their rape by blaming themselves and excusing their aggressive partner. Hence, although they enacted the women's relationship maintenance role, these young women simultaneously supported the male role of being in charge and used romantic ideals about relationships to discount the gravity of their experience.

Some additional unique qualities of dating roles might further contribute to acts of sexual aggression. One of these unique qualities is that although socially prescribed role expectations are gender-segregated, fulfillment of these demands is not related to the gender-role beliefs of the individuals (Christopher et al., 1998; Poppen & Segal, 1988). Put another way, the fact that a person who dates is male or female is a better predictor of the sexual behaviors in which the person will engage than is the individual's level of masculinity or femininity. This indicates how rule-bound and potentially rigid gender-based dating roles may be. Another indication of a lack of flexibility comes from the realization that these role expectations have changed very slowly compared to other societal male and female roles such as those found in the workplace.

There are likely a number of reasons why dating roles have changed so slowly. To review, the role demands themselves provide participants a degree of comfort in that they know what is expected of them. This comfort may be particularly needed for individuals who are at an age where they are exploring different adult role options and who may feel unsure of what the future holds for them. In addition, attempting to change the traditional role expectations can lead to experiencing negative sanctions. For instance, relationships are unlikely to last past three dates when single women ask single men for the first date (K. Kelley et al., 1981). Similarly, men who choose to wait for a woman to ask them for a date will spend many a lonely weekend night by themselves. Individuals may also be reluctant to vary from traditional roles if they are romantically interested in a person, but unable to predict his or her reactions to nontraditional behaviors because they do not know the person well enough. Finally, men may find being in control rewarding and might be unwilling to relinquish this position of power (Lloyd & Emery, 1999).

It is important to realize that these traditional roles put many single women in a bind as role expectations do not allow them to openly acknowledge a sexual interest in men without risking the negative positional labels of "loose" or "sexually easy" from peers or family. Muehlenhard and McCoy (1991) investigated the dynamics of this phenomenon by comparing women who openly acknowledged a sexual interest in a partner, women who followed traditional scripts by saying no to sex but in fact were interested, and women who experienced neither. The women from the three groups did not differ in their beliefs about women's roles. They did differ in that those who used scripted refusals were more likely to view their partners as holding a sexual double standard than were women who openly acknowledge a sexual interest. These women feared being punished for stepping out of traditional female dating roles.

Finally, the restrictiveness of these gender roles is apparent in how individuals perceive males and females interacting in normal, daily life. When presented with vignettes depicting cross-sex interactions in a variety of interpersonal contexts, both single men and women judge female characters in the vignettes as more sexy, seductive, and promiscuous than male characters independent of the emotional closeness of the characters (Abbey Cozzarelli, McLaughlin, & Harnish, 1987; Abbey & Melby, 1986). Moreover, women's clothing is used as an indicator of sexual interest by both men and women, whereas men's clothing is not (Abbey et al., 1987; Abbey & Melby, 1986). Use of clothing as an indicant of sexual interest starts young. These beliefs exist even among early and late adolescents (Goodchilds & Zellman, 1984).

These findings illustrate the societal level of support that exists for traditional, gender-based dating roles. They additionally highlight how constrictive this role can be for women. The women's role is viewed as sexual in nature, yet it is the man who initiates and increases sexual intimacy. Without doing anything except interacting with a man, others are inclined to perceive these women as sexual. This may be especially so with their dates, given that men tend to look at interactions with "sex-colored glasses" (Abbey & Melby, 1986). If a woman dresses attractively, she runs the additional risks of her date taking this as a cue of sexual interest and of others judging her as sexually loose.

Social Support for Aggression

Some scholars have proposed that there is general cultural support for men sexually aggressing against women, especially in the context of close relationships. Burt (1980, 1983) was among the first to advance this proposition. She felt the basis of this support was a belief in myths about the dynamics of rape; myths such as maintaining that many women have an unconscious wish to be raped, believing it is the woman's fault if she kisses or allows petting and things get out of hand, or feeling that any healthy woman can resist rape if she wants. In her first investigation, Burt showed that in a group of randomly selected adults, belief in rape myths was predicted by a collection of other attitudes. For both men and women, these predictive attitudes included believing in traditional gender-role stereotypes, accepting interpersonal violence, and defining the sexual relationship between men and women as adversarial. Other investigators have replicated Burt's findings (Check & Malamuth, 1983; Jenkins & Dambrot, 1987; Lonsway & Fitzgerald, 1995) although Lonsway and Fitzgerald questioned whether misogyny is an underlying dimension to this collection of interrelated attitudes.

Research efforts after Burt's seminal work focused on identifying the type of individual who would hold attitudes that support single men's use of sexual assault and coercion. A consistent finding across studies has been that men are more accepting of sexual aggression than women (see Lonsway & Fitzgerald, 1994, for a review). When young men, and to a lesser extent young women, believe in traditional gender-role stereotypes, they are even more likely to endorse men's use of sexual assault or coercion under some of the commonly experienced conditions that arise in normal dating (G. Fisher, 1986; Lonsway & Fitzgerald, 1994; Muehlenhard, 1988). These include men paying for the date and couples going to the man's apartment during their dates. Moreover, men who accept rape myths see women depicted in dating relationship vignettes as more sexual as a person, and more sexually interested in their partners, than men who are not as accepting of rape myths and women regardless of their rape myth beliefs (Abbey & Harnish, 1995). Not surprisingly, accepting rape myths appears to be linked to feelings of hostility toward women (Lonsway & Fitzgerald, 1995).

Other scholars have tried to identify the cues used by individuals to judge whether a single male has raped his dating partner. How much resistance the woman used is one cue (L. Schultz & DeSavage, 1975; Shotland & Goodstein, 1983). More forceful resistance by women results in young adults defining the interaction as rape. How much sexual intimacy occurred prior to the forced intercourse is another cue. If women wait until they have removed their clothing before protesting further sexual involvement, others are less likely to see forced intercourse as rape. The amount of force used by the male is a third critical cue. Consistent with the conceptualization of two forms of sexual aggression, individuals will judge the interaction as rape when force is utilized. When less forceful, but clearly malicious means of influence are employed, individuals will see the behavior as wrong, but fail to define the experience as rape (Shotland & Goodstein, 1983).

Similar types of cues are used to assign blame to victims in date rape scenarios. Female victims in the scenarios are held more responsible if they wear revealing clothing, if they are described as being of questionable moral character, and if they know their assailant (see Whatley, 1996, for a meta-analysis). Women in these scenarios are also blamed if they allow sexual interaction to progress but draw the line on further sexual involvement before coitus (Kopper, 1996), and if both the woman the perpetrator have been drinking (Norris & Cubbins, 1992). Again, these beliefs are learned at an early age. Goodchilds and Zellman (1984) found many of these same attitudes operating among a group of adolescents between the ages of 14 and 18.

Thus, there appears to be widespread support for defining sexual assault as rape, but this is not the case for sexual coercion. Sexual coercion is much more of a gray area; it lacks a symbolic consensus about its meaning. Evaluating its meaning when it occurs is therefore difficult for the men and women involved.

Media reports on sexual aggression may aid in maintaining these cultural perceptions. Berger et al. (1988) examined how a community's campus and local newspapers reported sexual aggression. These news reports gave the misleading perception that cases of sexual aggression were rare. They also tended to spotlight cases that involved brutality and perversion, and focused on the pathology of the offender. When articles centered on nonforceful aggression, they stressed that the women involved were unharmed. Thus, the media is liable to focus more on cases of sexual assault then on instances of sexual coercion.

These findings show that being the sexual gatekeeper in the relationship is one of the primary sexual roles in dating for single women. Many single men see their dating partners fulfilling this role, especially if they hold traditional gender-role beliefs. This role has a darker side, one that relieves men of responsibility of their behaviors in achieving sexual involvement when women consent to more advanced stages of precoital involvement. The general acceptance of these views implies that they are a part of the role expectations many adolescents and young adults are socialized to hold.

Immediate Social Influences on Aggression

Cultural expectations are often taught in the socialization experiences of individuals. This would imply that others in the individual's social environment influence the person's use of sexual aggression. As with sexual behavior in general, the most likely candidates for socializing individuals are parents and peers. Researchers have highlighted the means by which parents increase the chance that their children will eventually engage in sexual aggressive practices. For instance, experiencing family violence during childhood is associated with later use of sexual aggression (Dean & Malamuth, 1997; Malamuth, Linz, Heavey, Barnes, & Acker, 1995). Specifically, witnessing parents abusing one another, and/or being a victim of child physical or sexual abuse, leads to a greater probability of men sexually aggressing against a dating partner (Gwartney-Gibbs, Stockard, & Bohmer, 1987; Koss & Dinero, 1988; Stets & Pirog-Good, 1989; Wilson et al., 1983). Such early experiences possibly lead these men to link issues of control in close relationships to the use of aggression, such that the aggression eventually becomes symbolic of the male's control.

Peers can provide support for acts of sexual aggression. Kanin's (1970) seminal work revealed that aggressive men surround themselves in a male subculture. This subculture emphasizes erotic achievements and provides status for members who succeed in erotic adventures. Although these peers may not reward unsolicited use of force, they see sexual assault and coercion as acceptable if women "lead men on" sexually.

Similar and more recent results point toward differential reinforcement of sexual aggression by peers (Koss & Dinero, 1988). Use of nonphysical coercion to obtain coitus is predicted by associating with other men who were also coercive and by receiving reinforcement from one's peers for engaging in these behaviors (Boeringer et al., 1991; Christopher et al., 1998; DeKeseredy & Kelly, 1995; Garrett-Gooding & Senter, 1987). DeKeseredy and Kelly's analysis of a national probability sample of Canadian college students provides further insights into the role of peers. In their work, two forms of peer support predicted sexual aggressiveness. The first was an attachment or friendship bond with similarly coercive men. The second involved using one's peers to give meaning to and provide positive social sanctions for single men's coercive behavior.

Investigations of fraternities, a group supportive of traditional masculine dating roles, provide parallel findings. Fraternity members, more than independents, use coercive means to engage in sexual intercourse with women (Lackie & de Man, 1997; Tyler, Hoyt, & Whitbeck, 1998). Correspondingly, sorority members report a disproportionately high number of sexually coercive incidents connected with fraternity functions and involving fraternity members (Copenhaver & Grauerholz, 1991).

Given this set of findings, it is not surprising that aggressive men have a higher need for social recognition than nonaggressive men, suggesting that social reinforcers provided by peers may be particularly potent for this population (Petty & Dawson, 1989). Moreover, having male friends who are similarly aggressive may not be the only type of role behavior to which premaritally sexual aggressive men are exposed. Other investigations suggest that peer groups of aggressive males include victimized females (Christopher et al., 1998; Gwartney-Gibbs & Stockard, 1988). Thus, both the role of aggressor and the corresponding victim role exist in these single men's social environments.

Peer groups are likely to do two things for sexually aggressive single men. First, they are apt to provide meaning to sexually aggressive acts (DeKeseredy & Kelly, 1995). This meaning probably emphasizes traditional male characteristics—that women should be viewed as sexual objects (DeKeseredy & Kelly, 1995; Koss & Dinero, 1988) and that engaging in sexual conquests is a strong litmus test of one's manliness. Second, they provide social status for these men, status that reinforces their actions and feeds into a sexual aggressor self-definition. This self-definition is liable to become the vehicle by which males guide the development of their future role expectations of how they and their dating partners should act.

Contributions of Setting and Circumstances

Certain social settings and circumstances are associated with and provide a context for sexual aggression. Although Ward et al. (1991) reported that many women are victimized by men they meet at parties, it is doubtful that acts of aggression occur in such public settings. In fact, most findings indicate that privacy is an important prerequisite for sexual aggression to occur (e.g., Gwartney-Gibbs & Stockard, 1989). Depending on the type of private setting asked about, coercion is most likely to take place while parking with an aggressive male (Muehlenhard & Linton, 1987), in a house or apartment (B. Miller & Marshall, 1987), or in a fraternity house (Copenhaver & Grauerholz, 1991). Not surprisingly, physical isolation is negatively related to the success with which women have resisted sexual aggression (Amick & Calhoun, 1987). Undoubtedly, these findings reflect the usual requirement of privacy needed for sexual interaction.

Alcohol and illicit drug use are frequently a part of sexual aggression. Reports of men being sexual aggressors while under the influence of these intoxicants during incidents fall between 71% and 80%; whereas reports of female victims' usage fall between 54% and 79% (Copenhaver & Grauerholz, 1991; Harrington & Leitenberg, 1994; Ward et al., 1991). Not all investigations, however, have found differences in victims and offenders use (Amick & Calhoun, 1987). Alcohol use has an independent role in sexual aggression, multivariate analyses show that it is related when considering the effects of other variables (Koss & Dinero, 1989; Muehlenhard & Linton, 1987), including among early adolescents (Small & Kerns, 1991). Using alcohol and drugs can be part of an overall influence strategy of sexual coercion, but may serve a differential role depending on who is consuming them (Christopher & Frandsen, 1990). Specifically, alcohol and drugs can serve as a disinhibitor for those who are considering aggression and can be used to cloud the judgment of their partners so they will be more susceptible to sexual advances. This can lead to women engaging in risky behavior. When women and their assailants are at least somewhat drunk, compared to couples who are not drunk, they are more apt to engage in more intimate and consensual sexual involvement prior to being victim of their dating partner's sexual coerciveness (Harrington & Leitenberg, 1994).

Relationship Conditions Associated With Sexual Aggression

Sexual aggression occurs within the context of a relationship, underscoring the importance of examining relationship dynamics. Only a few scholars, however, have considered the role of relationship properties in premarital sexual aggression, and only a limited range of properties have been investigated.

Power and influence strategies are elements of normal intimate relationships and their use provides cues about how they may be related to sexual aggression. In intimate heterosexual relationships, men use direct and bilateral means of influencing, whereas women use indirect and unilateral strategies (Falbo & Peplau, 1980). Women additionally feel less powerful in their relationships when, relative to their partner, they perceive themselves as contributing more and feel more in love and involved (Sprecher, 1985). These power differences between men and women may be inherit in romantic relationships and likely lay the groundwork for sexual aggression. Power differentials are associated with sexual aggression. Muehlenhard and Linton (1987) concluded from their investigation that indicators of differences in power were more common in women's dates where sexual aggression took place compared to dates where it had not. For example, men were more likely to ask the women out, drive, and pay for the expenses on dates involving sexual aggression. Not surprisingly, sexually aggressive men are more attuned to the power dimension of their relationships (Lisak & Roth, 1988).

The goal of using aggression as a power assertion in a relationship may be to gain control. Stets and Pirog-Good (1989) examined predictors of inflicting sexual aggression for both males and females. Men's use of mild and severe sexual aggression, and women's use of severe forms, were positively predicted by the level of their interpersonal control in the relationship. They posited that in these instances, men and women use sexual aggression as a means of getting their partners to comply with their wishes in the relationship. Hence, sexual aggression was symbolic of their power in and control of the relationship. Christopher and McQuaid's (1998) findings support this. Their analysis showed that interpersonal control mediated the relationship of relational conflict and use of sexual coercion for sexually aggressive men.

Besides power, other qualities of the dating relationship are associated with sexual aggression. Kanin (1969, 1970) found that male perpetrators and female victims differed from one another in their religious background, social and educational status, age, and intelligence. He believed that these partner differences led sexually aggressive men to conclude that their dates were inferior and undesirable, especially when they considered them as future relationship prospects, thereby justifying their aggression.

He additionally found that there was a failure in cross-sex communication in many, but not all of these couples (Kanin, 1969, 1970; Kanin & Parcell, 1977). This failure began in the consensual sexual behaviors they engaged in prior to acts of aggression. These behaviors included kissing

(7% of the cases), fondling breasts (23%), and genital petting (70%). Kanin postulated that the men perceived these behaviors as erotic encouragement in these incidents, whereas the women may not have understood the symbolic meaning their dates assigned to these acts. Furthermore, Kanin concluded that the men were unable to understand the women's rejection of further sexual intimacy. It is conceivable that many of these men believed that women say "no" but mean "yes." Muehlenhard and Linton (1987) found that sexually aggressive men often felt led on, even though women report that they do not intend to do so. Some of this miscommunication may happen because men are prone to interpret male–female interactions as sexual even when sexual cues are not meant to be sent by the women involved (Abbey & Melby, 1986; Shotland & Craig, 1988). Some of it also occurs because sexually aggressive men appear to question the truthfulness of women's sexual refusals, especially when women offer clear and direct messages of not being interested (Malamuth & Brown, 1994).

Kanin's findings further intimate that dyadic commitment plays a role. Although male aggression was common in casually dating couples (Kanin, 1970), it was more common in seriously dating couples when acts of aggression were paired with prior consensual sexual intimacy (Kanin, 1969). Current research substantiates these early findings. Christopher (1998) and his colleagues (Christopher, Owens, Stecker, 1993b), for example, found women more liable to be pressured into oral genital contact and coitus while seriously dating. Additionally, use of a pressure and manipulation strategy was more likely when individuals were in a monogamously committed relationship and wanted more sexual involvement, when compared to those who were satisfied with their level of sexual intimacy, or who wished that less sexual involvement had occurred. Furthermore, women in committed relationships used the antisocial acts influence strategy when they wanted greater sexual intimacy. Being in a committed relationship possibly leads both men and women to believe that they have a greater license in how they can pursue their sexual goals (Burke, Stets, & Pirog-Good, 1988; Koss & Cleveland, 1997; Muehlenhard, Goggins, Jones, & Satterfield, 1991). Commitment may also lead coercive men to act on their beliefs about love; beliefs that see love as having a gamelike quality with little emotional depth and sexual intimacy as something that exists for pleasure (Kalichman et al., 1993; Sarwer, Kalichman, Johnson, Early, & Ali, 1993).

Poor relationship experiences are also connected with acts of sexual aggression. Dyadic conflict and ambivalence are positively related to sexual assault and coercion for both aggressive men and women (Christopher et al., 1993a; Christopher et al., 1998; Christopher & McQuaid, 1998). Structural equation analyses of men's reports of their dating relationships reveal a direct path between poor relationship experiences and sexual aggression, and that these dyadic experiences mediate the effect of a number of individual and relational variables (Christopher et al., 1993b; Christopher & McQuaid, 1998). These findings may have two, noncompeting explanations. Conflict and ambivalence may lead to the use of sexual aggression as a way to maintain interpersonal control of the relationship, a hypothesis already explored in the discussion of power in this section. Second, these relationship experiences may lead aggressive individuals to devalue their partners and their relationships, and to not care if the relationship eventually ends. Sexual aggression, then, could achieve a self-defined positive outcome, such as sexual intercourse, in a relationship offering few alternative rewards to the individual in the present or foreseeable future.

Ironically, in dating relationships involving an aggressive male, it may fall to the female partner and victim to attempt to repair the relationship after aggressive incidents. Women victims often may blame themselves for what occurred (Lloyd & Emery, 1999; Muehlenhard et al., 1991) and their romantic involvement may keep them from defining their experiences as rape or sexual aggression (Lloyd, 1991; Lloyd & Emery, 1999). Furthermore, women are relied on to instigate relationship repair and to maintain relationship quality. Hence, these women may change their behavior in an attempt to decrease the chances of future aggression. Such attempts would most likely be unsuccessful.

Individual Contributions of the Aggressor

Attitudes. Burt (1980), as has been reviewed, found attitudinal support within society for sexual aggression against women. She identified three sets of beliefs that sustained sexual aggression, including believing in rape myths, believing that men's and women's sexual relationships were adversarial in nature, and accepting interpersonal violence. Burt's (1983) later work led her to compare convicted rapists to a sample of the general public. She found rapists much more accepting of rape myths and interpersonal violence. She surmised that rapists used their attitudes to justify their actions.

Burt's (1980, 1983) work provided a solid foundation for many researchers who investigated whether attitudes were related to sexual aggression in dating relationships. Concurrent findings across investigations provide strong evidence that aggressive males believe in rape myths, with multivariate analyses indicating that this association holds true even when considering other variables (Christopher et al., 1993a; Dean & Malamuth, 1997; Koss & Dinero, 1988; Muehlenhard & Linton, 1987). Aggressive males further believe that men's and women's sexual interactions are inherently adversarial. Moreover, these men, when compared to sexually nonaggressive men, are more accepting of interpersonal violence (Byers & Eno, 1991; Malamuth, 1986; Muehlenhard & Linton, 1987; Stets & Pirog-Good, 1989), endorse the use of force (Garrett-Gooding & Senter, 1987; Rapaport & Burkhart, 1984), see force as a legitimate means of gaining sexual access (Koss & Dinero, 1988), indicate a higher likelihood of raping if they would not be caught (Petty & Dawson, 1989), and endorse male sexual dominance (Muehlenhard & Falcon, 1990). Taken as a whole, these findings establish that sexually aggressive men have an attitude complex that strongly endorses and supports the use of interpersonal violence.

Disinhibitors. Hall and Hirschman (1991) theorized that normal socialization experiences include the internalization of inhibitions that control anger and aggressive urges. They posit that sexual aggression becomes more likely when individuals experience affective or emotional states that weaken these inhibitions. They labeled these *states of affective dyscontrol.* Partial support for their conceptualization comes from Lisak and Roth (1988), who found sexually aggressive single men more disinhibited than nonaggressive men. In a similar vein, these men have greater impulsivity (Petty & Dawson, 1989) and are more likely to be sensation seekers (Lalumière & Quinsey, 1996) when compared to their nonaggressive counterparts.

Further support comes from work that suggests that these males posses some antisocial characteristics. Rapaport and Burkart (1984) found sexually aggressive men less likely to understand social rules, feel personal responsibility for their actions, and internalize prosocial values. Christopher et al. (1993b) showed that low levels of empathy were indirectly related to sexual aggression (see also Lisak & Ivan, 1995). These findings indicate that normal concerns about the potential impact of one's aggressive behavior on a partner are not present in these men to the degree that they are in nonsexually aggressive men.

Additional support for this view comes from researchers who have identified two specific states of affective dyscontrol related to engaging in sexual aggression. Anger plays a role (Mosher & Anderson, 1986), but this is not the quick arousal form of anger. It is a long-standing, brooding type of anger (Christopher et al., 1993b) that may have its origins in these men's perceptions that they were poorly treated by women in their past (Kanin, 1970; Lisak & Roth, 1988). In a similar vein, feeling hostile toward women is also characteristic of these men (Kanin, 1970; Malamuth et al., 1995) and has been linked to their feelings of anger (Christopher et al., 1993). Check (1988) defined hostility toward women as a predisposition to be aggressive, with the aggression focused on women. Multivariate tests consistently find that this form of hostility contributes to sexual aggression (Koss & Dinero, 1988; Malamuth, 1986), although structural equation analyses have differed in whether this is a direct or an indirect relationship (Christopher et al., 1993b; Malamuth et al., 1995; Malamuth, Sockloski, Koss, & Tanaka, 1991).

Dominance. Although power and influence are usually conceptualized as qualities inherent in relationships (Huston, 1983), dominance is a personality trait that predisposes individuals to use aggressive influence strategies. Dominance is predictive of sexual aggression, albeit not as strong as other individual factors. However, when *sexual* dominance is measured, the relationship between these two variables becomes much stronger (Muehlenhard & Falcon, 1990).

Gender-Role Beliefs. Earlier in this chapter, research findings were reviewed that suggested being a man or a woman was more predictive of sexual aggression than one's gender-role beliefs. This should not be construed, however, to mean that gender-role beliefs are unrelated to using sexual aggression. Kanin's (1969) early work revealed that men holding a double sexual standard are more liable to be sexually aggressive than men who did not hold this standard. More recent investigations provide concurrent support (Wilson et al., 1983) and additionally show that aggressive men have traditional beliefs about women's place in society (Koss et al., 1985; Muehelenard & Falcon, 1990; Muehlenhard & Linton, 1987; Walker, Rowe, & Quinsey, 1993).

Not all investigators come to the same conclusion. Rapaport and Burkhart (1984) included measures of gender-role stereotyping and gender-role satisfaction and found neither was related to sexual aggression. Similarly, Koss and Dinero's (1988) measure of negative masculinity failed to discriminate between aggressors and nonaggressors. Christopher et al. (1998) found masculinity and femininity unrelated to sexual aggression in multivariate tests. Even more puzzling is Burke et al.'s (1988) finding that less masculine and more feminine males are likely to be aggressive.

The divergence in findings is probably an artifact of measurement differences. Investigators who used either a measure of sexual attitudes, or the Attitudes Toward Women scale, have consistently found aggressive men more traditional in their gender-role beliefs. Researchers using alternative instruments to tap into gender-role attitudes have not found such a relationship (i.e., Christopher et al., 1998; Koss & Dinero, 1988; Rapaport & Burkhart, 1984). Moreover, Burke et al.'s (1988) measure of gender identity is somewhat suspect. Contrary to the usual conceptualization of gender being composed of separate masculine and feminine components, these investigators used a unidimensional measure with the two poles representing the two gender orientations. Hence, their investigation may be flawed on theoretical and measurement grounds.

Outlook on Sexuality. A number of scholars have explored different aspects of the sexuality of sexually aggressive men. Their efforts provide a clear indication that these men, when compared to nonaggressive men, possess a different expectation about how sexuality fits into their lives. Kanin (1967) first reported that sexually aggressive men were more sexually focused than nonaggressive men. They were more sexually experienced and resolute in their search for new sexual encounters. More recent researchers similarly found these men to have greater numbers of sexual partners (Koss & Dinero, 1988; Koss et al., 1985), to begin their sexual experiences earlier in life (Koss & Dinero, 1988; Malamuth et al., 1995), and to be more sexually experienced (Dean & Malamuth, 1997) especially in uncommitted sexual relationships (Lalumière, Chalmers, Quinsey, & Seto, 1996; Lalumière & Quinsey, 1996).

Furthermore, sexually aggressive single men engage in behaviors that result in orgasm more frequently. Men who self-identified themselves as having raped a dating partner experienced an average of 1.5 orgasms a week compared to .8 a month for nonrapists (Kanin, 1983). Ironically, these same aggressive men feel sexually frustrated (Kanin, 1967, 1970, 1983). Fully 71% of the rapists, but only 38% of the nonrapists, rate their sex life as unsatisfactory. The rapists believe they would only be sexually satisfied if they experienced 4.51 orgasms a week, compared to 2.8 for nonrapists.

Additional differences exist in what is sexually arousing. Arousal has been hypothesized to play a role in sexual aggression, especially if violence is seen as sexually stimulating (Hall & Hirschman, 1991). There is evidence that this is the case with sexually aggressive men. When compared to nonaggressive men, aggressive men report greater sexual arousal when listening to a guided imagery of rape (Mosher & Anderson, 1986). Similarly, Malamuth (1986) found the degree of penile tumescence experienced to a story of a woman being raped was predictive of using sexual aggression independent of attitudes, past sexual experience, and dominance ratings. These findings may explain why Koss and Dinero (1988) discovered that aggressive men are more likely to watch violent pornography.

This collection of findings paints a picture of single sexually aggressive men having an almost predatory approach to their sexuality. They are easily aroused, seek novel and frequent sexual interactions with a number of partners, prefer to have little commitment with their sexual partners, but often find their sexual encounters less than satisfying. This dissatisfaction may motivate them to seek their next sexual conquest.

Sexually Aggressive Women

As has been reviewed, there are sexually aggressive single women, women who achieve their sexual goals by aggressive means. Only a handful of researchers have attempted to identify correlates of women's sexual aggression. Several individual-level variables are associated. Similar to sexually aggressive men, women who abuse are likely to have experienced abuse as a child (Stets & Pirog-Good, 1989). As adults, these women's belief systems also coincide with aggressive men; both accept rape myths and interpersonal aggression and believe that men and women are adversaries in their sexual relationships (Burke et al., 1988; Christopher et al., 1993a).

Although the latter two of these beliefs is consistent with these women's actions, their belief in rape myths is more difficult to understand. Christopher et al. (1993a) speculated that many rape myths have a common theme, that of the women in control of their sexual interactions, if not the relationship as a whole. Hence, women who accept rape myths may use sexual aggression to gain interpersonal control of the relationship. Stets and Pirog-Good (1989) supported this proposition, finding female's interpersonal control related to their use of sexual aggression.

Additional individual characteristics are associated with women's aggression. Number of coital partners, hostility toward men, brooding anger, and past acts of aggression are all positively related (Christopher et al., 1993a; Christopher et al., 1998). Self-esteem is negatively related to women's aggression according to Stets and Pirog-Good's (1989) findings. Christopher et al. (1993a), however, failed to find this relationship, although self-esteem was negatively correlated with brooding anger in their investigation. This suggests that self-esteem may act indirectly on aggression through anger.

Finally, single women's relationship experiences are linked to their use of aggression. Women's aggression is more probable in committed relationships (Christopher et al., 1993a; Stets & Pirog-Good, 1989). Moreover, using aggressive influence strategies is positively related to engaging in relational conflict, experiencing sexual conflict, and having feelings of ambivalence (Christopher et al., 1993a; Christopher et al., 1998; Christopher, McQuaid, & Updegraff, 1999). Similar to men, sexually coercive women are sexually dissatisfied and evaluate their sexual interactions as involving costs. Being in a committed relationship may allow some women to be sexually aggressive without worrying about others outside of the relationship judging them negatively. Experiencing dyadic conflict is understandable if these women hold a long-standing anger, feel hostile toward men, and accept violence. Moreover, experiences of sexual conflict are understandable given their use of sexual coercion. The coercion is likely to assert their control over the sexual interaction with their partner. Feelings of ambivalence about the relationship are also not surprising. However, given these women's attitudes and women's usual dating roles, feelings of ambivalence may reflect larger questions about the role of sexual expression in their dating relationships.

Victims and Risk

Victims' experiences have received some attention by scholars in this area. Factors have been identified that put women, and to a lesser extent men, at risk for sexual abuse. These factors should not be construed as markers of victims' responsibility for their plight. No woman wants to serve as prey for sexual aggressors. It can be valuable, however, to construe these variables as risk indicators. Women who have certain early experiences, believe in the indicated attitudes, or have the identified relationship experiences are at greater risk of being sexually victimized in their dating relationships.

Early Influences. Early adolescents who have experienced sexual aggressiveness in their dating relationships share certain commonalties. Using alcohol, illegal drugs, or both is more characteristic of victimized than nonvictimized teens (Erickson & Rapkin, 1991; Small & Kerns, 1991). Parental monitoring of teens' activities is also lower among victims (Small & Kerns, 1991). Additionally, disproportionately more adolescent victims report being sexually abused earlier in their life (Erickson & Rapkin, 1991; Small & Kerns, 1991).

Retrospective reports of young adults further indicate that childhood experiences of physical and/or sexual abuse puts both men and women at risk for being victims of sexual abuse at this later developmental stage (Burke et al., 1988; Koss & Dinero, 1989). In fact, Koss and Dinero (1989) found that 66% of women in their sample who were raped, or were victims of attempted rape, had childhood sexual experiences, with 13% experiencing attempted or completed acts of coitus. Comparatively, only 20% of the nonvictimized women had childhood sexual experiences of whom only 3% experienced attempted or completed acts of coitus. Similarly, Himelein's (1995) longitudinal investigation revealed that precollege sexual victimization was a strong predictor of victimization while at college.

Using anecdotal data, Lundberg-Love and Geffner (1989) speculated why these women may be more apt to be victims of sexual aggression while dating. They posit that when women experience cues that aggression is forthcoming, they ignore these cues because of their past. They wrongfully believe they are being overly sensitive because of their prior ordeals. When these women are actually confronted with aggression, they become incapacitated because they re-experience and are overwhelmed by emotions linked with their earlier abusive episodes, and therefore offer little resistance. Aggressive males may see the lack of resistance as a tacit approval of their actions. The early abuse experiences, therefore, lay the foundation for these women falling into the role of victim as an adult.

Individual Factors.   Investigations into the individual factors in victimization experiences are limited. Women's attitudes toward female societal roles appear unrelated to their victimization status (Korman & Leslie, 1982; Muehlenhard & Cook, 1988). Female victims have lower self-esteem and male victims are more accepting of violence in interpersonal relationships. The cross-sectional nature of these findings makes it difficult to establish the cause–effect relationship between these variables (Stets & Pirog-Good, 1989).

Differences in the dating history, sexual history, and sexual attitudes exist for victimized and nonvictimized single women. Early work in this area revealed that victimized women date more frequently, were more likely to make dates spontaneously, and, for those who reported more serious aggression, were more likely to be nonvirgins (Kanin & Parcell, 1977; Kirkpatrick & Kanin, 1957). Koss et al.'s (1985) more recent and encompassing investigation confirms that victimized women have more sexual partners and hold more liberal sexual attitudes. Similarly, Himelein (1995) reported that women who were victimized were less likely to endorse sexually conservative attitudes.

Relationship Conditions and Experiencing Aggression. Certain qualities of victimized women's relationship experiences put them at increased risk. Being in a more involved relationship is one of them (Burke et al., 1988; Stets & Pirog-Good, 1989). As commitment is a part of most meaningful relationships, this may be a demonstration of the principle of least interest. Simply put, this principle states that the partner who has the least interest has the greatest power in the relationship. If the woman is highly committed, but the partner is not, this may open the door for her partner to use abuse and coercion as a means of demonstrating his power over her. It is not surprising, then, that victims assign more responsibility to a perpetrator in stranger rapes than in acquaintance rapes (Koss et al., 1988). Commitment does not always play a role though. Ward et al. (1991) found aggression was frequently associated with a women being picked up at a party by a man she did not know well.

Although previously reviewed, it bears repeating that consenting to engage in precoital sexual intimacy puts women at risk for men using aggression to achieve greater sexual intimacy. Furthermore, the more involved the consented sexual intimacy, the greater the risk, and the more justified peers will judge a man's actions. Hence, consensual sexual activity is liable to become symbolic of the woman's overall sexual willingness in the male's eyes. It also bears repeating that moderate or heavy use of alcohol by women and their dating partners also puts women at risk (Abbey et al., 1996; Gross & Billingham, 1998; Harrington & Leitenberg, 1994).

Women's efforts at resistance may not always affect the outcome of the aggression. Fully 73% of unwanted acts of intercourse took place even though the women resisted in some way according to Ward et al. (1991). Women use a number of methods in their attempts to stop aggressors. Most directly say no, but may also fight, cry, turn cold, reason or plead, run away, or physically struggle (Koss et al., 1988). All of these strategies are used as frequently with stranger rapes as they are with acquaintance rapes with one exception, that women are less likely to scream for help with acquaintance rapes.

Amick and Calhoun's (1987) investigation provides additional insight into the effectiveness of resistance attempts. They divided women into three victim groups: low victimization women (attempts at kissing or fondling), moderate victimization women (verbal, nonphysically threatening means to achieve intercourse), and high victimization women (threats and/or force used to achieve intercourse). Low and high victim groups more likely utilized physical tactics to resist sexual aggression, whereas moderate victims were apt to use verbal tactics. In fact, the moderate group was much more liable to convey messages of clear nonconsent than women in the other two groups. Differences existed between successful resistors and nonsuccessful resistors. Successful resistors in the low victimization group showed initiative and persistence. In the moderate victimization group, successful resistors were more poised and had greater social skills. As a group, unsuccessful resistors were more apt to be in an established relationship and have a higher frequency of prior experiences of genital fondling and/or coitus.

Women's Reactions

Women react very negatively to their victimization experiences (Lloyd & Emery, 1999). Some feel anger, disgust, disillusionment, and guilt (Kirpatrick & Kanin, 1957). Koss et al. (1988) found female victims markedly higher than nonvictims on depression and anxiety, and experienced lower levels of relationship quality and sexual satisfaction. Koss and her colleagues concluded that "the responses . . . indicated a lingering, potentially clinically significant impact of rape" (p. 22).

Other investigators support this. Zweig, Barber, and Eccles (1997) reported that when women who experienced sexual coercion are compared to women who have not had such an experience, the victimized women suffer from depressed mood, lowered self-esteem, increased anger, and a greater degree of social isolation. Santello and Leitenberg (1993) similarly found that sexually coerced women coped with their aggression experiences by avoiding the problem, socially withdrawing, and criticizing themselves. In their study, women's scores on the Brief Symptom Checklist indicated that 22% of the sexually coerced women scored in the clinical range, whereas only 9% of the noncoerced women's scores were this high.

Youthful experiences with sexual aggression while dating have similar long-term impacts. Zweig, Crockett, Sayer, and Vicary (1999) followed a group of women from ninth grade to their early 20s. Adolescent experiences with sexual coercion involving other youth resulted in young adult women suffering from greater sexual depression when compared to nonvictimzed peers. When adolescent experiences included sexual assault, the effects on early adulthood were more pervasive. They included depression, low self-esteem, low sexual-esteem, poor body image, and poor quality romantic relationships.

One of the reasons women experience such pervasive effects may have to do with how they assign blame. Lloyd and Emery (1999) found there were two themes in how young women construed responsibility and blame. First, they found excuses for their partner's aggression by focusing on his upbringing, his attitudes about women or violence, or the influence of his friends or his alcohol use. Second, they identified ways that they themselves were to blame for the coercion—they put themselves in the situation, they should have seen the signs of what was coming, they led him on until he could not control himself, or they should have said "no" with greater strength. Undoubtedly, such self-blame is apt to be at least partly responsible for the range of emotional reactions and symptoms revealed by researchers.

Given these strong reactions, it is surprising who women tell of their experiences. Women very often do not tell anyone of their victimization. If they do tell, they choose to confide in friends more so than counselors or police (B. Miller & Marshall, 1987; Ogletree, 1993; Ward et al., 1991). Even with forced intercourse, only a minority seek medical attention (Copenhaver, & Grauerholz, 1991; B. Miller & Marshall, 1987). Berger et al. (1988) reported some of the reasons why women tell so few professionals about their experiences. Some indicate that too many days followed the incident before they were ready to speak with a professional; others were concerned that they would not be taken seriously. A number felt some responsibility for what happened, especially in cases where they knew the perpetrator. Finally, there were those who wanted to protect their lovers and boyfriends, and offered excuses for their assaultive and coercive behavior. Lloyd and Emery (1999) also cited the fact that perpetrators are rarely charged, and even more rarely convicted, as playing a role in these women's silence.

This review again reflects the complexity of any form of sexual expression, including sexual aggression. A range of cultural, social, dyadic, and individual factors contribute to this phenomenon. In the next chapter I propose a model that integrates these findings utilizing the concepts proposed in previous chapters.

8

A Theoretical Model
of Premarital
Sexual Aggression

The symbolic interactional concepts used in the previous, theory-focused chapters provide the foundation for integrating the body of literature on premarital sexual aggression. This literature, however, suffers from a major drawback—far more is known about male aggression than female aggression in dating. I found the lack of empirical investigations into female sexual aggression a major obstacle to theory building. Although the limited findings suggest parallels exist between aggressive individuals of both sexes, it would be foolish to believe that all male-related findings can generalize to women. Thus, I begin this chapter with a caveat. The relationships between variables I propose in this chapter apply predominantly to male premarital sexual aggression. I point out instances when findings for women exist, but more research into the phenomenon of female premarital sexual aggression is necessary before full models can be proposed.

The Self and Sexual Aggression
Role Enactment

Recall from previous chapters that one's *self* is the center of a number of activities. These activities include building a sexual self-identity and assigning meaning to one's own and one's partner's role enactments. An individual's sexual attitudes, values, and norms play a key role in this process as they represent the different meaning structures that are integrated into one's normative sexual roles. As individuals mature, their sexual attitudes become more complex reflecting their deeper understanding of sexuality. In the previous chapter, the findings of scholars provided a detailed look at the sexual attitudes and norms of single, sexually aggressive men. Conceptually, these attitudes can be organized into a complex composed of three interrelated components.

The first component reflects aggressive men's acceptance of interpersonal violence (Byers & Eno, 1991; Malamuth, 1986) and endorsement of using force (Garrett-Gooding & Senter, 1987). These attitudes are grounded in values that legitimize sexually aggressive behavioral acts. The second component of the attitude complex centers on the gender-role beliefs of sexually aggressive men. These men are traditional in their beliefs about the place women in society in general (Koss et al., 1985; Muehlenhard & Falcon, 1990; Walker et al., 1993) and their acceptance of the double sexual standard demonstrates their beliefs about women's sexual roles specifically (Kanin, 1969). The double standard allows men to categorize the women whom they date into those worthy of a future relationship, to be treated sexually with respect, and those unworthy of this status, who do not deserve sexual respect. Both views of women reflect a *role position* to which dating partners are assigned. Thus, one manifestation of the double standard allows aggressive men to devalue women with whom they see no possible relationship future. This explains why sexually aggressive men take an inferior view of the dating partners they aggress against (Kanin, 1969, 1970). Such an attributional status characterizes the assigned dating role position for the partner. This position does not require aggressive men to respect their dating partner's wishes and these men's attitudes, in turn, allow them to value and justify their own aggressive behaviors.

The third component of the attitude complex integrates the first two components. The more general finding that men with traditional gender-role beliefs are more accepting of sexual aggression (G. Fisher, 1986; Lonsway & Fitzgerald, 1994; Muehlenhard, 1988) hints that the first two attitude components are related for aggressive men. Researchers demonstrate these ties exist. On one level, sexually aggressive men view men's and women's sexual relationships as adversarial (Christopher et al., 1993b). More specifically, however, these men see force as a legitimate means for gaining sexual access (Koss & Dinero, 1988; Muehlenhard & Linton, 1987), endorse sexual dominance (Muehlenhard & Falcon, 1990), and believe in myths about rape (Christopher et al., 1993b; Koss & Dinero, 1988). Belief in rape myths such as "women say no but mean yes" or that "any women can resist a rape if she wants" focuses the control of and blame for sexual aggression on the female partner (Christopher et al., 1993b). This allows sexually aggressive men to assign meaning to their own and their partners' sexual role behaviors that purge themselves of personal responsibility. It is not surprising, therefore, that they feel less responsibility for their actions in their dating relationships (Rapaport & Burkhart, 1984). Thus, the general hypothesis from previous chapters, that youths' sexual attitudes and values have a direct relationship to their sexual role enactments, can be applied to acts of sexual aggression. Moreover, the proposed relation between violent attitudes and sexually aggressive role enactment is supported by structural equation analyses (Christopher et al., 1993b; Malamuth et al., 1991; Malamuth et al., 1995).

Because acceptance of sexual aggression is characteristic to some degree of many men (cf. Jenkins & Dambrot, 1987; Lonsway & Fitzgerald, 1994; Muehlenhard, 1988), especially when they endorse traditional gender-roles (cf. Fisher, 1986; Lonsway & Fitzgerald, 1994), it is legitimate to question what separates aggressive from nonaggressive single men. The answer may lie in other personality traits that contribute to the assignment of meaning in the aggressive male's self. Hall and Hirschman (1991) speculated that nonaggressive individuals learn inhibitions that control aggression through socialization. Aggressive individuals, however, possess disinhibitors that either block or eliminate these controls. Rapaport and Burkhart's (1984) finding that aggressive men are less likely to have internalized prosocial values in comparison to nonaggressive men support this reasoning. I hypothesize that these disinhibitors are a part of the self.

Low levels of empathy in the context of dating relationships characterize the first disinhibitor. Empathy helps individuals understand the ramifications of their actions by cognitively and/or emotionally putting themselves in another person's position. Thus, empathy is vital to role taking and role making. Empathy is negatively and directly related to possessing violent attitudes in sexually aggressive single men (Christopher et al., 1993b; Lisak & Ivan, 1995). This suggests that the development of the attitude complex involves poor insight into the experiences of dating victims and helps to illuminate how sexually aggressive men can absolve themselves of responsibility for their actions (Rapaport & Burkhart, 1984). Their lack of understanding of their victim's plight supports their aggressive acts.

A second disinhibitor is an outcome of the attitudes. If the identified violent attitude complex operates on role choice, then individuals should develop a predisposition to behave violently toward women—to experience hostility toward them (Check, 1988). Concurrent structural equation analyses (Christopher et al., 1993b; Dean & Malamuth, 1997; Malamuth et al., 1991) support this hypothesis. Put another way, hostility toward women constitutes a role norm located in the self that, because of values inherit in their attitude complex, further sanctions the choice of sexually aggressive role enactments. The personality trait of dominance is likely to operate in a similar fashion. Although dominance is positively associated with being sexually aggressive (Muehlenhard & Falcon, 1990), its exact relation with the other variables in the model remains untested at this time. Its effect is liable to parallel hostility's by sanctioning aggressive acts as a means of exerting control over the relationship.

Anger is the third disinhibitor specifically identified by Hall and Hirschman (1991) that distinguishes sexually aggressive men. Styker and Statham (1985) speculated that emotions become part of a role by the same process of socialization through which individuals learn possible behavioral sequences that build role compliments. In this manner, the meaning assigned to different role sequences becomes paired with particular emotions and as the self engages in role making, these emotions become a part of one's role experience. Sexually aggressive men possess an anger that is related to their aggressive role enactments (Malamuth et al., 1991). This anger is a brooding one that may originate in past dating relationship experiences (Kanin, 1970; Lisak & Roth, 1988) thereby demonstrating one possible avenue of socialization (see Fig. 8.1).

Structural equation analyses highlight two additional points about this anger (Christopher et al., 1993b). First, it is negatively predicted by empathy. Stated another way, not being able to take an other's viewpoint is associated with higher levels of anger. Second, anger is additionally and positively predicted by hostility toward women. If this form of hostility contributes to the role norms that guide an individuals' role enactments, then the relationship between these two variables supports Stryker and

FIG. 8.1. *The self and male sexually aggressive role enactments.*

Statham's (1985) conceptualization that emotions are an integral part of role enactments.

Investigations of the sexuality of single, aggressive men illuminate ways these different facets of the self come together to give meaning to their sexuality. Sexually aggressive men find sexual interactions paired with violence arousing (Malamuth, 1986; Mosher & Anderson, 1986). They are sexually focused and strive for new sexual encounters (Kanin, 1967, 1970, 1983; Koss et al., 1985; Lalumière & Quinsey, 1996). At the same time, they feel more sexually frustrated than nonaggressive men even though they average more orgasms on a weekly basis (Kanin, 1983). Not surprisingly, they are coitally experienced (Christopher et al., 1993b; Koss & Dinero, 1988; Lalumière et al., 1996) and have been sexually aggressive in the past (Christopher et al., 1998). Expressions of sexual aggression in previous relationships demonstrate how role enactments can be learned over time and may include dyadic interactions gone awry that contribute to these men's brooding anger. This relationship is depicted in Fig. 8.1.

Emerging from this set of findings are two themes that characterize sexual role expectations and enactments of aggressive men. First, they view their role in a dating relationship as predatory in nature, they actively and continuously search for the next sexual conquest. Yet, conquest does not provide role satisfaction in terms of sexual fulfillment. The second theme more likely reflects the true goal of these men's role expectations. In this theme, sexual involvement is paired with coercion, assault, or both, found stimulating, and allows these individuals to gain control of and power over their dating partners. Experiencing stimulating sex, and successful exertion of control over their partners and relationships undoubtedly reinforces these role enactments and increases the chances these role sequences will occur in the future.

The Self and Female Sexual Aggression in Dating. Parallel research findings between sexually coercive and aggressive single men and women suggest similarities in their sexual selves. First, they posses similar attitudes (Burke et al., 1988; Christopher et al., 1993a). Sexually aggressive young women, for instance, believe men and women have adversarial sexual relationships, accept interpersonal aggression, and believe in rape myths. Believing these myths may reflect seeing themselves as women in control of the relationship—a theme that characterizes these myths (Christopher et al., 1993a). They therefore appear to have an attitude complex that, in part, parallels aggressive males' attitude complex. This complex would operate in a similar fashion in the self—providing meaning and justification for aggressive sexual role enactments. Concluding this, however, must be tempered by the limits of the findings in this area; not as much is known about the full range of sexually aggressive women's attitudes. Sexually aggressive women's gender-role beliefs, for example, are unrelated to their aggressive role enactments (Christopher et al., 1998).

Aggressive acts by single women are also associated with experiencing hostility toward men and holding a brooding anger (Christopher et al., 1993a; Christopher et al., 1998). If hostility toward men establishes potential role norms for these women, it is congruent with the attitudes they hold and the role actions they take. Together, their attitudes and hostility likely aid in role making by defining possible sexual role enactments. These women's brooding anger would operate in fashion similar to men as well, becoming a part of and giving meaning to their aggressive role behaviors.

Little is known about the sexuality of these women outside of the finding of a positive association between number of coital partners and being sexually coercive (Christopher et al., 1993a). This possibility is evidence of them being sexually aggressive in past relationships, a developmental influence on their use of sexual aggression in current relationships (Christopher et al., 1998). Thus, sexually aggressive role enactments for single women are learned, in part, through the socialization experiences of previous and similar role enactments. Again, similar to aggressive males, these role enactments are punctuated by the theme of relationship control (Stets & Pirog-Good, 1989). Successful attainment of control by using aggression reinforces these actions and increases the probability of their occurrence in the future.

Socialization Forces in Sexual Aggression

Consistent with models proposed in previous chapters, the self is hypothesized to be influenced by the social self and both the self and the social self are influenced by significant others through socialization. Socialization allows individuals to consider different possible meanings for role behavior compliments. It is also in the social self that individuals consider the role expectations of significant and generalized others. These perceived role expectations provide one source of potential role enactments from which to choose.

Socializing influences on individuals' sexual self and social self considered in previous chapters included parents and peers. Identified parental influences on male premarital sexual aggression primarily take place during childhood and early adolescence, and include being the victim of physical abuse, sexual abuse, or witnessing parents abusing one another (Dean & Malamuth, 1997; Koss & Dinero, 1988; Malamuth et al., 1995; Stets & Pirog-Good, 1989). These early experiences have a potentially lasting impact on close relationship schemas developed during these early developmental stages because of the intensity that characterizes them and because they are liable to be repeated on a number of occasions (Browne & Finkelhor, 1986). These early schemas may eventually become an integral part of older adolescents' and young adults' self, providing possible role choices for future romantic relationships. Certainly, the potential for modeling such early aggressive experiences in later life is present; being abused as a child or abusing one's partner in a romantic relationship both contain a theme of interpersonal control (Stets & Pirog-Good, 1989). Early victimization experiences, or viewing aggressor–victim role models, may lead to forming relational attitudes that value establishing control over a relationship partner. It is doubtful, however, if these early experiences are sufficient to trigger later sexual aggression in dating relationships by themselves (Christopher & Lloyd, 2000). Other variables, proposed to be a part of the self, likely mediate or moderate these earlier influences in current sexually aggressive role enactments (see Fig. 8.2).

Peer influences on male sexual aggression are much more immediate in their effect. Peer attitudes, norms, and role expectations mirror those held by premaritally sexually aggressive men (Boeringer et al., 1991; Christopher & McQuaid, 1998; DeKeseredy & Kelly, 1995; Garrett-Gooding & Senter, 1987). The role positions that peers assign single women and men who date highlight their aggressive role expectations and establish peer status rewards for engaging in these role compliments. In this socially constructed environment, women are viewed as sexual objects, so it is not surprising the erotic achievements of men are valued and positively sanctioned by peers (DeKeseredy & Kelly, 1995; Kanin, 1970; Koss & Dinero, 1988). This sexual role orientation reinforces the predatory sexuality single aggressive men display. It also establishes meanings to be assigned to behavioral acts that guide choices in role enactments. For instance, according to aggressive peer groups, women who sexually "lead men on" by dressing in a particular way, or engaging in precoital behaviors but not coitus, are to be punished by coercing them into intercourse, thereby "giving them what they deserve" (DeKeseredy & Kelly, 1995; Kanin, 1970). It is highly probable that aggressive men return to their peers and regale them with tales of their sexual conquests (Christopher & McQuaid, 1998). In this way, peer groups provide meaning and support for individual role enactments.

Men who act according to their peer group's role expectations achieve status (Koss & Dinero, 1988). This status may have a particularly strong effect on role enactment because sexually aggressive men have a greater need for social recognition than nonaggressive men (Petty & Dawson, 1989). Specifically, individuals may be more strongly motivated in their sexual role choices by anticipated peer rewards than they are by rewards offered by one's dating partner. This may be particularly true if the relationship is punctuated by conflict and ambiguity, relational experiences associated with sexual coercion and assault (Christopher & McQuaid, 1998; Christopher et al., 1993b). This dynamic is explored in greater depth in the next section.

Peer groups may not be confined only to men, they can include victimized females (Christopher et al., 1998; Gwartney-Gibbs & Stockard, 1988). It is unclear if these women are stable members of the group, or become members only while dating a particular male member. Nonetheless, the inclusion of female victims presents aggressive men with aggressor–victim complimentary role models. Having these complimentary models allows for better role making on the part of aggressive men. The models provide insight into possible relationship dynamics that may be involved with acts of sexual aggression.

These variables fit together theoretically in ways similar to those proposed in past chapters (see Fig. 8.2). Peer norms and role attitudes have a bi-directional influence with peer sexual role enactments. Being in a social group that contains aggressive males and victimized females sustains and reinforces continued sexual aggression within the group and supports the norms and role expectations of the group. Both peer aggressive role enactments and the accompanying sexual norms and role expectations are apt to also directly influence the self of the aggressive male by establishing possible meanings for his own aggressive sexual role behaviors and by providing role models.

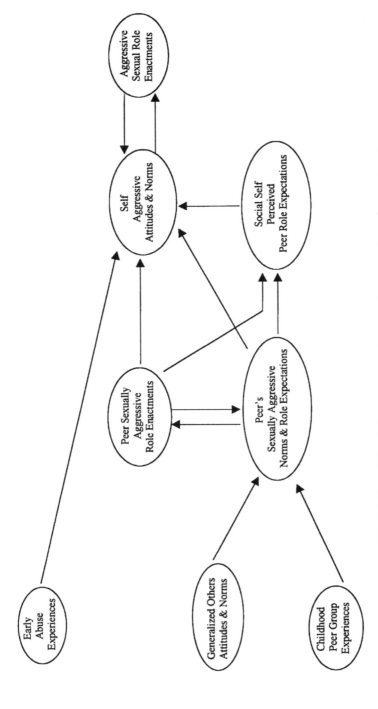

FIG. 8.2 Socializing influences on male sexually aggressive role enactments.

These aggressive peer role expectations and enactments are likely to be powerful influences on the social self of aggressive males. The parallels between peers' beliefs and actions, and sexually aggressive men's role enactments, suggests that peers may be stronger influences on their social self than what occurs among nonaggressive men. Hence, the role taking and role making within the aggressive man's self is heavily influenced by peers as aggressive males anticipate the reactions of their peers to their sexual role making in their social selves. They will seek the immediate reinforcement of sexual conquest in the relationship, and anticipate additional rewards from peers as they relate their experiences to them. In this manner, the peer group ascribes meaning to their role actions. Thus, when aggressive men role take potential behavioral choices in their dating relationships, the role expectations and reactions of peers are potentially more salient influences on their choices of behavior compliments than are the expectations and reactions of the dating partner.

Two influences on peer aggressive groups exist (see Fig. 8.2). First, the attitudes of the larger dating population of adolescents and young adults, or generalized others, reflects (a) disagreement about what constitutes sexual aggression, and (b) approval for sexual aggression in certain circumstances. These influence the self and social self of aggressive males indirectly by laying the foundation for aggressive peer norms and role expectations. In this more diffuse peer group, rape does not necessarily occur simply if a woman says no to coitus, but the partner ignores her and coerces her into sexual intercourse despite her wishes. Instead, this broader group considers such factors as how much the women resisted, how much force the man used, what the women was wearing, whether she was of moral character, and how much prior sexual intimacy occurred before the woman said "no," and then decides whether a rape occurred (Kopper, 1996; Shotland & Goodstein, 1983; Whatley, 1996). Sexual assault, with its accompanying threats or use of force, constitutes rape in this social discourse. Sexual coercion, although possibly seen as wrong, is less likely to be defined as rape and may even be believed to be justified under certain conditions. I hypothesize that aggressive peers use the lack of clarity in a social definition of sexual aggression to their advantage. It aids them in constructing justifications and peer rewards for coercive sexual behavior. Thus, male enclaves, such as fraternities, can be characterized by using and sanctioning sexual coercive behavior (Boeringer et al., 1991; Garrett-Gooding & Senter, 1987; Lackie & de Man, 1997; Tyler et al., 1998).

This group of generalized others attitudinally justifies sexual aggression under certain conditions.

For example, the majority of adolescents ages 14 to 18 in Goodchilds and Zellman's (1984) survey believed that a man was justified in forcing sexual intercourse on a date if he spent a lot of money on the woman, if she got him sexually excited, if she had engaged in intercourse with others, or if the couple had dated for a long time. In other research, young adults viewed women as responsible for their victimization if they became partially unclothed, allowed petting, or failed to forcefully resist sexual advances (Kopper, 1996; Shotland & Goodstein, 1983; Whatley, 1996). Sexually aggressive peer group norms are influenced by these cohort attitudes.

The second influence on peer group norms involves earlier socialization forces (see Fig. 8.2). The anticipation and receiving of status rewards from male peers for breaking social rules while pursuing erotic stimulation through sexual aggression have parallels to preadolescent rule breaking where pornography was viewed in all boy settings (see chapter 2). Both phenomena involve highly stereotypical masculine activities focused on breaking social rules and receiving peer reinforcement for one's actions. Both have similar outcomes, treating women as a sexual object depersonalizes them. In the earlier developmental setting, women shown in the pornographic materials are cast as objects of desire who readily and willingly serve the sexual needs of men. At the later stage of development, young aggressive men devalue their dating partners' wishes, thereby depersonalizing the women they date. This results in treating partners as sexual objects who should be controlled, rather than as persons with legitimate sexual wishes that need to be treated with respect. These parallels lead me to hypothesize that the earlier, all-boy settings provide learning experiences about how men can interact with one another, specifically, what role compliments they can use when interacting with one another. Stated another way, the early experiences of talking about the meaning of the viewed pornography, paired with the sharing of the viewing experience, establish complimentary male-friend roles focused on how men should interact with one another. For some men, these male roles contribute to forming later life peer groups that support sexual aggression among its members.

From this perspective, male peer groups provide meaning for aggressive men's sexual identity. Women can be described as "pieces of ass," "bitches," "whores," or as an object, "Wouldn't you like to get into *that*?"

These descriptions will be accepted and sanctioned by peers. Considering this acceptance and these sanctions in the social self is a strong source of influence on sexual role choices for these men.

Socializing Forces and Sexually Aggressive Women. Whether similar socialization forces operate for sexually aggressive women is not as clear at this time. Although similarities in socialization experiences have been found, these are findings of single studies rather than findings cross validated across studies. Thus, the fullness of the findings about socialization forces on female sexual aggression is missing. Nonetheless, some socialization forces are similar. For instance, sexually aggressive women are liable to have suffered abuse as a child (Stets & Pirog-Good, 1989). Hence, their choice of using sexually aggressive influence strategies may be a product of parental modeling. These early experiences may additionally foster adult relationship norms that value controlling relationship partners even if this requires using sexual aggression.

Aggressive women associate with peers who are similarly aggressive (Christopher et al., 1998). I hypothesize that these peer groups function in a similar manner to the peer groups of sexually aggressive males. They provide meaning to and support for aggressive women's sexual role enactments. However, influences on the groups themselves are less clear at this time. There does not appear to be social support among age cohorts, or generalized others, for female sexual aggression. Typical childhood experiences among girls that focus on building relationship skills would also not seem to foster aggressive role choices in later life for women. Thus, although incidences of early abuse, and having an aggressive peer group clearly operate as socializing forces in these women's sexually aggressive role choices, the influence of other variables has yet to be uncovered. Additional research is needed to more fully comprehend the dynamics of these forces.

Relationships and Sexually Aggressive Role Enactments

It is important to establish that sexually aggressive men are not liable to be aggressive in every dating relationship (Shotland, 1989). Consider a single man predisposed to be sexually aggressive. If this individual casually dates a woman, and this partner willingly engages in sexual intercourse, the man is unlikely to be aggressive toward her because she provides him ready access to his sexual goal. In a similar vein, some women may, after getting to know this individual, sense his potential to be aggressive and break off the relationship prior to becoming victims. Thus, these men may use aggression only when faced with certain relationship experiences.

These relationship experiences were reviewed in the previous chapter. Not surprisingly, many of these are characteristic of normal relational and sexual role enactments in dating. This contributes to the blurring of the line between what constitutes acceptable premarital sexual influence techniques and sexual coercion. Privacy, for example, is a contextual requirement for most dating couples' sexual role enactments as well as for acts of sexual aggression. Thus, when women consent to sharing a private setting, aggressive or nonaggressive partners alike can perceive it as a role cue of possible sexual access. Similarly, the use of alcohol or drugs by both dyad members is not uncommon in normal dating relationships and is positively related to sexual intimacy (Mongeau & Johnson, 1995). Using intoxicants can also be a part of sexually aggressive role enactments. Its use by a male aggressor likely involves a strategic role choice that relieves him of responsibility for his actions. He can blame his aggression on the intoxicants and/or hope to lower the resistance of his date, thereby shifting responsibility for any sexual outcome to her.

Other relational experiences associated with sexual aggressive role enactments are depicted in Fig. 8.3. Commitment is central to enactments, but may operate in different ways. Enacting a sexually aggressive role is more likely for some men because commitment is lacking in a relationship (Kanin, 1970; Ward et al., 1991). Under these circumstances, the aggressive man may use his belief in the double sexual standard to assign his date a role position that devalues and objectifies her. Her lower status is then used to justify his sexually aggressive role choices.

Commitment may be used in aggressive role making in an alternative way. As seen in previous chapters, commitment is viewed by most but not all young adults as a sufficient condition for engaging in coitus (Christopher & Cate, 1985a; Peplau et al., 1977). It could be concluded that this constitutes a normative sexual standard among many of today's youth. An aggressive male who adopts this as a personal standard may come to view sexual intercourse as his right, an integral part of forming a monogamous dating relationship. He may choose a sexually coercive role enactment in this relationship if he has engaged in precoital acts but not coitus with his partner, or if the couple has previously engaged in coitus but his partner is presently unwilling to do so again (Koss & Cleveland, 1997). He will feel justified in this role choice because his personal standard, that monogamous commitment equals coitus, resides

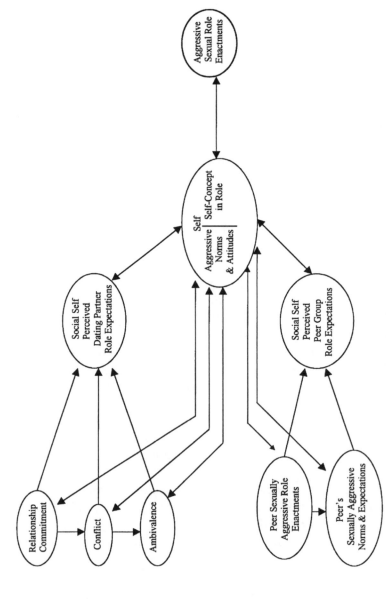

FIG. 8.3. *Relationship and peer influences on male sexually aggressive role enactments. (Note: The concept of social self is artificially divided into two for illustrative purposes)*

in his self and guides his sexual role enactments. Other personal standards, related to forming a relationship commitment, may come into play as well. Recall Lloyd and Emery's (Lloyd, 1991; Lloyd & Emery, 1999) proposition that men may feel they control different facets of the relationship as they increase relational involvement, including their partner's sexuality. Using sexually coercive techniques would be further justified by this particular relationship standard.

The symbolic value of engaging in precoital behaviors in this process cannot be overstated. Sexual intimacy is largely a nonverbal interaction for many dating couples (O'Sullivan & Byers, 1992). Even when verbal initiation cues are used, they tend to be ambiguous rather than direct. In making role choices, the female partner may see herself giving something symbolic of her feelings toward her partner with each step of sexual involvement, and that it is her right to limit sexual intimacy. In this interaction, the man may see each step of sexual interaction as symbolizing his partner's willingness to engage in coitus, his sexual role goal (Kanin & Parcell, 1977; Muehlenhard & Linton, 1987). Women may verbally or nonverbally say "no" if unwilling to engage in intercourse under these circumstances (Koss et al., 1988). Because of his acceptance of rape myths, there is a risk that an aggressive man will interpret a woman's "no" as symbolizing "yes," when analyzing his partner's role expectations in his social self, especially given the manner that he interprets precoital sexual involvement (Malamuth & Brown, 1994). This can result in his choice of sexually coercive or assaultive role behaviors.

Enacting a sexually aggressive role is associated with two additional relationship experiences—conflict and ambivalence. Relational conflict in dating involves dyad members disagreeing; power and control are inherit qualities in its experience. Stated another way, dating couples negotiate different power arrangements; either partner can be in control of relationship outcomes or control can be shared in an egalitarian power arrangement. Lloyd and Emery (Lloyd, 1991; Lloyd & Emery, 1999) hypothesized that normal dating roles have the complimentary role themes of man in control and woman dependent on the man. They speculated that sexual aggression is an extension of these normal role behaviors. Complementing their reasoning, Stets and Pirog-Good (1989) and Christopher and McQuaid (1998) revealed that interpersonal control is positively associated with male sexual aggression. Taken together, the works of these scholars suggest that sexually aggressive role behaviors are symbolic of men's efforts to exert power and take control their partners and of the relationship.

Consider one possible outcome of male premarital sexual aggression, the man being in a more powerful position in his dating relationships, a position many aggressive men hold (Lloyd & Emery, 1999; Muehlenhard & Linton, 1987). Christopher et al. (1993b) and Lisak and Ivan (1995) found that, in the context of their dating aggression, these men had low levels of empathy. Empathy allows an individual to take another's perspective on a cognitive and/or emotional level (Davis, 1980). This ability facilitates role taking, or considering a dating partner's reactions to possible role enactments, in the social self. In other words, possessing empathy allows a more accurate reading of a dating partner's potential reactions to one's role enactment (Hewitt, 1991). This, in turn, would effect the choices one makes in fulfilling a role. Although all individuals engage in role taking, individuals are less motivated to be accurate in their role taking when they are in a more powerful position whereas the reverse is true for those in a less powerful position (Hewitt, 1991). Because those in a position of greater power are more in control of a given situation, they need not be as accurate in considering the responses of those in a position of lesser power as the low power person's reactions have less of a consequence for them. From this perspective, men do not need to be empathetic when considering choices in their sexual role making because they have achieved control of their partner and the relationship. Instead, their partners are more likely to actively engage in role taking and making because of their power down position relative to the male member of the dyad. This final point is considered in greater depth later.

It is also possible that conflict and ambivalence about the future of the relationship become associated with each other across time (Braiker & Kelley, 1979; Christopher et al., 1993b). The aggressive male may find his relationship rewards diminishing under these circumstances (Christopher & McQuaid, 1998) and speculates that engaging in sexually coercive or assaultive role behaviors may result in sexual intercourse, a reward more easily attained than other relationship rewards that presently allude him. Additionally, the presence of relational conflict and ambivalence suggest that this man's present relationship role making is not going well. He and his partner are unable to negotiate compatible relational role enactments. Again, under these conditions, a man predisposed toward sexual aggression may consider alternative roles to achieve desired goals. A choice to use sexually aggressive role compliments may be based on the knowledge that although such action may not be rewarded by his partner, they will be by his peers.

In other words, in previous chapters I speculate that sexual role enactment in dating occurs as two individuals interpret each other's actions and consider each other's role expectations in their respective social selves. In these instances, choosing to engage in particular role acts is directly influenced by a partner's anticipated reactions. In some acts of sexual aggression, however, a different process may occur. Experiencing a decrease in relationship rewards as a result of conflict can result in increased ambivalence about the future of the relationships. The female partner may be devalued under these conditions and her ability to influence her partner's sexual role choice may become severely limited. Instead, the man turns toward aggressive peers, and the role choices they have offered through socialization, as viable and alternative sources of rewards and meaning for his aggressive role choices. Thus, choosing to be aggressive can result in the rewarding experiences of feeling in control of a relationship whose future has become uncertain, and while concurrently building stature among one's peers.

Victims and Risk Behaviors. What is a single woman's role-making response to her dating partner's sexual aggression? Lloyd and Emery (1999) found that a woman's dependency on her partner, paired with the romanticism that permeates the dating couple's relationship roles, leads many women to take a submissive posture to their partners' aggressive power assertions. These women downplay and reinterpret the importance of aggressive acts, often defining them in a manner that relieves their partners of responsibility for the aggression, while taking much of the responsibility for the aggression on themselves. Similarly recall that just over 70% of the women in Koss et al.'s (1988) survey who were casually or seriously dating did not define their experiences of legal rape as a crime. They also assigned less responsibility to their aggressive dating partners than was true of women raped by strangers. Thus, the female partner's role-making responses to aggression may inadvertently support her male partner's aggression.

This active reinterpretation of aggressive acts involves the self and social self of these women. In interpreting their own and their partner's behaviors, these women's selves use their own attitudes and values. It is undoubtedly difficult to face the fact that the object of their romantic interest has been sexually aggressive toward them. Instead, the value these women place on romanticism (a value possibly influenced by their own significant and generalize others), the standards inherit in establishing dependency on male partners, and being the partner largely responsible for relationship repair cause these women to assign a more acceptable meaning to her partner's actions. Unfortunately, this reinterpretation involves taking some of the responsibility for her partner's aggressive acts on herself. Under these circumstances, she will more carefully consider her partner's relational wishes when engaging in role taking in her social self. Her experiences of dependency will increase as his wishes become more of a motivational force in her role choices than her own. Ironically, I have postulated that at the same time, the male partner is becoming even less empathic to her relational wishes. This cycle is apt to eventually make its contribution to the conflict the couple experiences.

Other role-making behaviors in which victims engage can have the unintended outcome of contributing to their partners' sexual aggression. The potential consequences of using alcohol or drugs, and of consenting to certain sexual acts, have already been reviewed. In the previous chapter, I also outlined Lundberg-Love and Geffner's (1989) hypothesis that previous incidents of sexual abuse may lead a victim to underestimate her partner's preaggressive cues as she evaluates herself as being excessively sensitive. She questions her assignment of meaning to his cues in her role taking. When she experiences aggression, she becomes overwhelmed and fails to react. Her partner is likely to interpret her passivity as permission to continue.

The sexual standards and past sexual experiences of some women may additionally put them at risk. Koss et al. (1985) found that victims of aggression had more coital partners and held more sexually liberal attitudes than nonvictimized women (see also Himelein, 1995). According to my previously proposed model, such sexual standards can lead these women to more readily engage in precoital behaviors, or even sexual intercourse, without fully establishing whether their partner would be a good relationship prospect. This can have two consequences. First, the aggressive male can view such women as "easy," thereby devaluing them as individuals. This may result in the male making aggressive role choices when the woman wants to end the dating relationship or becomes unwilling to engage in coitus again. Second, in instances where the woman and man form a relationship, the lack of attention to interpersonal fit is apt to result in experiencing conflict and ambivalence by both partners, conditions already shown as contributing to men's acts of sexual coercion and assault.

Relationships and Sexually Aggressive Women's Role Enactments.
Although some men are sexually aggressive in casually dating relationships, this appears uncharacteristic of sexually aggressive women (Christopher et al., 1993a). Women's acts of sexual aggression are more apt to emerge when they are monogamously dating their partners. One possible explanation for this rests in the dynamics involved in making this commitment. Recall these women's beliefs in rape myths and that men and women are sexual adversaries (Burke et al., 1988; Christopher et al., 1993a). Interpersonal control is a common theme to these beliefs, either by seeing women in control of relationship outcomes or by perceiving dyad members as competing for control. Given that these attitudes likely influence relationship role choices, it is not surprising that women's sense of interpersonal control is positively related to their use of sexual aggression (Stets & Pirog-Good, 1989). Their sexual aggression is grounded in and symbolized by their need to control their partner and the relationship. These women may become more sexually aggressive as they become more committed because the potential impact of the relationship on their future becomes increasingly salient under these conditions. Stated another way, monogamous commitment carries with it the potential for further intimacy and even greater commitment. These women's relational and sexual attitudes may lead them to value being in control of the relationship when this occurs. Thus, their sexually aggressive role enactments represents a power assertion over their dating partners.

Increases in commitment may make a second, indirect contribution. Increases in commitment are linked to increases in conflict for dating couples in general (Braiker & Kelley, 1979). As reviewed in reference to aggressive men, conflict involves power assertions in attempts to gain control of the relationship. Thus, using sexually aggression may also be triggered by dyadic conflict—instances where the couple is struggling with who will control the relationship. If such conflict is intense enough, it is apt to be accompanied by ambivalence about the future of the relationship, an experience also positively related to women's sexually aggressive role enactments. Gaining control is apt to decrease ambivalence, therefore engaging in sexual aggression may again reflect these women's valuing being in control of relationship outcomes.

9

Last Steps:
Concluding Remarks

In the preface, I observed that our knowledge of premarital sexuality has been fragmented and lacked unity. Because of the limitations with which all researchers must work, investigations have often focused on a single group of sexual correlates while sampling youth from a single developmental stage. For example, attitudes or personality characteristics may have served as an investigative focus, without considering the important influence of peers, family, or relationship partners. Additionally, the majority of the work in sexuality could be characterized as atheoretical despite potentially useful and readily available theories (Weis, 1998, explores the issue of the use of theory in sexuality research). These two weaknesses in previous premarital sexuality work led me to establish two overarching goals that guided the development of this book.

First, I wanted to provide a broad-based review of the empirical literature on sexuality before marriage. To this end, individual chapters in this book reviewed the sexuality literature for childhood, early adolescence, older adolescence and young adulthood, and sexual aggression. No previous work offers an examination of each of these areas in a single publication. Considering it as a "body of literature" raises valuable questions about developmental changes, the interrelatedness of the diverse influences, and how the field can be advanced by multidisciplinary based research.

Such a review by itself, although useful to interested students and scholars, still fails to provide the degree of unity I wanted to achieve in this work. Hence, my second goal for the book was to propose a unifying model of premarital sexuality. Symbolic interactionism, in my estimation, offered the flexibility necessary to simultaneously consider individual, familial, peer, and dyadic influences on premarital sexuality. I find such theoretical constructs as roles, self, role taking, role making, significant and generalized others, and searching for meaning powerful, compelling, and ultimately very useful. The theory-based chapters offered my view of how these interrelated constructs can integrate the diversity of premarital sexuality research findings into a comprehensive model.

It is my hope that the reader complete this book with an appreciation of the complexity of the phenomenon known as premarital sexuality. Sexuality before marriage involves a dynamic, evolving expression of one's self, an expression resulting from a range of individual choices and influenced by myriad of forces. However, it is also my hope that readers do not take my word for how these forces are interrelated. Charles Caleb Colton penned the popular phrase "imitation is the sincerest form of flattery." I believe that for science this common adage is better stated as "The testing of one's ideas is the sincerest form of flattery."

This book offers a cornucopia of proposed relationships within and between constructs in an attempt to explain the sexual expression of youths at different stages of development. It is my hope that others find my ideas so thought-provoking that they want to test them. These tests could take many forms. Longitudinal research could investigate the developmental changes I propose as occurring in parental and peer influences as individuals move from early adolescence to young adulthood. I have also proposed that early childhood experiences have reaching effects into adolescent family and peer influences, as well as into male sexual aggression; propositions similarly suited to longitudinal investigations. My theoretical models need to be tested by examining the full range of potential influences on sexual expression within a given developmental period. For example, the inclusion of variables from the dyadic, parental, peer, and individual domains for early adolescence or young adulthood would provide insights into their relative contributions to youth's sexual role enactments.

The review of literature also establishes gaps in our knowledge of young individuals' sexual expression. Little is known about early adolescents' romantic relationships, female sexual aggression in dating, and how sexual meanings are constructed in peer groups. Similarly, I have hypothesize that peers have greater influence then dating partners on male sexually aggressive role enactments, especially when the dating relationship is conflicted and the aggressor's commitment is waning. Such hypothesized differences in the strength of the relationships of these variables need to be empirically tested. Moreover, some areas previously investigated need additional research to better clarify the relationship between variables. The contradictory findings about the impact of parent–adolescent communication on adolescent sexual involvement demonstrate the need for new, well-designed research in this area.

These are but a few of the possible ways this book can inform future research. If this work inspires others to follow these suggestions or to test my model in other ways, then I will genuinely believe I made a contribution to the study of premarital sexuality.

Appendix

Methodological Design, Statistical Issues, and Path Models

This appendix has a number of purposes. First, I include it so that readers with a limited knowledge in research design and statistical analysis can become familiar with the concepts that appear in the book. It is impossible to summarize in this limited space the knowledge needed to become conversant in the designs and analyses that characterize investigations into premarital sexuality. There are, however, issues in different chapters that may require more explanation for those less experienced in these areas. Hence, I hope to provide some insight into these matters in this appendix. Second, I gave more weight to some studies compared to others when making conclusions about whether and how certain variables are related to sexual involvement. Better designs and/or analyses characterize the favored studies. I explain in general terms why I favored one type of study over another. Finally, I use path models to illustrate the hypothesized relations between variables in the chapters focused on theory development and therefore review important path concepts.

SAMPLING

As is true of many areas of social science, the body of knowledge about premarital sexuality is largely built on samples of convenience. This type of sampling can result in a number of problems including selection biases and an underrepresentation of minorities. Much more is known, for example, about the sexuality of White, middle-class college students than working-class individuals of the same age because college students are readily accessible to most researchers. A better approach is to use *probability sampling* where random samples within subgroups reflect the majority and minority composition of the nation or of a given region. This approach has greater *external validity* or the ability to generalize a study's findings to a larger population. Since the late 1970s, a number of investigations into premarital sexuality have utilized national probability sampling. The majority, but not all, focused on early adolescents. The 1990s, for instance, saw an increase in national data sets that included young adults (Christopher & Sprecher, in press). For the most part, these investigations received more weight in my writings if equivocal findings existed from another study about whether or how variables were related to one another.

CROSS-SECTIONAL VERSUS
LONGITUDINAL DESIGNS

Collecting data at a single point in time characterizes *cross-sectional designs*. Surveys are good examples of this method of data collection. In contrast, *longitudinal designs* follow participants across time and collect data two or more times. Longitudinal designs may be short in duration, involving only a few weeks, or quite long, following the same sample over a number of years. Not surprisingly, most investigations into premarital sexuality have been cross-sectional as longitudinal work is more costly and involves a greater commitment on the part of all involved. One of the major advantages of longitudinal work is that it provides insight into causal relationships between variables. For instance, Thornton and Camburn's (1989) 18-year study showed that mothers who regularly attended religious services when their children were young had adolescents who also attended religious services regularly many years later. They concluded a causal relations might exist between these two events, that the religious attendance of the parents contributed to the attendance of their children. Such conclusions often need tempering by the realization that other unmeasured, or *third variables,* may contribute to such findings. Cross-sectional designs, although allowing questions about whether and how strongly variables are related to one another, preclude making such causal conclusions. Because theory development focuses on causal relationships between variables, I gave more weight to findings based on well-conducted longitudinal as opposed to cross-sectional designs when all other design and analysis considerations were equal.

LEVELS OF STATISTICAL ANALYSES

Understanding the intricacies of statistical analyses is a challenge to many students of premarital sexuality. Although more sophisticated analyses provide greater insight into how variables are related to one another, these analyses are often the most difficult to comprehend. In the following paragraphs, I attempt to illuminate the meaning behind many of the statistical terms I use. I refer interested readers to Tabachnick and Fidell's (1996) excellent text for a more in-depth discussion of the many faucets of statistical analysis.

One of the more basic of analyses is a *bivariate correlation.* This statistic assesses whether two variables are related to one another and the *strength* and *direction* of the relationship if one exists. Rarely in real life, however, do we encounter such a simple relationship between two events. Consider the presently popular belief that low self-esteem is a root cause of teen sexual exploration. Although such simplistic reasoning has its attractions, it inadvertently ignores a host of other variables associated with adolescent sexual activity. As reflected in chapter 3, these include the quality of parent–child relationships, the sexual attitudes of the teens, and the perceived sexual activity of peers to name a few. Thus, a conclusion based on a bivariate relationship may be overly simplistic in representing how two variables are related to one another.

Asking a series of questions, with an appropriate analysis to answer them, provides a more meaningful understanding about the relation between variables. Consider the following set of questions that a researcher may pose. Which variables in a group, when considered concurrently, are related to sexual activity (in statistical jargon this is called *predicting a variable*)? What is the direction and strength of the relationship between each variable and teen sexual activity when tested against one another? Is a variable of interest, such as self esteem, related to an *outcome variable*, such as teen sexual exploration, when simultaneously considering other potential life influences (usually stated as *controlling for the effects* of other variables)? How much change in sexual activity can be accounted for individually and collectively by the predictor variables (refereed to as accounting for variance)? Because answering these questions involves multiple variables, the analyses are called *multivariate analyses*. Moreover, *multiple regression* is the statistic most frequently used to explore such questions.

Greater confidence can be put in scholars' conclusions that are based on multivariate rather than bivariate analyses. In these instances, the test of a relationship between a set of predictor variables and an outcome variable is more stringent and more closely approximates real-life experiences. Often in these tests some but not all predictors are related to the outcome variable. Such was the case for self-esteem when Rosenbaum and Kandel (1990) included it in a regression with other potential predictors of adolescent coital activity. A statistically significant relationship between self-esteem and engaging in coitus failed to emerge because other variables had stronger relationships to coital activity. Stated another way, these other variables better explained why teens engaged in sexual intercourse.

Regression analysis allows for additional insights into the relationship between variables. It is also possible to examine how much change or *variance* a set of predictor variables accounts for in an outcome variable. When analyses account for greater levels of variance, they provide scholars with an indication of the strength of the relationship between the predictors and the outcome variable. Variables that account for more variance are more strongly related to the outcome variable of interest. Researchers therefore conclude that they gain a greater understanding about why a particular outcome occurs in these instances.

PATH MODELS

In the previous paragraphs, I introduced the idea that an outcome variable, such as sexual activity, may be related to a number of different variables. I take this idea one step further by introducing the concept of *path models*. First, let us switch to a different outcome variable for the sake of variety—premarital sexual aggression. Let us say that multiple regression analysis shows that believing in certain rape myths, such as women can resist a rape if they want, is positively related to being sexually aggressive while dating for single men. This is, in fact, a common

FIG. A.1. *Belief in rape myths predicts premarital sexual aggression.*

research finding (Koss & Cleveland, 1997). Figure A.1 depicts the relation between these two variables.

A possible question that may follow this finding is what predicts the belief in rape myths. This question is investigated in Christopher, Owens, and Strecker (1993b). We found empathy negatively related to a belief in rape myths and we confirmed that believing in rape myths negatively predicted sexual aggression. Figure A.2 illustrates the relation between these three variables. In the language of path models, belief in rape myths *mediates* the relation of the other two variables and has a *direct effect* on sexual aggression, whereas empathy has an *indirect effect*.

It is possible to test whether proposed paths actually exist using *path analysis*. Two forms of path analysis exist. The first involves using a series of multiple regressions. The second utilizes structural equation analysis and has become increasingly popular in recent years. It allows researchers to simultaneously test all proposed paths in a path model while also allowing for multiple measures of a theoretical variable. Hence, structural equation modeling is a powerful and conservative test of path models.

Other types of relations between variables can exist and be portrayed in a path diagram. Consider the variable of locus of control. Individuals with an external locus of control believe that fate, circumstances, and other individuals determine what happens to them in life. Contrastingly, individuals with an internal locus of control believe that they are in charge of their outcomes. In chapter 4, I hypothesize that early adolescents with an external locus of control likely adapt their peers' sexual attitudes, whereas those early adolescents with an internal locus of control do not. Thus, in the parlance of path modeling, locus of control *moderates* the relationship between peer and self sexual attitudes. This type of relationship is pictured in Fig. A.3.

FIG. A.2. *Belief in rape myths mediates the relationship of empathy to premarital sexual aggression.*

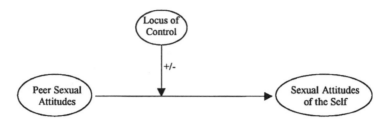

FIG. A.3. *Locus of control moderates the relationship between peer sexual attitudes and the sexual attitudes of the self.*

Two final points need to be made about diagramming models. First, in all three of these illustrations the arrows between variables are pointed in a single direction. It is possible, however, for two variables to influence each other thereby forming a *bi-directional* or *reciprocal* relation with one another. This is pictured with arrows pointing in both directions. Second, I kept my examples of path models quite simple. Many of the path models I propose in the theoretically based chapters are more complex. They involve a greater number of variables with direct and indirect relationships to each other and to one or more outcome variables. The principles behind the figures I used in the present section still apply to these more complex models.

Path models, with their proposed causal relationships between variables, are required to be solidly grounded in theory. Although previous empirical findings can aid in building path models, often such past work lacks a theoretical focus. Thus, integrating these findings into a defensible, theoretical model can be a challenge. The chapters in this book are my attempt to meet this challenge by using symbolic interaction theory to inform the corpus of our present knowledge about premarital sexuality.

References

Abbey, A., Cozzarelli, C., McLaughlin, K., & Harnish, R. J. (1987). The effects of clothing and dyad sex composition on perceptions of sexual intent: Do women and men evaluate these cues differently. *Journal of Applied Social Psychology, 17,* 108–126.

Abbey, A., & Harnish, R. J. (1995). Perception of sexual intent: The role of gender, alcohol consumption, and rape supportive attitudes. *Sex Roles, 32,* 297–313.

Abbey, A., & Melby, C. (1986). The effects of nonverbal cues on gender differences in perceptions of sexual intent. *Sex Roles, 15,* 283–298.

Abbey, A., Ross, L. T., McDuffie, D., & McAuslan, P. (1996). Alcohol and dating risk factors for sexual assault among college women. *Psychology of Women Quarterly, 20,* 147–169.

Adams, G., & Gullotta, T. (1983). *Adolescent life experiences.* Monterey: Brooks/Cole.

Allgeier, E. R. (1992). *School-based education.* Geneva, Switzerland: World Health Organization.

Amick, A. E., & Calhoun, K. S. (1987). Resistance to sexual aggression: Personality, attitudinal, and situational factors. *Archives of Sexual Behavior, 16,* 153–163.

Aneshensel, C. S., Fielder, E. P., & Becerra, R. M. (1989). Fertility and fertility-related behavior among Mexican-American and non-Hispanic White female adolescents. *Journal of Health and Social Behavior, 30,* 56–76.

Aral, S. O., & Holmes, K. K. (1991). Sexually transmitted diseases in the AIDS era. *Scientific American, 264*(2), 62–69.

Aron, A., & Aron, E. N. (1991). Love and sexuality. In K. McKinney & S. Sprecher's (Eds.), *Sexuality in close relationships* (pp. 25–48). Hillsdale, NJ: Lawrence Erlbaum Associates.

Asmussen, L., & Shehan, C. L. (1992, November). *Gender expectations and behavior in dating relationships.* Paper presented at the annual conference of the National Council on Family Relations, Orlando, FL.

Baker, S. A., Thalberg, S. P., & Morrison, D. M. (1988). Parents' behavioral norms as predictors of adolescent sexual activity and contraceptive use. *Adolescence, 90,* 265–282.

Bauman, K. E., & Udry, J. R. (1981). Subjective expected utility and adolescent sexual behavior. *Adolescence, 63,* 527–534.

Bauman, K. E., & Wilson, R. R. (1974). Sexual behavior of unmarried university students in 1968 and 1972. *Journal of Sex Research, 10,* 327–333.

Bell, R. R., & Chaskes, J. B. (1970). Premarital sexual experience among coeds, 1958 and 1968. *Journal of Marriage and the Family, 32,* 81–84.

Bell, R. R., & Coughey, K. (1980). Premarital sexual experience among college females, 1958, 1968, 1978. *Family Relations, 29,* 353–357.

Bell-Scott, P., & McKenry, P. C. (1986). Black adolescents and their families. In G. K. Leigh & G. W. Peterson (Eds.), *Adolescents in family* (pp. 410–432). Cincinnati, OH: Southwestern.

Berger, R. J., Searles, P., Salen, R. G., & Pierce, B. A. (1988). Sexual assault in a college community. *Sociological Focus, 19,* 1–26.

Berscheid, E. (1983). Emotion. In H. Kelley, E. Berscheid, A. Christensen, J. Harvey, T. Huston, G. Levinber, E. McClintock, L. A. Peplau, & D. R. Peterson (Eds.), *Close relationships* (pp. 110–168). New York: Freeman.

Billy, J. O. G., Brewster, K. L., & Grady, W. R. (1994). Contextual effects on the sexual behavior of adolescent women. *Journal of Marriage and the Family, 56,* 387-404.

Billy, J. O. G., Tanfer, K., Grady, W. R., & Klepinger, D. H. (1993). The sexual behavior of men in the United States. *Family Planning Perspectives, 25,* 52–60.

Billy, J. O. G., & Udry, J. R. (1985). Patterns of adolescent friendship and effects on sexual behavior. *Social Psychology Quarterly, 48,* 27–41.

Bingham, C. R., Miller, B. C., & Adams, G. R. (1990). Correlates of age at first sexual intercourse in a national sample of young women. *Journal of Adolescent Research, 5,* 18–33.

Boeringer, S. B., Shehan, C. L., & Akers, R. L. (1991). Social context and social learning in sexual coercion and aggression: Assessing the contribution of fraternity membership. *Family Relations, 40,* 58–64.

Braiker, H. B., & Kelley, H. H. (1979). Conflict in the development of close relationships. In R. L. Burgess & T. L. Huston (Eds.) *Social exchange in developing relationships* (pp. 135–168). New York: Academic.

Brewster, K. L., Cooksey, E. C., Guilkey, D. K., & Rindfuss, R. R. (1998). The changing impact of religion on the sexual and contraceptive behavior of adolescent women in the United States. *Journal of Marriage and the Family, 60,* 493–504.

Browne, A., & Finkelhor, D. (1986). Initial and long-term effects: A review of the research. In D. Finkelhor (Ed.), *A sourcebook on child sexual abuse* (pp. 143–179). Newbury Park, CA: Sage.

Burke, P. J., Stets, J. E., & Pirog-Good, M. A. (1988). Gender identity, self-esteem, and physical and sexual abuse in dating relationships. *Social Psychology Quarterly, 51,* 272–285.

Burkhart, B. R., & Stanton, A. L. (1988). Sexual aggression in acquaintance relationships. In G. W. Russel (Ed.), *Violence in intimate relationships* (pp. 43–65). New York: PMA.

Burt, M. R. (1980). Cultural myths and supports for rape. *Journal of Personality and Social Psychology, 38,* 217–230.

Burt, M. R. (1983). Justifying personal violence: A comparison of rapists and the general public. *Victimology, 8,* 131–150.

Buss, D. M. (1989). Sex differences in human mate preferences: Evolutionary hypotheses tested in 37 cultures. *Behavioral and Brain Sciences, 12,* 1–49.

Buss, D. M. (1998). Sexual strategies theory: Historical origins and current status. *The Journal of Sex Research, 35,* 19–31.

Byers, E. S., & Demmons, S. (1999). Sexual satisfaction and sexual self-disclosure within dating relationships. *The Journal of Sex Research, 36,* 180–189.

Byers, E. S., Demmons, S., & Lawrence, K. (1998). Sexual satisfaction within dating relationships: A test of the interpersonal exchange model of sexual satisfaction. *Journal of Social and Personal Relationships, 15,* 257–267.

Byers, E. S., & Eno, R. J. (1991). Predicting men's sexual coercion and aggression from attitudes, dating history, and sexual response. *Journal of Psychology and Human Sexuality, 4,* 55–70.

Byers, S. E., & Lewis, K. (1988). Dating couples' disagreements over the desired level of sexual intimacy. *Journal of Sex Research, 24,* 15–29.

Calderone, M. (1983). Fetal erection and its message to us. *SIECUS Report, 11,* 9–10.

Carns, D. (1973). Talking about sex: Notes on first coitus and the double standard. *Journal of Marriage and the Family, 35,* 677–687.

Carroll, L. (1988). Concern with AIDS and the sexual behavior of college students. *Journal of Marriage and the Family, 50,* 405–411.

Carroll, J. L., Volk, D. K., & Hyde, S. J. (1985). Differences between males and females in motives for engaging in sexual intercourse. *Archives of Sexual Behavior, 14,* 131–139.

Catania, J. A., Dolcini, M. M., Coates, T. J., Kegeles, S. M., Greenblatt, R. M., Puckett, S., Corman, M., & Miller, J. (1989). Predictors of condom use and multiple partnered sex among sexually-active adolescent women: Implications for AIDS-related health interventions. *Journal of Sex Research, 26,* 514–524.

Cate, R. M., Long, E., Angera, J. J., & Draper, K. K. (1993). Sexual intercourse and relationship development. *Family Relations, 42,* 158–164.

Cate, R. M., Lloyd, S. A., Henton, J. M., & Larson, J. H. (1982). Fairness and reward level as predictors of relationship satisfaction, *Social Psychology Quarterly, 45,* 177–181.

Check, J. V. P. (1988). Hostility toward women: Some theoretical considerations (pp. 29–42). In G. W. Russel (Ed.), *Violence in intimate relationships.* New York: PMA.

Check, J. V. P., & Malamuth, N. M. (1983). Sex role stereotyping and reactions to depictions of stranger versus acquaintance rape. *Journal of Personality and Social Psychology, 45,* 344–356.

Chilman, C. S. (1982). Adolescent childbearing in the United States: Apparent causes and consequences. In T. M. Field, A. Huston, H. C. Quay, L. Troll, & G. E. Finley (Eds.), *Review of human development* (pp. 418–431). New York: Wiley

Christopher, F. S. (1988). An initial investigation into a continuum of premarital sexual pressure. *Journal of Sex Research, 25,* 255–266.

Christopher, F. S. (1993, June). *Sexual involvement in dating: The role of relationship and individual variables.* Paper presented at the fourth International Network Conference on Personal Relationships, Milwaukee, WI.

Christopher, F. S. (1995). Adolescent pregnancy prevention. *Family Relations, 44,* 384–391.

Christopher, F. S., & Cate, R. M. (1984). Influences on sexual decision making. *Journal of Sex Research, 20,* 363–376.

Christopher, F. S., & Cate, R. M. (1985a). Anticipated influences on sexual decision making for first intercourse. *Family Relations, 34,* 265–270.

Christopher, F. S., & Cate, R. M. (1985b). Premarital sexual pathways and relationship development. *Journal of Personal and Social Relationships, 2,* 271–288.

Christopher, F. S., & Cate, R. M. (1988). Premarital sexual involvement: A developmental investigation of relational correlates. *Adolescence, 23,* 793–803.

Christopher, F. S., & Frandsen, M. M. (1990). Strategies of influence in sex and dating. *Journal of Social and Personal Relationships, 7,* 89–107.

Christopher, F. S., Johnson, D. C., & Roosa, M. W. (1993). Family, individual, and social correlates of early hispanic adolescent sexual expression. *Journal of Sex Research, 30,* 45–52.

Christopher, F. S., & Lloyd, S. (2000). Physical and sexual aggression in relationships. In C. Hendricks and S. Hendricks (Eds.), *Close relationships: A source book* (pp. 331–334). Thousand Oaks, CA: Sage.

Christopher, F. S., Madura, M. & Weaver, L. (1998). Premarital sexual aggressors: A multivariate analysis of social, relational, and individual variables. *Journal of Marriage and the Family, 60,* 56–69.

Christopher, F. S., & McQuaid, S. (1998, June). *Dating relationships and men's sexual aggression: A test of a relationship-based model.* Paper presented at the biennial meeting of the International Society for the Study of Personal Relationships, Saratoga Springs, NY.

Christopher, F. S., McQuaid, S., & Updegraff, K. (1999, November). *Single women's use of sexual coercion: A symbolic interactional investigation.* Annual meeting of the Society for the Scientific Study of Sexuality, St. Louis, MO.

Christopher, F. S., Owens, L. A., & Stecker, H. L. (1993a). An examination of men and women's premarital sexual aggressiveness. *Journal of Social and Personal Relationships, 10,* 511–527.

Christopher, F. S., Owens, L. A., & Stecker, H. L. (1993b). Exploring the darkside of courtship: A test of a model of male premarital sexual aggressiveness. *Journal of Marriage and the Family, 55,* 469–479.

Christopher, F. S., & Sprecher, S. (in press). Sexuality in marriage, family, and other relationships: A decade review. *Journal of Marriage and the Family.*

Clark, S. D., Zabin, L. S., & Hardy, J. B. (1984). Sex, contraception, and parenthood: Experiences and attitudes among urban black young men. *Family Planning Perspective, 16,* 77–82.

Clayton, R. (1969). Religious orthodoxy and premarital sex. *Social Forces, 47,* 469–474.

Clayton, R. (1972). Premarital sexual intercourse: A substantive test of the contingent consistency model. *Journal of Marriage and the Family, 34,* 273–279.

Cohen, L. L., & Shotland, R. L. (1996). Timing of first sexual intercourse in a relationship: Expectations, experiences, and perceptions of others. *The Journal of Sex Research, 33,* 291–299.

Coker, A. L., Richter, D. L., Valois, R. F., McKeown, R. E., Garrison, C. Z., & Vincent, M. L. (1994). Correlates and consequences of early initiation of sexual intercourse. *Journal of School Health, 64,* 372–377.

Copenhaver, S., & Grauerholz, E. (1991). Sexual victimization among sorority women: Exploring the link between sexual violence and institutional practices. *Sex Roles, 24,* 31–41.

Cupach, W. R., & Metts, S. (1991). Sexuality and communication in close relationships. In K. McKinney & S. Sprecher's (Eds.), *Sexuality in close relationships* (pp. 93–110). Hillsdale, NJ: Lawrence Erlbaum Associates.

Curran, J. P., Neff, S., & Lippold, S. (1973). Correlates of sexual experience among university students. *Journal of Sex Research, 9,* 124–134.

Cvetkovich, G., & Grote, B. (1980). Psychosocial development and the social problem of teenage illegitimacy. In C. Chilman (Ed.), *Adolescent pregnancy and childbearing: Findings from research* (pp. 15–41). Washington, DC: U.S. Department of Health and Human Services.

Cyranowski, J. M., & Anderson, B. L. (1998). Schemas, sexuality, and romantic attachment. *Journal of Personality and Social Psychology, 74,* 1364–1379.

D'Augelli, J. F., & Cross, H. J. (1975). Relationship of sexual guilt and moral reasoning to premarital sex in college women and in couples. *Journal of Consulting and Clinical Psychology, 43,* 40–47.

D'Augelli, J. F., & D'Augelli, A. R. (1977). Moral reasoning and premarital sexual behavior: toward reasoning about relationships. *Journal of Social Issues, 33,* 46–66.

Daugherty, L. R., & Burger, J. M. (1984). The influence of parents, church, and peers on the sexual attitudes and behaviors of college students. *Archives of Sexual Behavior, 13,* 351–359.

Davidson, J. K., & Darling, C. A. (1993). Masturbatory guilt and sexual responsiveness among post-college-age women: Sexual satisfaction revisited. *Journal of Sex & Marital Therapy, 19,* 289–300.

Davidson, J. K., & Leslie, G. R. (1977). Premarital sexual intercourse: An application of axiomatic theory construction. *Journal of Marriage and the Family, 39,* 15–28.

Davidson, J. K., & Moore, N. B. (1994). Masturbation and premarital sexual intercourse among college women: Making choices for sexual fulfillment. *Journal of Sex and Marital Therapy, 20,* 178–197.

Davis, M. H. (1980). A multidimensional approach to individual differences in empathy. *Catalog of Selected Documents in Psychology, 10*(4), 85.

Day, R. D. (1992). The transition to first intercourse among racially and culturally diverse youth. *Journal of Marriage and the Family, 54,* 749–762.

Dean, K. E., & Malamuth, N. M. (1997). Characteristics of men who aggress sexually and of men who imagine aggressing: Risk and moderating variables. *Journal of Personality and Social Psychology, 72,* 449–455.

DeKeseredy, W. S., & Kelly, K. (1995). Sexual abuse in Canadian university and college dating relationships: The contribution of male peer support. *Journal of Family Violence, 10,* 41–53.

DeLamater, J. (1987). Gender differences in sexual scenarios. In K. Kelley (Ed.), *Females, males, and sexuality: Theories and research* (pp. 127–139). Albany: State University of New York Press.

DeLamater, J. D., & MacCorquodale, P. (1979). *Premarital sexuality: Attitudes, relationships, behavior.* Madison: University of Wisconsin Press.

Denney, N. W., Field, J. K., & Quadagno, D. (1984). Sex differences in sexual needs and desires. *Archives of Sexual Behavior, 13,* 233–245.

Denzin, N. (1970). Rules of conduct and the study of deviant behavior: Some notes on the rules of social relationships. In G. J. McCall (Ed.), *Social relationships* (pp. XXXX). Chicago: Aldine.

DiBalasio, F. A., & Benda, B. B. (1990). Adolescent sexual behavior: Multivariate analysis of a social learning model. *Journal of Adolescent Research, 5,* 449–466.

DiClemente, R. J. (1993). Confronting the challenge of AIDS among adolescents: Directions for future research. *Journal of Adolescent Research, 8,* 156–166.

Dorius, G. L., Heaton, T. B., & Steffen, P. (1993). Adolescent life events and their association with the onset of sexual intercourse. *Youth and Society, 25,* 3–23.

Dornbusch, S. M., Carlsmith, J. M., Gross, R. T., Martin, J. A., Jennings, D., Rosenberg, A., & Duke, P. (1981). Sexual development, age, and dating: A comparison of biological and social influences upon one set of behaviors. *Child Development, 52,* 179–185.

Driscoll, R. H., & Davis, K. E. (1971). Sexual restraints: A comparison of perceived and self-reported reasons for college students. *Journal of Sex Research, 7,* 253–262.

Duck, S. W. (1994). *Meaningful relationships: Talking sense and relating.* Thousand Oaks, CA: Sage.

Dyk, P. H. (1993). Anatomy, physiology, and gender issues in adolescence. In T. P. Gullotta, G. R. Adams, & R. Montemayor (Eds.), *Adolescent sexuality* (pp. 35–56). Newbury Park: Sage.

Earle, J. R., & Perricone, P. J. (1986). Premarital sexuality: A ten-year study of attitudes and behavior on a small university campus. *Journal of Sex Research, 22,* 304–310.

East, P. L. (1996). The younger sisters of childbearing adolescents: Their attitudes, expectations, and behaviors. *Child Development, 67,* 267–282.

East, P. L., Felice, M. E., & Morgan, M. C. (1993). Sisters' and girlfriends' sexual and childbearing behavior: Effects on early adolescent girls' sexual outcomes. *Journal of Marriage and the Family, 55,* 953–963.

Ehrman, W. (1959a). *Premarital dating behavior*. New York: Henry Holt.

Ehrman, W. (1959b). Premarital sexual behavior and sex codes of conduct with acquaintances, friends, and lovers. *Social Forces, 38,* 158–164.

Elo, I. T., King, R. B., & Furstenberg, F. F. (in press). Adolescent females: Their sexual partners and the fathers of their children. *Journal of Marriage and the Family.*

Erickson, P. I., & Rapkin, A. (1991). Unwanted sexual experiences among middle and high school youth. *Journal of Adolescent Health, 12,* 319–325.

Falbo, T., & Peplau, L. A. (1980). Power strategies in intimate relationships. *Journal of Personality and Social Psychology, 38,* 618–628.

Faulkenberry, J. R., Vincent, M., James, A., & Johnson, W. (1987). Coital behaviors, attitudes, and knowledge of students who experience early coitus. *Adolescence, 86,* 321–332.

Fisher, G. J. (1986). College student attitudes toward forcible date rape: I. Cognitive predictors. *Archives of Sexual Behavior, 15,* 457–466.

Fisher, T. D. (1986). An exploratory study of parent–child communication about sex and the sexual attitudes of early, middle, and late adolescents. *The Journal of Genetic Psychology, 147,* 543–557.

Flannery, D. J., Rowe, D. C., & Gulley, B. L. (1993). Impact of pubertal status, timing, and age on adolescent sexual experience and delinquency. *Journal of Adolescent Research, 8,* 21–40.

Fletcher, A., Darling, N., Steinberg, L., & Dornbusch, S. (1995). The company they keep: Relation of adolescents' adjustment and behavior to their friends' perceptions of authoritative parenting in the social network. *Developmental Psychology, 31,* 300–310.

Forste, R. T., & Heaton, T. B. (1988). Initiation of sexual activity among female adolescents. *Youth and Society, 19,* 250–268.

Forste, R. T., & Tanfer, K. (1996). Sexual exclusivity among dating, cohabitating, and married women. *Journal of Marriage and the Family, 58,* 33–47.

Fox, G. L. (1980). The mother adolescent relationship as a sexual socialization structure: A research review. *Family Relations, 29,* 21–28.

Fox, G. L., & Inazu, J. K. (1980). Patterns of outcomes of mother–daughter communication about sexuality. *Journal of Social Issues, 36,* 7–29.

Franzoi, S. L., & Herzog, M. E. (1987). Judging physical attractiveness: What body aspects do we use? *Personality and Social Psychology Bulletin, 13,* 19–33.

Furstenberg, F. F., Herceg-Baron, R., Shea, J., & Webb, D. (1984). Family communication and teenagers' contraceptive use. *Family Planning Perspectives, 16,* 163–170.

Furstenberg, F. F., Morgan, S. P., Moore, K. A., & Peterson, J. L. (1987). Race differences in the timing of adolescent intercourse. *American Sociological Review, 52,* 511–518.

Garcia, L. T., & Kushnier, K. (1987). Sexual inferences about female targets: The use of sexual experience correlates. *Journal of Sex Research, 23,* 252–257.

Gargiulo, J., Attie, I., Brooks-Gunn, J., & Warren, M. P. (1987). Dating in middle school girls: Effects of social context, maturation, and grade. *Developmental Psychology, 23,* 730–737.

Garrett-Gooding, J., & Senter, R. (1987). Attitudes and acts of sexual aggression on a university campus. *Sociological Inquiry, 57,* 348–371.

Gecas, V. (1979). The influence of social class on socialization. In W. Burr, R. Hill, I. Nye, and I. Reiss (Eds.), *Contemporary theories about the family* (Vol. 1, pp. 365–404). New York: The Free Press.

Gecas, V. (1981). Contexts of socialization. In M. Rosenberg & R. H. Turner (Eds.), *Social psychology: Sociological perspectives* (pp. 165–199). New York: Basic Books.

Gecas, V., & Seff, M. A. (1990). Families and adolescents. *Journal of Marriage and the Family, 52,* 941–958.

Geer, J. H., & Broussard, D. B. (1990). Scaling heterosexual behavior and arousal: Consistency and sex differences. *Journal of Personality and Social Psychology, 58,* 664–671.

Gfellner, B. M. (1988). Relations between sexual attitudes, gender, and sexual behavior concepts of older adolescents. *Journal of Adolescent Research, 3,* 305–316.

Gibson, J. W., & Kempf, J. (1990). Attitudinal predictors of sexual activity in hispanic adolescent females. *Journal of Adolescent Research, 5,* 414–430.

Goldman, R., & Goldman, S. (1982). *Children's sexual thinking.* London: Routledge & Kegan Paul.

Goodchilds, J. D., & Zellman, G. L. (1984). Sexual signaling and sexual aggression in adolescent relationships. In N. M. Malamuth & E. Donnerstein (Eds.), *Pornography and sexual aggression* (pp. 233–243). Orlando, FL: Academic Press.

Gross, W. C., & Billingham, R. E. (1998). Alcohol consumption and sexual victimization among college women. *Psychology Reports, 82,* 80–82.

Gundersen, B., Melas, P. S., & Skar, J. E. (1981). Sexual behavior of preschool children. In L. L. Constantine & F. M. Martinson (Eds.), *Children and sex: New findings, new perspectives* (pp. 45–62). Boston: Little, Brown.

Gwartney-Gibbs, P., & Stockard, J. (1989). Courtship aggression and mixed sex peer groups. In M. A. Parage-Good & J. E. Stets (Eds.), *Violence in dating relationships: Emerging social issues* (pp.185–204). New York: Praeger.

Gwartney-Gibbs, P. A., Stockard, J., & Bohmer, S. (1987). Learning courtship aggression: The influence of parents, peers, and personal experiences. *Family Relations, 36*, 276–282.

Hall, G. C. N., & Hirschman R., (1991). Toward a theory of sexual aggression: A quadripartite model. *Journal of Consulting and Clinical Psychology, 59*, 662–669.

Harrington, N. T., & Leitenberg, H. (1994). Relationship between alcohol consumption and victim behaviors immediately preceding sexual aggression by an acquaintance. *Violence and Victims, 9*, 315–324.

Harris, Louis, and Associates. (1986). *American teens speak: Sex, myths, TV, and birth control.* New York: Author.

Hayes, C. D. (1987). *Risking the future: Adolescent sexuality, pregnancy, and childbearing* (Vol 1). Washington DC: National Academy Press.

Hendrick, S. S., & Hendrick, C. (1995). Gender differences and similarities in sex and love. *Personal Relationships, 2*, 55–65.

Hendrick, S., Hendrick, C., Slapion-Foote, M. J., & Foote, F. H. (1985). Gender differences in sexual attitudes. *Journal of Personality and Social Psychology, 48*, 1630–1642.

Henshaw, S. K., & Van Vort, J. (1989). Teenage abortion, birth, pregnancy statistics: An update. *Family Planning Perspectives, 21*, 85–88.

Herold, E. S., & Goodwin, M. S. (1981). Adamant virgins, potential nonvirgins, and nonvirgins. *Journal of Sex Research, 17*, 97–113.

Herold, E. S., Maticka-Tyndale, E., & Mewhinney, D. (1998). Predicting intentions to engage in casual sex. *Journal of Social and Personal Relationships, 15*, 502–516.

Herold, E. S., & Mewhinney, D. M. K. (1993). Gender differences in casual sex and AIDS prevention: A survey of dating bars. *Journal of Sex Research, 30*, 36–42.

Herold, E. S., & Way, L. (1988). Sexual self-disclosure among university women. *Journal of Sex Research, 24*, 1–14.

Hewitt, J. P. (1991). *Self and society : a symbolic interactionist social psychology* (5th Ed.). Boston: Allyn & Bacon.

Hill, C. A., & Preston, L. K. (1996). Individual differences in the experience of sexual motivation: Theory and measurement of dispositional sexual motives. *The Journal of Sex Research, 33*, 27–45.

Himelein, M. J. (1995). Risk factors for sexual victimization in dating: A longitudinal study of college women. *Psychology of Women Quarterly, 19*, 31–48.

HIV/AIDS Surveillance Report (1997). *Year-end 1997 Edition, 9(2)* [online publication]. Available: http://www.cdc.gov/nchstp/hiv_aids/stats/hasrlink.htm.

Hoefferth, S. L., Kahn, J. R., & Baldwin, W. (1987). Premarital sexual activity among U.S. teenage women over the past three decades. *Family Planning Perspectives, 19,* 46–53.

Hobgen, M., & Byrne, D. (1998). Using social learning theory to explain individual differences in human sexuality. *Journal of Sex Research, 35,* 58–71.

Hogan, D. P., & Kitagawa, E. M. (1985). The impact of social status, family structure, and neighborhood on the fertility of Black adolescents. *American Journal of Sociology, 90,* 825–855.

Hovell, M., Sipan, C., Blumberg, E., Atkins, C., Hofstetter, C. R., & Kreitner, S. (1994). Family influences on Latino and Anglo adolescents sexual behavior. *Journal of Marriage and the Family, 56,* 973–986.

Huston, T. L. (1983). Power. In H. Kelley, E. Berscheid, A. Christensen, J. Harvey, T. Huston, G. Levinber, E. McClintock, L. A. Peplau, & D. R. Peterson (Eds.), *Close Relationships* (pp. 169–219). New York: Freeman.

Inazu, J. K., & Fox, G. L. (1980). Maternal influence on the sexual behavior of teen-age daughters. *Journal of Family Issues, 1,* 81–102.

Jackson, E. D., & Potkay, C. R. (1973). Precollege influences on sexual experiences of coeds. *Journal of Sex Research, 9,* 143–149.

Jacoby, A. P., & Williams, J. D. (1985). Effects of premarital sexual standards and behavior on dating and marriage desirability. *Journal of Marriage and the Family, 47,* 1059–1065.

Jedlicka, D., & Robinson, I. E. (1987). Fear of venereal disease and other perceived restraints on the occurrence of premarital coitus. *Journal of Sex Research, 23,* 391–396.

Jemmott, L. S., & Jemmott, J. B. (1992). Family structure, parental strictness, and sexual behavior among inner-city Black male adolescents. *Journal of Adolescent Research, 7,* 192–207.

Jenkins, M. J., & Dambrot, F. H. (1987). The attribution of date rape: Observer's attitudes and sexual experiences and the dating situation. *Journal of Applied Social Psychology, 17,* 875–895.

Jesser, C. J. (1978). Male responses to direct verbal sexual initiatives of females. *Journal of Sex Research, 14,* 118–128.

Jessor, R., Costa, F., Jessor, L., & Donovan, J. E. (1983). Time of first intercourse: A prospective study. *Journal of Personality and Social Psychology, 44,* 608–626.

Jessor, S. L., & Jessor, R. (1974). Maternal ideology and adolescent problem behavior. *Developmental Psychology, 10,* 246–254.

Jones, E. F., Forrest, J. D., Goldman, N., Henshaw, S. K., Lincoln, R., Rosoff, J. I., Westoff, C. F., & Wuf, D. (1985). Teenage pregnancy in developed countries: Determinants and policy implications. *Family Planning Perspectives, 17,* 53–62.

Jorgensen, S. R. (1993). Adolescent pregnancy and parenting. In T. P. Gullotta, G. R. Adams, R. Montemayor (Eds.), *Adolescent sexuality* (pp. 103–140). Newbury Park, CA: Sage.

Jorgensen, S. R., King, S. L., & Torrey, B. A. (1980). Dyadic and social network influences on adolescent exposure to pregnancy risk. *Journal of Marriage and the Family, 42,* 141–155.

Jurich, A. P., & Jones, W. C. (1986). Divorce and the experience of adolescents. In G. K. Leigh & G. W. Peterson (Eds.), *Adolescents in family* (pp. 308–336). Cincinnati, OH: Southwestern.

Jurich, A. P., & Jurich, J. A. (1974). The effect of cognitive moral development upon the selection of premarital sexual standards. *Journal of Marriage and the Family, 36,* 736–741.

Kaats, G. R., & Davis, K. E. (1970). The dynamics of sexual behavior of college students. *Journal of Marriage and the Family, 32,* 390–399.

Kalichman, S. C., Sarwer, D. B., Johnson, J. R., Ali, S. A., Early, J., & Tuten, J. T. (1993). Sexually coercive behavior and love styles: A replication and extension. *Journal of Psychology and Human Sexuality, 6,* 93–106.

Kanin, E. J. (1967). An examination of sexual aggression as a response to sexual frustration. *Journal of Marriage and the Family, 29,* 428–433.

Kanin, E. J. (1969). Selected dyadic aspects of male sex aggression. *Journal of Sex Research, 5,* 12–28.

Kanin, E. J. (1970). Sex aggression by college men. *Medical Aspects of Human Sexuality, 4,* 28–40.

Kanin, E. J. (1983). Rape as a function of relative sexual frustration. *Psychological Reports, 52,* 133–134.

Kanin, E. J., & Parcell, S. R. (1977). Sexual aggression: A second look at the offended female. *Archives of Sexual Behavior, 6,* 67–76.

Kantor, D., & Lehr, W. (1975). *Inside the family: Toward a theory of family process.* New York: Harper Colophon.

Kellar-Guenther, Y., & Christopher F. S. (1997, July). *How effective are sexual history discussions?* Paper presented at the International Network on Personal Relations Conference, Oxford, OH.

Kellar-Guenther, Y., & Christopher F. S. (1998, June). *The role of romantic relationship variables play in the decision to use a condom.* Paper presented at the International Conference on Personal Relationships, Saratoga.

Kelley, J. (1978). Sexual permissiveness: Evidence for a theory. *Journal of Marriage and the Family, 40,* 165–181.

Kelley, J. A. (1995). Advances in HIV/AIDS education and prevention. *Family Relation, 44,* 345–352.

Kelley, K., Pilchowicz, E., & Byrne, D. (1981). Responses to female-initiated dates. *Bulletin of the Psyhonomic Society, 17,* 195–196.

King, K., Abernathey, T. J., Robinson, I. E., & Balwsick, J. O. (1976). Religiosity and sexual attitudes and behavior among college students. *Adolescence, 11,* 535–539.

King, K., Balswick, J. O., & Robinson, I. E. (1977). The continuing premarital sexual revolution among college females. *Journal of Marriage and the Family, 39,* 455–459.

Kinnaird, K. L., & Gerrard, M. (1986). Premarital sexual behavior and attitudes toward marriage and divorce among young women as a function of their mother's marital status. *Journal of Marriage and the Family, 48,* 757–765.

Kinsey, A., Pomeroy, W., & Martin, C. (1948). *Sexual behavior in the human male.* Philadelphia: Saunders.

Kirkendall, L. A. (1961). *Premarital intercourse and interpersonal relationships.* New York: Gramercy.

Kirkendall, L. A. (1967). Characteristics of sexual decision making. *The Journal of Sex Research, 3,* 201–211.

Kirkpatrick, C., & Kanin, E. (1957). Male sex aggression on a university campus. *American Sociological Review, 22,* 52–58.

Knox, D., & Wilson, K. (1981). Dating behaviors of university students. *Family Relations, 30,* 255–258.

Koch, P. B. (1988). The relationship of first intercourse to later sexual functioning concerns of adolescents. *Journal of Adolescent Research, 3,* 345–362.

Kopper, B. A., (1996). Gender, gender identity, rape myth acceptance, and time of initial resistance on the perception of acquaintance rape blame and avoidability. *Sex Roles, 34,* 81–93.

Korman, S. K., & Leslie, G. R. (1982). The relationship of feminist ideology and date expense to perceptions of sexual aggression in dating. *Journal of Sex Research, 18,* 114–129.

Koss, M. P., & Cleveland, H. H. (1997). Stepping on toes: Social roots of date rape lead to intractability and politicization. In M. D. Schwartz (Ed.), *Researching sexual violence against women: Methodological and personal perspectives* (pp. 4–21). Thousand Oaks, CA: Sage.

Koss, M. P., & Dinero, T. E. (1988). Predictors of sexual aggression among a national sample of male college students. In R. A. Prentky & V. L. Quinsey (Eds.), *Human sexual aggression: Current perspectives. Annals of the New York Academy of Sciences* (Vol. 528, pp.133–146). New York: New York Academy of Sciences

Koss, M. P., & Dinero, T. E. (1989). Discriminant analysis of risk factors for sexual victimization among a national sample of college women. *Journal of Consulting and Clinical Psychology, 57,* 242–250.

Koss, M. P., Dinero, T. E., Seibel, C. A., & Cox, S. L. (1988). Stranger and acquaintance rape. *Psychology of Women Quarterly, 12,* 1–24.

Koss, M. P., Gidycz, C. A., & Wisneiwski, N. (1987). The scope of rape: Incidence and prevalence of sexual aggression and victimization in a national sample of higher education students. *Journal of Consulting and Clinical Psychology, 55*, 162–170.

Koss, M. P., Leonard, K. E., Beezley, D. A., & Oros, C. J. (1985). Nonstranger sexual aggression: A discriminant analysis of the psychological characteristics of undetected offenders. *Sex Roles, 12*, 981–992.

Koss, M. P., & Oros, C. J. (1980, August). *The "unacknowledged" rape victim.* Paper presented at the American Psychological Association meeting, Montreal Canada.

Lackie, L., & de Man, A. F. (1997). Correlates of sexual aggression among male university students. *Sex Roles, 37*, 451–457.

Lally, C. F., & Maddock, J. W. (1994). Sexual meaning systems of engaged couples. *Family Relations, 43*, 53-60.

Lalumière, M. L., Chalmers, L. J., Quinsey, V. L., & Seto, M. C. (1996). A test of the mate deprivation hypothesis of sexual coercion. *Ethology and Sociobiology, 17*, 299–318.

Lalumière, M. L., & Quinsey, V. L. (1996). Sexual deviance, antisociality, mating effort, and the use of sexually coercive behaviors. *Personality and Individual Differences, 21*, 33–48.

LaPlante, M. N., McCormick, N., & Brannigan, G. G. (1980). Living the sexual script: College students' views of influence in sexual encounters. *Journal of Sex Research, 16*, 338–355.

Laumann, E. O., Gagnon, J. H., Michael, R. T., & Michaels, S. (1994). *The social organization of sexuality: Sexual practices in the United States.* Chicago: The University of Chicago Press.

Lawrence, K., & Byers, E. S. (1995). Sexual satisfaction in long-term heterosexual relationships: The interpersonal exchange model of sexual satisfaction. *Personal Relationships, 2*, 267–285.

Leigh, G. K., Weddle, K. D., & Loewen, I. R. (1988). Analysis of the timing of transition to sexual intercourse for black adolescent females. *Journal of Adolescent Research, 3*, 333–344.

Leukefeld, C. G., & Haverkos, H. W. (1993). Sexually transmitted diseases. In T. P. Gullotta, G. R. & Adams, R. Montemayor (Eds.), *Adolescent sexuality* (pp. 161–180). Newbury Park, CA: Sage.

Lewis, R. A. (1973). Parents and peers: Socialization agents in the coital behavior of young adults. *Journal of Sex Research, 9*, 156–170.

Lewis, R. A., & Burr, W. R. (1975). Premarital coitus and commitment among college students. *Archives of Sexual Behavior, 4*, 73–79.

Lewis, R. J., Gibbons, F. X., & Gerrard, M. (1986). Sexual experiences and recall of sexual vs. nonsexual information. *Journal of Personality, 54,* 676–693.

Lisak, D., & Ivan, C. (1995). Deficits in intimacy and empathy in sexually aggressive men. *Journal of Interpersonal Violence, 10,* 296–308.

Lisak, D., & Roth, S. (1988). Motivational factors in nonincarcerated sexually aggressive men. *Journal of Personality and Social Psychology, 55,* 795–802.

Lloyd, S. (1991). The darkside of courtship: Violence and sexual exploitation. *Family Relations, 40,* 14–20.

Lloyd, S. A., & Emery, B. C. (1999). *The darkside of dating: Physical and sexual violence.* Thousand Oaks, CA: Sage.

Long, E. C. J., Cate, R. M., Fehsenfeld, D. A., & Williams, K. M. (1996). A longitudinal assessment of a measure of premarital sexual conflict. *Family Relations, 45,* 302–308.

Longmore, M. A., (1998). Symbolic interactionism and the study of sexuality. *Journal of Sex Research, 35,* 44–51.

Lonsway, K. A., & Fitzgerald, L. F. (1994). Rape myths in review. *Psychology of Women Quarterly, 18,* 133–164.

Lonsway, K. A., & Fitzgerald, L. F. (1995). Attitudinal antecedents of rape myth acceptance: A theoretical and empirical reexamination. *Journal of Personality and Social Psychology, 68,* 704–711.

Lundberg-Love, P., & Geffner, R. (1989). Date rape: Prevalence, risk factors, and a proposed model. In M. Pirog-Good & J. States (Eds.), *Violence in dating relationships: Emerging social issues* (pp. 169–184). New York: Praeger.

Luster, T., & Small, S. A. (1994). Factors associated with sexual risk-taking behaviors among adolescents. *Journal of Marriage and the Family, 56,* 622–632.

MacCorquodale, P. (1989). Gender and sexual behavior. In K. McKinney & S. Sprecher (Eds.), *Human sexuality: The societal and interpersonal context* (pp. 91–112). Norwood, NJ: Ablex.

Mahoney, E. R. (1980). Religiosity and sexual behavior among heterosexual college students. *Journal of Marriage and the Family, 29,* 119–113.

Malamuth, N. M. (1986). Predictors of naturalistic sexual aggression. *Journal of Personality and Social Psychology, 50,* 953–962.

Malamuth, N. M., & Brown, L. M. (1994). Sexually aggressive men's perceptions of women's communications: Testing three explanations. *Journal of Personality and Social Psychology, 67,* 699–712.

Malamuth, N. M., Linz, D., Heavey, C. L., Barnes, G., & Acker, M. (1995). Using the confluence model of sexual aggression to predict men's conflict with women: A 10–year follow-up study. *Journal of Personality and Social Psychology, 69,* 353–369.

Malamuth, N. M., Sockloski, R. J., Koss, M. P., & Tanaka, J. S. (1991). Characteristics of aggressors against women: Testing a model using a national sample of college students. *Journal of Consulting and Clinical Psychology, 59,* 670–681.

Mare, R. D. (1991). Five decades of educational assortative mating. *American Sociological Review, 56,* 15–31.

Mark, M. M., & Miller, L. M. (1986). The effects of sexual permissiveness. Target gender, subject gender, and attitude toward women and social perception: In search of the double standard. *Sex Roles, 15,* 311–322.

Maticka-Tyndale, E., Herold, E. S., & Mewhinney, D. (1998). Casual sex on spring break: Intentions and behaviors of Canadian Students. *Journal of Sex Research, 35,* 254–264.

McCabe, M. P. (1984). Toward a theory of adolescent dating. *Adolescence, 29,* 159–170.

McCabe, M. P., & Collins, J. K. (1983). The sexual and affectional attitudes and experiences of Australian adolescents during dating: The effects of age, church attendance, type of school, and socioeconomic class. *Archives of Sexual Behavior, 12,* 525–539.

McCormick, N. B. (1979). Come-ons and put-offs: Unmarried students' strategies for having and avoiding sexual intercourse. *Psychology of Women Quarterly, 4,* 194–211.

Mercer, G. W., & Kohn, P. M. (1979). Gender differences in the integration of conservatism, sex urge, and sexual behaviors among college students. *Journal of Sex Research, 15,* 129–142.

Miller, B., & Marshall, J. C. (1987). Coercive sex on the university campus. *Journal of College Student Personnel, 47,* 38–47.

Miller, B. C., & Bingham, C. R., (1989). Family configuration in relation to the sexual behavior of female adolescents. *Journal of Marriage and the Family, 51,* 499–506.

Miller, B. C., Christensen, R. B., & Olson, T. D. (1987). Adolescent self-esteem in relation to sexual attitudes and behaviors. *Youth & Society, 19,* 93–111.

Miller, B. C., & Heaton, T. B. (1991). Age at first sexual intercourse and the timing of marriage and childbirth. *Journal of Marriage and the Family, 53,* 719–732.

Miller, B. C., Higginson, R., McCoy, J. K., & Olson, T. D. (1987). Family configuration and adolescent sexual attitudes and behavior. *Population and Environment, 9,* 111–123.

Miller, B. C., McCoy, J. K., Olson, T., Wallace, C. M. (1986). Parental discipline and control attempts in relation to adolescent sexual attitudes and behaviors. *Journal of Marriage and the Family, 48,* 503–512.

Miller, B. C., & Moore, K. A. (1990). Adolescent sexual behavior, pregnancy, and parenting: Research through the 1980s. *Journal of Marriage and the Family, 52,* 1025–1044.

Miller, B. C., & Olson, T. D. (1988). Sexual attitudes and behavior of high school students in relation to background and contextual factors. *Journal of Sex Research, 24,* 194–200.

Miller, K. S., Forehand, R., & Kotchick, B. A. (1999). Adolescent sexual behavior in two ethnic minority samples: The role of family variables. *Journal of Marriage and the Family, 61,* 85–98.

Miller, P. Y., & Simon, W. (1974) Adolescent sexual behavior: Context and change. *Social Problems, 22,* 58–76.

Mirandé, A. (1968). Adolescence and Chicano families. In G. K. Leigh & G. W. Peterson (Eds.), *Adolescents in family* (pp. 433–455). Cincinnati, OH: Southwestern.

Mirande, A. M. (1986). Reference group theory and adolescent sexual behavior. *Journal of Marriage and the Family, 30,* 572–577.

Mongeau, P. A., & Johnson, K. L. (1995). Predicting cross-sex first-date sexual expectations and involvement: Contextual and individual difference factors. *Personal Relationships, 2,* 267–286.

Moore, K. A. (1989). *Facts at a glance.* Washington DC:, Child Trends Inc.

Moore, K. A. (1996). *Facts at a glance.* Washington DC:, Child Trends Inc.

Moore, K. A., Nord, C. W., & Peterson, J. L. (1989). Nonvoluntary sexual activity among adolescents. *Family Planning Perspectives, 21,* 110–114.

Moore, K. A., Peterson, J. L., & Furstenberg, F. F. (1986). Parental attitudes and the occurrence of early sexual activity. *Journal of Marriage and the Family, 48,* 777–782.

Moore, M. M. (1985). Nonverbal courtship patterns in women: Context and consequence. *Ethology and Sociobiology, 6,* 237–247.

Moore, M. M. (1995). Courtship signaling and adolescents: ''Girls just wanna have fun''? *Journal of Sex Research, 32,* 319-328.

Moore, S. M., & Barling, N. R. (1991). Developmental status and AIDS attitudes in adolescence. *Journal of Genetic Psychology, 152,* 5–16.

Morbidity and Mortality Weekly Report. (1998, September 18). Trends in sexual risk behaviors among high school students. *Centers for Disease Control* [online], *47*(36), 749–751.

Mosher, D. L. (1966). The development and multitrait-multimethod matrix analysis of three measures of three aspects of guilt. *Journal of Consulting and Clinical Psychology, 30,* 25–29.

Mosher, D. L. (1968). Measurement of guilt in females by self-report inventories. *Journal of Consulting and Clinical Psychology, 32,* 690–695.

Mosher, D. L. (1979). Sex guilt and sex myths in college men and women. *Journal of Sex Research, 15,* 224-234.

Mosher, D. L., & Anderson, R. D. (1986). Macho personality, sexual aggression, and reactions to guided imagery of realistic rape. *Journal of Research in Personality, 20,* 77–94.

Mosher, D. L., & Cross, H. J. (1971). Sex guilt and premarital sexual experiences of college students. *Journal of Consulting and Clinical Psychology, 36,* 27–32.

Mott, F. L., Fondell, M. M., Hu, P. N., Kowaleski-Jones, L., & Menaghan, E. G. (1996). The determinants of first sex by age 14 in a high-risk adolescent population. *Family Planning Perspectives, 28,* 13–18.

Muehlenhard, C. L. (1988). Misinterpreted dating behaviors and the risk of date rape. *Journal of Social and Clinical Psychology, 6,* 20–37.

Muehlenhard, C. L., & Cook, S. W. (1988). Men's self-reports of unwanted sexual activity. *Journal of Sex Research, 24,* 58–72.

Muehlenhard, C. L., & Falcon, P. L. (1990). Men's heterosocial skill and attitudes toward women as predictors of verbal sexual coercion and forceful rape. *Sex Roles, 23,* 241–259.

Muehlenhard, C., Goggins, M. F., Jones, J. M., & Satterfield, A. T. (1991). Sexual violence and coercion in close relationships. In K. McKinney & S. Sprechers (Eds.), *Sexuality in close relationships* (pp. 155–175). Hillsdale, NJ: Lawrence Erlbaum Associates.

Meuhelenhard, C. L., & Hollabaugh, L. C. (1988). Do women sometimes say no when they mean yes? The prevalence and correlates of women's token resistance to sex. *Journal of Personality and Social Psychology, 54,* 872–879.

Muehlenhard, C. L., & Linton, M. A. (1987). Date rape and sexual aggression in dating situations: Incidence and risk factors. *Journal of Counseling Psychology, 34,* 186–196.

Muehlenhard, C. L., & McCoy, M. (1991). Double standard/double bind: The sexual double standard and women's communication about sex. *Psychology of Women Quarterly, 15,* 447–461.

Muehlenhard, C. L., & Rodgers, C. S. (1998). Token resistance to sex. *Psychology of Women Quarterly, 22,* 443–463.

Myers, D. R., Kilmann, P. R., Wanlass, R. L., & Stout, A. (1983). Dimensions of female sexuality: A factor analysis. *Archives of Sexual Behavior, 12,* 159–166.

Newcomb, M. D., Huba, G. J., & Bentler, P. M. (1986). Determinants of sexual and dating behaviors among adolescents. *Journal of Personality and Social Psychology, 50,* 428–438.

Newcomer, S. F., & Udry, J. R. (1984). Mother's influence on the sexual behavior of their teenage children. *Journal of Marriage and the Family, 46,* 477–485.

Newcomer, S., & Udry, J. R., (1987). Parental marital status effects on adolescent sexual behavior. *Journal of Marriage and the Family, 49,* 235–240.

Nix, L. M., Pasteur, A. B., & Servance, M. A. (1988). A focus group study of sexually active Black male teenagers. *Adolescence, 23,* 741–751.

Norris, J., & Cubbins, L. A. (1992). Dating, drinking, and rape: Effects of victim's and assailant's alcohol consumption on judgments of their behavior and traits. *Psychology of Women Quarterly, 16,* 179–191.

Ogletree, R. J. (1993). Sexual coercion experience and help-seeking behavior of college women. *College Health, 41,* 149–153.

Ohannessian, C. M., & Crockett, L. J. (1993). A longitudinal investigation of the relationship between educational investment and adolescent sexual activity. *Journal of Adolescent Research, 8,* 167–182.

Okami, P., Olmstead, R., & Abramson, P. R. (1997). Sexual experiences in early childhood: 18-year longitudinal data from the UCLA family lifestyles project. *Journal of Sex Research, 34,* 339-347.

Okami, P., Olmstead, R., Abramson, P. R., & Pendleton, L. (1998). Early childhood exposure to parental nudity and scenes of parental sexuality ("primal scenes"): An 18-year longitudinal study of outcome. *Archives of Sex Behavior, 27,* 361-384.

Oliver, M. B., & Hyde, J. S. (1993). Gender differences in sexuality: A meta-analysis. *Psychology Bulletin, 114,* 341–359.

O'Sullivan, L. F., & Allgeier, E. R. (1994). Disassembling a stereotype: Gender differences in the use of token resistance. *Journal of Applied Social Psychology, 24,* 1035–1055.

O'Sullivan, L. F., & Byers, E. S. (1992). College students' incorporation of initiator and restrictor roles in sexual dating interactions. *Journal of Sex Research, 29,* 435–446.

O'Sullivan, L. F., Byers, E. S., & Finkelman, L. (1998). A comparison of male and female college students' experiences of sexual coercion. *Psychology of Women Quarterly, 22,* 177–195.

O'Sullivan L. F., & Gaines, M. E. (1998). Decision-making in college students' heterosexual dating relationships: Ambivalence about engaging in sexual activity. *Journal of Social and Personal Relationships, 15,* 347–363.

Peplau, L. A., Rubin, Z., & Hill, C. T. (1977). Sexual intimacy in dating relationships. *Journal of Social Issues, 33,* 86–109.

Perper, T. L., & Weis, D. L. (1987). Proceptive and rejective strategies of U.S. and Canadian college women. *Journal of Sex Research, 23,* 455–480.

Peterson, G. W. (1986). Family conceptual frameworks and adolescent development. In G. K. Leigh & G. W. Peterson (Eds.), *Adolescents in family* (pp. 12–36). Cincinnati, OH: Southwestern.

Peterson, G. W. (1995). Autonomy and connectedness in families. In R. D. Day, K. R. Gilbert, B. H. Settles, & M. R. Burr (Eds.) *Research and theory in family science* (pp. 20-41). New York: Brooks/Cole Publishing Company.

Petty, G. M., & Dawson, B. (1989). Sexual aggression in normal men: Incidence, beliefs, and personality characteristics. *Personality and Individual Differences, 10*, 355–362.

Poitras, M., & Lavoie, F. (1995). A study of the prevalence of sexual coercion in adolescent heterosexual dating relationships in a Quebec sample. *Violence and Victims, 10*, 299–313.

Poppen, P. J., & Segal, N. J. (1988). The influence of sex and sex role orientation on sexual coercion. *Sex Roles, 19*, 689–701.

Propper, S., & Brown, R. A. (1986). Moral reasoning, parental sex attitudes, & sex guilt in female college students. *Archives of Sexual Behavior, 15*, 331–340.

Radke-Yarrow, M., Zahn-Waxler, C., & Chapman, M. (1983). Children's prosocial dispositions and behavior. In P. H. Mussen (Ed.) *Handbook of child psychology* (4th ed., pp. 469–545). New York: Wiley.

Rapaport, K., & Burkhart, B. R. (1984). Personality and attitudinal characteristics of sexually coercive college males. *Journal of Abnormal Psychology, 93*, 216–221.

Reed, D., & Weinberg, M. S. (1984). Premarital coitus: Developing and establishing sexual scripts. *Social Psychology Quarterly, 47*, 129–138.

Reiss, I. L. (1960). *Premarital sexual standards in American.* Glencoe, IL: The Free Press.

Reiss, I. L. (1964). The scaling of premarital sexual permissiveness. *Journal of Marriage and the Family, 26*, 188–198.

Reiss, I. L. (1967). The social context of premarital sexual permissiveness. New York: Holt, Rinehart, & Winston.

Roberts, E. J., Kline, D., & Gagnon, J. (1978). *Family life and sexual learning.* Cambridge: MA: Populuation Education Inc.

Robinson, I., Ziss, K., Ganza, B., Katz, S., & Robinson, E. (1991). Twenty years of sexual revolution, 1965–1985: An update. *Journal of Marriage and the Family, 53*, 216–220.

Roche, J. P. (1986). Premarital sex: Attitudes and behavior by dating stage. *Adolescence, 21*, 107–121.

Roche, J. P., & Ramsbey, T. W. (1993). Premarital sexuality: A five-year follow-up study of attitudes and behavior by dating stage. *Adolescence, 28*, 67–80.

Rosenbaum, E., & Kandel, D. B. (1990). Early onset of sexual behavior and drug involvement. *Journal of Marriage and the Family, 52*, 783–798.

Ruble, D. N., & Martin, C. L. (1998). Gender development. In W. Damon (Ed.), *Handbook of child psychology* (5th Ed., pp. 933–1016). New York: Wiley.

Rusbult, C. (1980). Commitment and satisfaction in romantic associations: A test of the investment model. *Journal of Experimental Social Psychology, 16*, 172–186.

Russo, T. J., Barnes, H. L., & Wright, D. W. (1991). *Parental factors influencing parent–child communication about general and specific human sexuality topics.* Paper presented at the annual conference of the National Council on Family Relations, Denver, CO.

Santello, M. D., & Leitenberg, H. (1993). Sexual aggression by an acquaintance: Methods of coping and later psychological adjustment. *Violence and Victims, 8,* 91–104.

Sarwer, D. B., Kalichman, S. C., Johnson, J. R., Early, J., & Ali, S. A. (1993). Sexual aggression and love styles: An exploatory study. *Archives of Sexual Behavior, 22,* 265–275.

Schultz, B., Bohrnstedt, G. W., Borgatta, E. F., & Evans, R. R. (1977). Explaining premarital sexual intercourse among college students: A casual model. *Social Forces, 56,* 148–165.

Schultz, L. G., & DeSavage, J. (1975). Rape and rape attitudes on a college campus. In L. G. Schultz (Ed.), *Rape victimology* (pp. 77–90). Springfield, MA: Charles C. Thomas.

Sexually Transmitted Disease Surveillance. (1996). Centers for Disease Control and Prevention [online publication]. Available: http://cdc3.cdc.gov/Wonder/.

Shah, F., & Zelnik, M. (1981). Parent and peer influence on sexual behavior, contraceptive use, and pregnancy experience of young women. *Journal of Marriage and the Family, 43,* 339–348.

Sheppard, V. J., Nelson, E. S., & Andreoli-Mathie, V. (1995). Dating relationships and infidelity: Attitudes and behaviors. *Journal of Sex & Marital Therapy, 21,* 202–212.

Sherwin, R. & Corbett, S. (1985). Campus sexual norms and dating relationships: A trend analysis. *Journal of Sex Research, 21,* 258–274.

Shotland, R. L. (1989). A model of the causes of date rape in developing and close relationships. In C. Hendrick (Ed.), *Close Relationships: Review of personality and social psychology* (Vol. 10, pp. 247–270). Newbury Park, CA: Sage.

Shotland, R. L., & Craig, J. M. (1988). Can men and women differentiate between friendly and sexually interested behavior? *Social Psychology Quarterly, 51,* 66–73.

Shotland, R. L., & Goodstein, L. (1983). Just because she doesn't want to doesn't mean it's rape: An experimentally based causal model of the perception of rape in a dating situation. *Social Psychology Quarterly, 46,* 220–232.

Shotland, R. L., & Hunter, B. A. (1995). Women's "token resistant" and compliant sexual behaviors are related to uncertain sexual intentions and rape. *Personality and Social Psychology Bulletin, 21,* 226–236.

Simkins, L., & Rinck, C. (1982). Male and female sexual vocabulary in different interpersonal contexts. *Journal of Sex Research, 18,* 160–172.

Simpson, J. A., & Gangestad, S. W. (1991). Personality and sexuality: Empirical relations and an integrative theoretical model. In K. McKinney & S. Sprecher (Eds.), *Sexuality in close relationships* (pp. 71–92). Hillsdale, NJ: Lawrence Erlbaum Associates.

Singer, D. G. (1983). A time to reexamine the role of television in our lives. *American Psychologist, 38,* 815–816.

Small, S. A., & Kerns, D. (1991, November). *Sexual coercion in adolescent relationships.* Paper presented at the annual meeting of the National Council on Family Relations, Denver, Col

Small, S. A., & Kerns, D. (1993). Unwanted sexual activity among peers during early and middle adolescence: Incidence and risk factors: *The Journal of Marriage and the Family, 55,* 941–952.

Small, S. A., & Luster, T. (1994). Adolescent sexual activity: An ecological, risk-factor approach. *The Journal of Marriage and the Family, 56,* 181–192.

Smith, E. A., & Udry, J. R. (1985). Coital and non-coital sexual behaviors of white and black adolescents. *American Journal of Public Health, 75,* 1200–1230.

Smith, E. A., Udry, J. R., & Morris, N. M. (1985). Pubertal development and friends: A biosocial explanation of adolescent sexual behavior. *Journal of Health and Social Behavior, 26,* 183–192.

Smith, T. W. (1994). Attitudes toward sexual permissiveness: Trends, correlates, and behavioral connections. In A. S. Rossi (Ed.), *Sexuality across the life course* (pp. 63–97). Chicago: The University of Chicago Press .

Snyder, M., & Simpson, J. A. (1984). Self-monitoring and dating relationships. *Journal of Personality and Social Psychology, 47,* 1281–1291.

Snyder, M., Simpson, J. A., & Gangestad, S. (1986). Personality and sexual relations. *Journal of Personality and Social Psychology, 54,* 181–190.

Sonnerstein, F. L., Pleck, J. H., & Leighton, C. K. (1991). Levels of sexual activity among adolescent males in the United States. *Family Planning Perspectives, 23,* 162–167.

Spanier, G. (1976). Formal and informal sex education as determinants of premarital sexual behavior. *Archives of Sexual Behavior, 5,* 39–67.

Spanier, G. B. (1977). Sources of sex information and premarital sexual behavior. *Journal of Sex Research, 13,* 73–88.

Sprecher, S. (1985). Sex differences in bases of power in dating relationships. *Sex Roles, 12,* 449–462.

Sprecher, S. (1990). The impact of the threat of AIDS on heterosexual dating relationships. *Journal of Psychology and Human Sexuality, 3,* 3–23.

Sprecher, S. (1998). Social exchange theories and sexuality. *Journal of Sex Research, 35,* 32–43.

Sprecher, S., Hatfield, E., Cortese, A., Potapova, E., & Levitskaya. (1994). Token resistance to sexual intercourse and consent to unwanted sexual intercourse:

College students' dating experiences in three countries. *Journal of Sex Research, 31,* 125–132.

Sprecher, S., & McKinney, K. (1993). *Sexuality and close relationships.* Newbury Park, CA: Sage.

Sprecher, S., McKinney, K., & Orbuch, T. L. (1987). Has the double standard disappeared? An experimental test. *Social Psychological Quarterly, 50,* 24–31.

Sprecher, S., McKinney, K., & Orbuch, T. L. (1991). The effect of current sexual behavior on friendship, dating, and marriage desirability, *Journal of Sex Research, 28,* 387–408.

Sprecher, S., McKinney, K. Walsh, R., & Anderson, C. (1988). A revision of the Reiss premarital sexual permissiveness scale. *Journal of Marriage and the Family, 50,* 821–828.

Sprecher, S., & Regan, P. C. (1996). College virgins: How men and women perceive their sexual status. *Journal of Sex Research, 33,* 3–15.

Stebleton, M. J., & Rothenberger, J. H. (1993). Truth or consequences: Dishonesty in dating and HIV/AIDS-related issues in a college-age population. *Journal of American College Health, 42,* 51–54.

Steinberg, L, Lamborn, S., Dornbusch, S., & Darling, N. (1992). Impact of parenting practices on adolescent achievement: Authoritative parenting, school involvement, and encouragement to succeed. *Child Development, 63,* 1266–1281.

Steinberg, L., & Silverberg, S. (1986). The vicissitudes of autonomy in early adolescence. *Child Development, 57,* 841–851.

Stets, J. E., & Pirog-Good, M. A. (1989). Sexual aggression and control in dating relationships. *Journal of Applied Social Psychology, 19,* 1392–1412.

Strouse, J. S., & Fabes, R. A. (1987). A conceptualization of transition to nonvirginity in adolescent females. *Journal of Adolescent Research, 2,* 331–348.

Struckman-Johnson, C. (1988). Forced sex on dates: It happens to men, too. *Journal of Sex Research, 24,* 234–241.

Struckman-Johnson, C., & Struckman-Johnson, D. (1994). Men pressured and forced into sexual experience. *Archives of Sexual Behavior, 23,* 93–114.

Stryker, S., & Statham, A. (1985). Symbolic interaction and role theory. In G. Lindzey & E. Aronson (Eds.), *Handbook of social psychology* (pp. 311–377). New York: Random House.

Tabachnick, B. G., & Fidell, L. S. (1996). *Using multivariate statistics* (3rd Ed.). New York: Harper & Row.

Tanfer, K., & Cubbins, L. A. (1992). Coital frequency among single women: Normative constraints and situational opportunities. *Journal of Sex Research, 29,* 221–250.

Tanfer, K., & Schoorl, J. J. (1992). Premarital sexual careers and partner change. *Archives of Sexual Behavior, 21,* 45–68.

Taris, T. W., Semin, G. R., & Bok, I. A. (1998). The effect of quality of family interaction and intergenerational transmission of values on sexual permissiveness. *Journal of Genetic Psychology, 159,* 237–251.

Teevan, J. (1972). Reference groups and premarital sexual behavior. *Journal of Marriage and the Family, 34,* 283–291.

Thorne, B., & Luria, Z. (1986). Sexuality and gender in children's daily worlds. *Social Problems, 33*(3), 176–190.

Thornton, A. (1990). The courtship process and adolescent sexuality. *Journal of Family Issues, 11,* 239–273.

Thornton, A., & Camburn, D. (1987). The influence of the family on premarital sexual attitudes and behavior. *Demography, 24,* 323–340.

Thronton, A., & Camburn, D. (1989). Religious participation and adolescent sexual behaviors. *Journal of Marriage and the Family, 51,* 641–653.

Tracy, K., Craig, R. T., Smith, M., & Spisak, F. (1984). The discourse of requests: Assessment of a compliance-gaining approach. *Human Communication Research, 10,* 513–538.

Treboux, D., & Busch-Rossnagel, N. A. (1990). Social network influences on adolescent sexual attitudes and behaviors. *Journal of Adolescent Research, 5,* 175–189.

Tyler, K. A., Hoyt, D. R., & Whitbeck L. B. (1998). Coercive sexual strategies. *Violence and Victims, 13,* 47–61.

Udry, J. R. (1979). Age at menarche, at first coitus, and at first pregnancy. *Journal of Biosocial Science, 11,* 433–441.

Udry, J. R., & Billy, J. O. G. (1987). Initiation of coitus in early adolescence. *American Sociological Review, 52,* 841–855.

Udry, J. R., Billy, J. O. G., Morris, N. M., Groff, T. R., & Raj, M. H. (1985). Serum androgenic hormones motivate sexual behavior in adolescent boys. *Fertility and Sterility, 43,* 90–94.

Udry, J. R., & Talbert, L. M. (1988). Sex hormone effects on personality at puberty. *Journal of Personality and Social Psychology, 54,* 291–295.

Udry, J. R., Talbert, L. M., & Morris, N. M. (1986). Biosocial foundations for adolescent female sexuality. *Demography, 23,* 217–227.

Upchurch, D. M., Levy-Storms, L., Sucoff, C. A., & Aneshensel, C. S. (1998). Gender and ethnic differences in the timing of first sexual intercourse. *Family Planning Perspectives, 30,* 121–127.

Ventura, S. J., Martin, J. A., Curtin, S. C., & Mathews, T. J. (1998). Report of final natality statistics, 1996. *Monthly Vital Statistics Report, 46(11)* [online publication]. Available: http://www.cdc.gov/nchswww/releases/98news/98news/natal96.htm.

Victor, J. S. (1980). *Human sexuality: A social psychological approach.* Englewood Cliffs, NJ: Prentice-Hall.

Waldner-Haugrud, L. K., & Magruder, B. (1995). Male and female sexual victimization in dating relationships: Gender differences in coercion techniques and outcomes. *Violence and Victims, 10,* 203–215.

Walker, W. D., Rowe, R. C., & Quinsey, V. L. (1993). Authoritarianism and sexual aggression. *Journal of Personality and Social Psychology, 65,* 1036–1045.

Waller, W. (1951). *The family: A dynamic interpretation.* New York: Holt, Rinehart & Winston.

Walsh, R. H., Ferrell, M. Z., & Tolone, W. L. (1976). Selection of reference group, perceived reference group permissiveness, and personal permissiveness attitudes and behavior: A study of two consecutive panels (1967–1971; 1970–1974). *Journal of Marriage and the Family, 38,* 495–508.

Walster, E., Walster, G. W., & Traupmann, J. (1978). Equity and premarital sex. *Journal of Personality and Social Psychology, 36,* 82–92.

Ward, S. K., Chapman, K., Cohn, E., White, S., & Williams, K. (1991). Acquaintance rape and the college social scene. *Family Relations, 40,* 65–71.

Warren, C. W., Santelli, J. S., Everett, S. A., Kann, L., Collines, J. L., Cassell, C., Morris, L., & Kolbe, L. J. (1998). Sexual behavior among U.S. High School Students, 1990–1995. *Family Planning Perspectives, 30,* 172–200.

Whatley, M. A. (1996). Victim characteristics influencing attributes of responsibility to rape victims: A meta-analysis. *Aggression and Violent Behavior, 1,* 81–95.

Weinberg, M. S., Lottes, I., & Shaver, F. M. (in press). Influences on egalitarian and permissive sexuality: A test of Reiss's hypotheses about Sweden and the United States. *Journal of Sex Research.*

Weinstein, M., & Thornton, A.. (1989). Mother-child relations and adolescent sexual attitudes and behavior. *Demography, 26,* 563–577.

Weis, D. L. (Ed.). (1998). The use of theory in research and scholarship on sexuality [Special issue]. *Journal of Sex Research, 35*(1).

Whitbeck, L. B., Simons, R. L., & Kao, M. (1994). The effects of divorced mothers' dating behaviors and sexual attitudes on the sexual attitudes and behaviors of their adolescent children. *Journal of Marriage and the Family, 56,* 615–621.

White, C. P., Wright, D. W., & Barnes, H. L. (1995). Correlates of parent-child communication about specific sexual topics: A study of rural parents with school-aged children. *Personal Relationships, 2,* 327–344

Whitfield, M. (1989). Development of sexuality in female-children and adolescents. *Canadian Journal of Psychiatry, 34,* 879-883..

Wilson, K., Faison, R., & Britton G. M. (1983). Cultural aspects of male sexual aggression. *Deviant Behavior, 4,* 241–255.

Zabin, L. S., Hirsch, M. B., Smith, E. A., & Hardy, J. B. (1984). Adolescent sexual attitudes and behavior: Are they consistent? *Family Planning Perspectives, 16,* 181–185.

Zabin, L. S., Smith, E. A., Hirsch, M. B., Hardy, J. B. (1986). Ages of physical maturation and first intercourse in black teenage males and females. *Demography, 23,* 595–605.

Zelnick, M., & Shah, F. K. (1983). First intercourse among young Americans. *Family Planning Perspective, 15,* 64–70.

Zweig, J. M., Barber, B. L., & Eccles, J. S. (1997). Sexual coercion and well-being in young adulthood. *Journal of Interpersonal Violence, 12,* 291–308.

Zweig, J. M., Crockett, L. J., Sayer, A., & Vicary, J. R. (1999). A longitudinal examination of the consequences of sexual victimization for rural young adult women. *Journal of Sex Research, 36,* 396–409.

Author Index

Subject Index

A

Attitudes, 51-52, 56, 99–101
 early adolescence and, 51–52,
  60–61
 older adolescents and young
  adults and, 99–101, 106,
  108–110
 standards, 100–101

B

Biology, 30–34, 97–99
 early adolescence and, 30–34
 hormonal influences, 33–34
 menarche, 31-32
 older adolescents and young
  adults and, 97–99, 106
 puberty, 30–34, 46, 68,
  71
 sociobiology, 98

C

Childhood, 11–23
 adolescent sexuality and, 12
 capacity for pleasure, 12–13
 cognitive development and,
  13–14
 cultural bias and restricting
  knowledge, 14–15
 definition of sexuality and,
  12
 family discussion rules and,
  17–18, 20–21
 hedonic value of sexual
  knowledge, 20–21, 22–23,
  58
 interest in sexuality 12–13
 media influences, 22
 peer influences on sexuality,
  15–17, 18, 21–22, 167